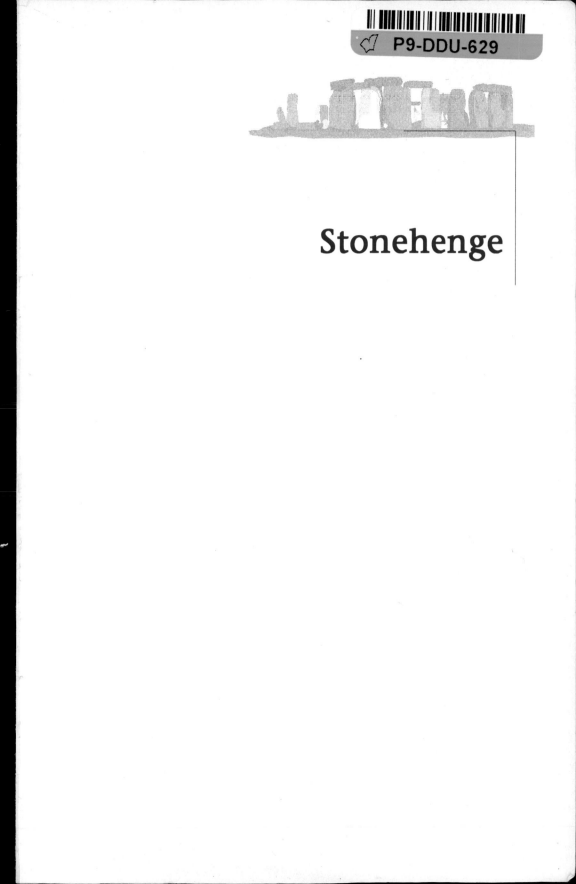

Stonehenge

MATERIALIZING CULTURE
. . . .

Series Editors: Paul Gilroy, Michael Herzfeld and Daniel Miller

Gen Doy, *Materializing Art History*

Laura Rival (ed.), *The Social Life of Trees: Anthropological Perspectives on Tree Symbolism*

Stonehenge

Making Space

BARBARA BENDER

with

Paul Aitken, Wesley Burrage, Mark Edmonds, Ian Hodder,
Ronald Hutton, Hilary Jones, Nick Merriman, Dolores Root,
Chris Tilley, Ruth Tringham and Peter Ucko

Oxford • New York

First published in 1998 by
Berg
Editorial offices:
150 Cowley Road, Oxford, OX4 1JJ, UK
70 Washington Square South, New York, NY 10012, USA

Berg is an imprint of Oxford International Publishers Ltd.

Library of Congress Cataloging-in-Publication Data

A catalogue record for this book is available from the Library of Congress.

British Library Cataloguing-in-Publication Data

A catalogue record for this book is available from the British Library.

Cover photograph: © Alan Lodge

ISBN 1 85973 903 2 (Cloth)
      1 85973 908 3 (Paper)

Typeset by JS Typesetting, Wellingborough, Northants.
Printed in the United Kingdom by Biddles Ltd, Guildford and King's Lynn.

For my extended family

– all the Farquharsons, Benders and Rowes –

Contents

Acknowledgements

I would like to thank the following people:

The editor of *The Journal of the Royal Anthropological Institute* (formerly *Man*) for permission to reprint Chapters 1 & 2; Kathryn Earle at Berg Publications for permission to reprint Chapter 4; and Eyre Methuen Ltd. for permission to reprint the quotation from Brecht at the beginning of Chapter 7.

My colleagues in the department of Anthropology at University College, for years of friendship, help and intellectual stimulation. In particular, John Gledhill, Danny Miller, Mike Rowlands and Chris Tilley.

Julian Richards who first introduced me properly to the *landscape* of Stonehenge.

The Stonehenge Campaign Group at Torriano Avenue, who welcomed me and nurtured the making of the exhibition. I would particularly like to thank Sue and John Rety who run the Torriano Meeting House in Camden Town and who created a wonderful ambience for the first showing of the exhibition, George Dice (htt://www.geocities.com/soho/9000/dicegeor.htm, or, for more about the Stonehenge Campaign, stonehenge@stones.com), Willie X, and, of course, most of all, Hilary, Wes, and Paul who worked with me on the exhibition and have been friends ever since. Hilary and Wes also loaded up their beat-up old van to take the exhibition to different venues around the country, put it up and took it down, and, at Glastonbury, the Rainbow Centre and the Hackney Festival for the Homeless, tended and protected it.

All the other people who worked closely on the exhibition: Arch Druid Rollo Maughfling, Annabel Edwards, Vicky Larkin, and Mandy Walker. Jan Farquharson who (leg in plaster) did nearly all the lay-out. Also Peter Stone, Nicole Segre, Mark Edmonds, Ewart Johns, Sam Farquharson (great tee-shirts), John Mitchell, Peter Dunn, Stephanie, George Firsoff, Brian Jones and many other students from the Anthropology Department, all of whom were involved in different ways in creating, making, setting up and looking after the exhibition.

Polly Farquharson, who photographed the exhibition, and Jack Oakley who turned the photos into illustrations.

Alan Lodge (Tash) for the photographs used on the cover and for figures 1c, 12, 25, 26, and 27. Pete Loveday who let me use many cartoons from *Russell, the Saga of a Peaceful Man* and drew two new cartoons for the book. And Dave Robinson who took my roughed-out autobiography and created something that, I hope, will show that it's OK to laugh and learn at the same time.

And, of course, all the people who enthusiastically got involved in the dialogues – by phone, letter, email, tape, conversation, and by walking the landscape with me: Mark Edmonds, Hilary, Wes and Paul, Ian Hodder, Ronald Hutton, Nick Merriman, Dolores Root, Chris Tilley, Ruth Tringham, and Peter Ucko.

The two (not so) anonymous readers who made many helpful suggestions – many of which are incorporated in the text.

Tom, for private reasons.

And most of all Jan for all his – critical – help, and his love.

List of Figures

Introduction: Time, Place and People

No subject in history is intrinsically 'micro' or 'macro', mainstream or marginal, big or small. The local study may be myopic, but then it is possible to hold eternity in a grain of sand.

Raphael Samuel 1975: xix

This book started life about twelve years ago. Three things happened that made me want to think more carefully about landscape and, almost immediately, about the landscapes of Stonehenge.

The first was moving from the city to the country and looking out of the window onto the shadowed slope of a deep Devon valley. The strange shapes and the sizes of the hedged fields bore no relationship to the present-day needs of the small dairy farmer who worked the land (Figure 1a). My first reaction was that I wanted to know how they had come to be that way, wanted to understand the historical palimpsest of activities and relationships. It took a while to recognise that not just the landscape, but my reaction, my desire to unpack a sequence of events, was quite culturally specific. Just as it took a while to realise that looking through the window – framing, looking out, standing back from, eliminating, in ways that are easily done, all the bits of landscape that did not conform to my vision, was also part of an historically specific way of 'seeing'. And indeed, it took a while to realise that rather mindlessly celebrating the escape from town to country left a lot of questions about attitudes, class, and money unattended to.[1]

---

1. See Harvey (1996: 404) for a brief comment on the flight from the city by those with 'power and money'.

1

(a)

(b)

(c)

Figure 1(a) Branscombe – view from the window (photo B. Bender);
(b) Mithinari painting on the beach at Yirrkala, northern Australia,1976. The
painting represents themes from the Macassan mythology (photo H.Morphy);
(c) Stonehenge at the Summer Solstice (photo Alan Lodge)

So: questions about a sedimented past that is cumulative but also always in process of being re-worked and re-constituted in the present-future.

It so happened that, at about the same time, I read Bruce Chatwin's *The Songlines*, and, like most people (though not Australians, who, on the whole, seem to find the book rather patronising),[2] I was swept up into this utterly different Aboriginal landscape. A landscape made by the ancestral beings for the people, who, in their turn – through ritual, painting, dance and song – nurtured both ancestors and land (Figure 1b).[3] Another way, not just of seeing, but of *being in* the landscape, one in which the divide that we create between nature and culture becomes meaningless. There is a moment in the book when Chatwin hears about the songline:

'Christ!' I said. 'Are you telling me that Old Alan here would know the songs for a country a thousand miles away?'
'Most likely.'
  'How the hell's it done?'
'No one', he said, 'could be sure . . . [but perhaps] the melodic contour of the song described the nature of the land over which the song passes. So, if the Lizard Man were dragging his heels across the salt-pans of Lake Eyre, you could expect a succession of long flats, like Chopin's 'Funeral March'. If he were skipping up and down the MacDonnell escarpments, you'd have a series of arpeggios and glissandos, like Liszt's 'Hungarian Rhapsodies'. Certain phrases, certain combinations of musical notes,

2. Howard Morphy (1996) analyses some of the reasons why Australian anthropologists, finding themselves placed in the unaccustomed role of becoming Chatwin's informants, might well have felt uneasy. He also points out that some of Chatwin's comments on white Australian women are more than a little sexist.
3. This is not the place to explain how Australian Aboriginal landscapes 'work', but here is Ingold talking about the Pintupi understanding of landscape:
First, it is not a given substrate, awaiting the imprint of activities that may be conducted upon it, but is itself the congelation of past activity – on the phenomenal level, of human predecessors, but more fundamentally of ancestral beings. Secondly, it is not so much a continuous surface as a topologically ordered network of places, each marked by some physical feature, and the paths connecting them. Thirdly, the landscape furnishes its human inhabitants with all the lineaments of personal and social identity, providing each with a specific point of origin and a specific destiny, and therefore, fourthly, the movement of social life is itself a movement *in* (not *on*) a landscape, and its fixed reference points are physically marked localities or 'sites' (Ingold 1996).

... describe the action of the Ancestor's *feet*. One phrase would say, 'Salt-pan', another 'Creek-bed', 'Spinifex', 'Sand-hill', 'Mulga-scrub', 'Rock-face' and so forth. An expert song-man . . . would count how many times his hero crossed a river, or scaled a ridge – and be able to calculate where, and how far along, a songline he was . . .

'So a musical phrase', I said, 'is a map reference?'

'Music', said Arkady, 'is a memory bank for finding one's way about the world'.

'I shall need some time to digest that.' (Chatwin 1988: 119–20)

I too would need time to digest, and try to understand a wholly different way of being in the world, and of engaging with the land.

Chatwin does not make the mistake of trying to restore the Australian Aborigines to some pre-contact Arcadian time. He does not try to airbrush out the last few hundred years of history. He recognises that their lives and landscapes are intimately bound up with those of White Australians (see also Morphy 1993; Strang 1997). But when I first read the book I was too entranced by their way of living *in* the land to worry much about the issues of politics and power, negotiation and subversion that formed part of these unequal relationships.

So: an acknowledgement – celebration – of difference. Landscapes to be thought about in terms of people's very different understandings and engagements with their world.

It was my third experience that hammered home that landscapes are not just differently understood and experienced but are differently *privileged*. Driving up and down the A303 between London and Devon in the Summer of 1985 I passed Stonehenge. Shrouded in barbed wire, arc-lights shining, police and dogs patrolling (Figure 1c). It was the year of the Battle of the Beanfield, when the free festivalers, making their way to the stones for the Solstice, were ambushed and set upon by the police. People were badly hurt and vans were trashed.[4] It was an extraordinarily powerful reminder of how passionately, and differently, people can feel about a place and a landscape. And of the importance of property, power, and the ownership of the past.

4. Stone (1996: 153–60) for a powerful evocation of the Battle of the Beanfield.

So: differential empowerment; the attempted suppression of 'view-points' that question the dominant 'way of seeing'.

It was not really quite so simple. I look back and these experiences seem important, but, of course, they are also pegs to hang my story on. Signposts for something that was in the wind, for I soon found that other archaeologists and anthropologists were also beginning to think about landscape. Why has landscape suddenly become so important? Is it to do with the greening of our consciousness? Or part of the post-modern questioning of the divide that we have created between culture and nature, and of the controlling sensibility of the western gaze? Is it a chafing at neat disciplinary boundaries and the discovery that explorations of landscape blow them wide open? (Bender 1993). Landscape – people's engagement with the material world – not only works between fields of knowledge, but also incorporates everyday life and contemporary politics, and highlights institutional constraints. It offers a holism: parts of life that are often compartmentalised spill over in a satisfactorily untidy way. And once you start to think your way into landscape you discover that it permeates everything. Our language is saturated with landscape metaphors. Look at this last paragraph: 'sign-posts', 'boundaries', 'divides', 'wide open', 'exploration' and more (Salmond 1982). We talk and walk landscape every moment of our lives.

So: this book is also an acknowledgement that what I write is subjective. All knowledge bears the fingerprints of its particular time, place and community (Harding 1993). But I also believe in what Donna Haraway calls 'situated knowledges' or Sandra Harding calls 'standpoint epistemology' (Haraway 1991; Harding 1993). That is: one cannot be objective but, rather than float on a sea of relativity, one can position oneself so as to ask questions and propose interpretations that seem relevant to contemporary concerns. I would even suggest, following Harding, that 'some situations are better placed than others as places from which to start knowledge projects' (Harding 1993).

The following chapters are the result of two separate, but entangled, enterprises. The first two-thirds (Chapters 1 to 5) were conceived first. The last third (Chapters 6 to 8) followed on as an unexpected consequence.

Let me explain. I wanted, very much as a result of what I had witnessed in 1985, to think about the Stonehenge landscape, and about why it had become such a contested contemporary icon. But first I needed to understand why the concept of landscape provides such a powerful entry-point for an understanding of how people relate to their world. So Chapter 1 focuses on three ways of thinking about landscape: landscape as *palimpsest*; landscape as *structure of feeling;* and landscape as *embodied*. All three have marked implications for how we relate to the land, and how we choose to 'protect', use, and interpret it.

W.G. Hoskins, famous for his *Making of the English Landscape*, thought of the landscape as a palimpsest (Hoskins 1985, first published 1955). It embodied the traces of people's past activities (this was the way in which I had first looked at my village landscape). This is a very seductive way of visualising the land; it permits a grounded and intimate sense of a sedimented past. But Hoskins's exploration of an English landscape palimpsest presents a history that pickles the past, negates the present, and excludes very large numbers of people from the story. Hoskins's past acts as a brake on the present and the future. It is overly reverential. We tiptoe among the ruins (Bender 1997b; Cosgrove 1994). We can take from Hoskins the celebration of the local, 'the bylines of history', but we need to work with more dynamic, more potentially democratic theoretical insights. So the work of Raymond Williams is discussed. His *structure of feeling* moves back and forth between people's understanding and perception of their worlds and the social and economic and political conditions that they live in (Williams 1973; 1994). Williams's exploration of multivocality and of people's sense of identity can be further explicated using recent feminist theory. Williams is good on class relations, much less good on gender and ethnicity, and he does not really explore the *fluidity* of identity. His ideas on power and resistance, following Gramsci, need to be pondered (see Chapter 6). And there are other areas that he hardly touched on that have to be wound into the discussion. There has to be more on every-day perception and action (Giddens's *Structuration,* Bourdieu's *habitus,* Ingold's *taskscape*); on *being in* rather than *looking at* the landscape (Tilley 1994; Thomas 1996) . Much more on the creation and negotiation of spaces (Barrett 1994).

Meshing Williams's insights with these more phenomenological approaches creates, I believe, a robust way of thinking about landscape. It permits questions about heritage and identity, allows people to *place themselves,* explores the social, cultural, economic and political relationships within which people's experiences of the world are embedded, and posits many ways of engaging, imagining, and contesting.

I wanted next – Chapter 2 – to mesh the theory with an analysis of the prehistoric making of the landscapes of Stonehenge. Roped off, fenced in, set in their polite green sward, the stones today are viewed by the visitor in isolation. The landscape is simply the backdrop to the photograph. But to understand the stones in the past or present, they have to be returned to the landscape.

Just as the Australian Aboriginal landscapes had stretched my imagination and understanding, so I wanted to be stretched by the prehistoric Stonehenge landscapes. The making of the Neolithic and Early Bronze Age landscapes, is both like and unlike anything that we can imagine. It is like because, at the end of the day, people have always worked on and thought about their relationships to each other and to the land, stayed put and moved around, attached meanings to places, had memories, made histories, negotiated and protested. It is unlike because what was happening five, six thousand years ago has no contemporary parallels (though that does not stop us using contemporary ethnographic analogies to feed our imaginings). Prehistoric Stonehenge is almost beyond our imagining, and yet, peering back through the lens of our own subjectivities, we continue to try to create, not *the* past, but *our* past.

It is our history and not theirs, and unlike many other contemporary people (Australian Aborigines, Native American Indians) who have their myths of origin, and know their pasts without needing to dig and probe (indeed, who feel that to do so is to dishonour their ancestors) (Deloria 1995), we still want to work back and forward between our interpretations, our imaginings, and the material remains. It was not so long ago that archaeologists felt that they had to 'stay with the evidence' – if it could not be proven, it should not be discussed. Now, fortunately, we have come to recognise that we *have* to go beyond the evidence, that 'the evidence' does not of itself deliver an understanding, and that it is open to any number of interpretations. So we still mix and match and get satisfaction from making physical contact with the past. That is *our* way, and that is what I have tried to do in Chapter 2.

One of the themes of Chapter 2 is that prehistoric people used the past – appropriated it and contested it – as part of the way in which they created a sense of identity and an understanding of their world. We dig up 'our' ancestors, the Neolithic people in the Stonehenge area dug up theirs and moved them around the landscape. What we do in the name of science to legitimate our knowledges, they did in the name of the sacred to legitimate theirs.

But the archaeological information is very piecemeal and ambiguous. We always write as though we know a great deal. We do not. The history of archaeological undertakings in the Stonehenge area is particularly

Figure 2 Colt Hoare and his daughter carrying home the archaeological spoils (Wiltshire Archaeological and Natural History Society)

poignant. In the nineteenth century archaeologists 'robbed' hundreds of burial mounds (Figure 2). In the twentieth century, we 'excavated' large parts of the Stonehenge site but failed miserably to annotate or publish the findings. When finally, two years ago, all the excavation material of this century was laboriously assembled, there was an agreement not to dwell on the ineptitude of the excavators. But anyone reading the five hundred page volume will catch glimpses of barely-suppressed outrage at the amount of evidence lost, fudged or (almost wilfully) misinterpreted (Cleal et al. 1995). Given a prehistoric landscape central to our sense of national identity, we have astonishingly little evidence. I say this now because once I begin to weave my story the continual uncertainties will tend to get lost or relegated to footnotes in the narrative.

In trying to understand the complexities of prehistoric landscapes, the question of how the past is constantly brought forward into the present, and is often contested, was only one among many themes. Prehistoric people appropriated the past through rhetoric and ritual, in their everyday activities, and by investing places in the landscape with changing meaning. Different people, differently placed in society, or at different times in their lives, would have thought about and used the past in different ways. As then, so now: multiple, and, sometimes, contested pasts.

In Chapter 4, this theme of appropriation and contestation becomes the focus. In most books on Stonehenge, although Chippindale's *Stonehenge Complete* (1983), and *Who Owns Stonehenge?* (1990) are obvious exceptions, the story of Stonehenge ends when the last stone is put in place – or, rather, fails to be put in place. But this only marks one sort of ending. The stones, the landscapes go on being used in peoples' lives and imaginations. In Chapter 4, the story moves from prehistoric, through medieval, seventeenth, eighteenth centuries, and then concentrates on the contemporary period. And that was where the first part of my research ended.

The final part of the book is rather different. Chapter 4 ends with Stonehenge as a highly contentious contemporary symbol. Among the hugely varied responses to the site and the landscape, the designated custodians see it as something to be preserved, a museum piece, an artefact, a vital part of our rooted, stable, national identity. But for a small minority it is something quite different: a living site, a spiritual centre, an integral part of an alternative life-style. They are an awkward minority – despised but also threatening. They put in question people's right to own large tracts of countryside and to exclude others from them. And so, at huge cost and via an increasingly draconian legal paraphernalia, these alternative groups are denied access to the stones and the wherewithal to pursue their ways of life. The question is not whether huge free festivals should take place right next to the stones, to which the answer is probably no, but the much more general one about the way in which an increasingly intolerant society marginalises sections of the population and denies them a voice and a presence. At Stonehenge the denial is quite specific and materially manifested: their presence is not to be tolerated on site or in the neighbouring landscape.

In an overtly political scenario, seemingly far removed from academia, academics nonetheless play their part. At Stonehenge, the archaeologists provide the raison d'être for the conservation politics. And their sequential narratives of the past, in which Stonehenge gets boxed into a bygone, over-and-done-with period, invalidate the notion of Stonehenge as a place which is continually renewed – a living site. So academics – in this case archaeologists – are, whether they like it or not, dragged into contemporary politics. They can shrug and say that their role is simply to provide the information, that what is done with it is not their concern, or they can take some responsibility – which

may mean getting involved in complicated, and sometimes contradictory, activities.

A group of archaeologists, including myself, protested at the impos-
ition of a four mile exclusion zone at the Summer Solstice. We were
protesting not just on behalf of the free festivalers, travellers, pagans
and so on, but, in a more general way, in favour of opening up the
past, opening up the landscape, and creating multiple ways of telling
and of experiencing the past.

One can protest, write about the politics of the past, or attempt other
forms of intervention. As will emerge in Chapter 6, almost accidentally,
I became involved in creating a travelling exhibition, *Stonehenge Belongs
to You and Me*, with a group of people which included free festivalers
and a Druid. The exhibition drew on the work that I have discussed in
Chapters 2 and 4 on appropriations and contestations in the Stonehenge landscape from prehistoric to contemporary times, then moved
on to create spaces and places for people to put their differing points
of view, and to a discussion of how dissenting views and people are
marginalised and crushed.

So Chapter 6 is about a contested place and about unequal power,
and about one way of creating a space for people to be heard. It seemed
worthwhile recounting the experience of working outside academia
with people with different interests and agendas, and suggesting – as
many others have done before me (see Dialogues 4, p. 209) – that small-
scale, inexpensive, flexible exhibitions offer a potential entry point for
working with others on some of the issues, often very context specific,
that surround the politics of the past.

The chapter has a more personal and more polemic style. Perhaps
the reader will feel that it sits uneasily with the more academic,
measured presentation of the first part. The change in style was not
entirely intentional. There came a moment where the more hands-on
experience involved in putting together the exhibition and taking it
around the country, getting responses, witnessing intolerance and
conservative prejudice at first hand, and recognising the entrenched
nature of a landscape of property, did not seem to permit of a distant,
more abstract style. Perhaps it is as well to underline quite forcibly,
through the change in style, the tensions that can occur between theory
and practice.

Just as the earlier chapters in the book concern themselves with
multivocality, and as the *Stonehenge Belongs to You and Me* exhibition
was also about multivocality, so, too, this book opens into dialogues
with other people. In Chapters 3, 5, 7 and 8 I talk with colleagues,

friends, free festivalers and a few opponents. I wanted to use the dialogues to question and to open up discussion of matters raised in the different chapters. I found the dialogues exhilarating precisely because they were dialogues, the arguments could move backwards and forwards, they could be critical and constructive, could offer alternative ways of thinking about things, bring in other case-studies, and they could also – although the people involved could not appreciate this – play off each other. Mark Edmonds and Chris Tilley, in Dialogues 1, talk to each other as well as to me. Likewise, in Dialogues 3, Ian Hodder's doubts about the nature of the contemporary Stonehenge alternative politics are in some measure addressed by the free festivalers themselves. Of course I edited the conversations, although I tried to retain people's idiosyncratic ways of talking (though I found that email noticeably flattens their voices). It is my book, I take responsibility, I set the agenda, but while I structure the dialogues and ask the questions, I cannot control the answers. So, although there are closures, things go off in unpredicted directions and expose the possibilities of other agendas, other books . . .[5]

As with the dialogues, so with the illustrations. I wanted to use them to open up the book – to find other ways of telling. I worked with Dave Robinson to create the opening intellectual autobiography. We used a *Beginners' Guide* format.[6] It was partly done in order to send up any incipient pretentiousness; partly to suggest that theories are not that difficult or inexplicable; and partly, no doubt, as a rather English form of self-protection: 'I'll tell you something about myself, but don't take it too seriously!' And I have used newspaper cartoons. The nameless person who read the outline to this book, reported favourably to the publishers, but worried that using cartoons 'ran the risk of trivialising'. Do they have this effect? Cartoons and jokes can make you laugh *and* ponder, can serve to prick pretensions and – hopefully – consciences. Remember, in *The Name of the Rose*, how Jorges destroys the second book of Aristotle because it ennobled mockery, it raised 'the weapon of laughter to the condition of a subtle weapon', it allowed 'what had been marginal [to] leap to the centre. . . . The seriousness of opponents

5. There is always the risk with using dialogues that people will find them more interesting than the main chapters! I remember that when I first read Flannery's *The Early MesoAmerican Village* I did just that – skipped the chapters and read the brilliant (but in this case entirely made-up) dialogues! (Flannery 1976).

6. Dave Robinson worked with Chris Garrett on *Ethics for Beginners* (1996) and *Descartes for Beginners* (in press).

[could] be dispelled with laughter, and laughter opposed with seriousness' (Ecco 1980: 475). Just as the free festivals can be seen as the
'trangression and mocking in public [of] the temporal authority of
tradition', so too laughter is – or can be – subversive (Hetherington
1992).[7]

7. For Bakhtin, in *Rabelais and his World* (1984), carnival and laughter are the counter
to official power, proof of the futility of ruling efforts to hegemonise. Irony, he believes,
over-rides all official authority, including the interpreter's. Bakhtin was writing under
Stalin – and his work on carnival and laughter was suppressed . . .

Where Do (my) Ideas Come From?
(*or* – A Short Intellectual Autobiography)

Animated by Dave Robinson

AS I GET OLDER I DON'T MIND MAKING A FOOL OF MYSELF, OR LETTING DAVE HAVE FUN WITH SOME OF MY INTELLECTUAL PRETENSIONS. ANYWAY THIS IS BY THE WAY OF A QUICK INTELLECTUAL AUTOBIOGRAPHY...

Theories don't just explain academnic stuff - they help explain real everyday life, social relations, politics . . . And they don't just happen in a vacuum. They reflect – and affect – what's going on in society. They're implicated in contemporary political and cultural values. And they're hugely affected by personal autobiography.

THE FACT THAT I'M A WOMAN, HALF-JEWISH AND SECOND GENERATION REFUGEE, WHITE AND MIDDLE CLASS, HAD AN AUTHORITARIAN FATHER AND WAS POLITICALLY FORMED IN THE SIXTIES ARE ALL PART OF THE STORY...

In the mid-sixties, at the Institute of Archaeology in London, there wasn't any theory. Well, of course, there was, it's just that no-one ever told us. We thought that the trick was to accumulate more and more evidence. Once you'd worked out which pots went with which graves and so on, you'd found the archaeological equivalent of a *society* or a *culture*. The dots on the map equalled a *culture area*. Changes occurred through *innovation* or *diffusion*.

Later I discovered that this rather particular way of reading the past is called *culture history theory..*

With this sort of theory you don't take too much notice of social relationships or of how people think about their world. It fits quite well with a colonial mentality: you can go anywhere in the world and dig where you want. What the people whose ancestors you're digging up might be thinking is not relevant.

In the late sixties I got my first job: lecturer in Chicago at the State University (where the students regularly fell asleep because they'd worked night shifts to pay their way through college. Or was it my teaching?).

The New Archaeologists or *processuals* were storming the barricades. They said they wanted to know about prehistoric 'people' and what they did. But what people 'did' seemed to boil down to making a living (which, apparently, involved *minimising* labour and *maximising* returns) and churning out tools. Societies were environmentally adaptive. Change, when it occurred, happened because people were overtaken by outside events - like population pressure (which apparently had nothing to do with how people organised their lives), or changes in climate.

The New Archaeology was also full of pseudo-science and cybernetic jargon:

To me it all seemed quite alienating. Everything reduced down to environmental adaptation. Cultural variability was just extraneous noise. Quite a suitable neo-colonial world view.

By the mid-seventies I had a partner and a child and lectured in archaeology and anthropology at University College London. It involved typical gendered juggling of work and home life.

The Anthropology Department was in ferment. Rather belatedly, British anthropology had discovered *structural marxism.* It combined Levi-Strauss's Structuralism and Marxism.

I'd been trying to figure out why prehistoric gatherer-hunters took to farming. Processual explanations about population pressures and climatic change seemed very reductionist. With structural-marxist theory I could suggest that gatherer-hunters were not just feeding themselves, but also feeding their social relations. There were systems of gift exchange that involved gift-giving, feasting and ceremonies. Such exchanges put pressure on production. One way of easing the pressure was to exert more control over plants and animals – a possible scenario for the beginning of domestication . . .

In the early eighties I got more interested in the politics of the past. When I first started studying archaeology I thought it was 'safe' – that the past was over and done with, and that my academic interests were quite separate from the rest of my life. Well, I was wrong.

We make the past in the present. We set the agendas and often we use the past to justify the present. An example of this is the way we assume that gendered divisions of labour are 'natural' and have always been that way: 'Man the Hunter' – out in the world, fighting his corner, and 'Woman the Gatherer' – keeping the home fires burning. But why? There are no economic or biological reasons for hard and fast divisions – indeed, everything suggests that early hominids would have had to be ultra flexible . . .

I thought about *the roots of inequality* and suggested that divisions of labour were culturally imposed. Gatherer-hunters were just as sociable as everyone else, so they had to learn the right way, the right time and place to do things. Those who 'knew how' could begin to exert control . . .

DANGER!
Artist at Work
Men only area

I also suggested that the Upper Palaeolithic painted caves could have been an arena for male activities that centred symbolically round the hunt. It's an O.K. story except that, as so often, the women get lost in the telling . . .

In the mid-eighties we moved out of London into a Devon village in which every hedge and bend in the road talks someone's history. But I still trundle up to London to work. I go along the A303 which runs by Stonehenge. And, in the Summer of '85, Stonehenge was under siege. The police (and the pressure groups behind the police) were out to trash the Travellers. So I began to focus on the idea of landscape – the way in which different people at different times engage with the world, and, more particularly, on the *politics* of landscape. And this is what this book is all about. Stonehenge seems a good place to start to think about some of these issues . . .

In this book I've tried to pull together different strands of theory.

There's Raymond Williams's *cultural marxism*. He creates the link - the tensioned relationship between people's socio-economic relations and their perceptions. Different people, differently placed in society, have different ideas and different ways of doing things. But whilst the actions and thoughts of some groups are authorised and legitimated, others are marginalised. Williams is good on how this emerges from class relations, not so good on gender . . .

John Clare – the Ploughman poet

And then there's Giddens's *structuration*. We have to keep moving backwards and forwards between people doing things, thinking, resisting, creating the structures of society, but also hamstrung by those same structures.

And we have to recognise that there isn't one history, but multiple histories – and some are legitimised and others excluded...

Bourdieu's *habitus* helps us to recognise the way in which places, spaces and timings of everyday life socialise us into ways of doing and thinking . . .

And the *phenomenologists* talk us through the way in which people move around their world. How they use places and spaces - and how they're constrained by them. Gendered spaces, hierarchical spaces, formal and informal, back-stage and front-stage. And movement, of course, always involves time (right times, wrong times, clock time, seasonal and personal time).

Thinking about Landscapes[1]

A whole history remains to be written about spaces *– which would at the same time be the history of* powers *. . . from the great strategies of geopolitics to the little tactics of the habitat.*

Michel Foucault 1980: 149

Introduction

We use the word 'landscape' in any number of ways. 'An arable landscape', we say, or 'an industrial landscape'. Here we're talking in terms of land use. 'A wooded landscape' – we're talking about vegetation. 'A picturesque landscape' or 'a surreal landscape', and we are talking about aesthetics. But always we're describing or appreciating *the surface* of the land. We *scan* the land, and we talk about things *done* to it, changes wrought on it. We invoke the land as something passive and as something separate from us. We draw culture and nature apart. These ways of envisaging and experiencing the world are very particular – not to say peculiar. They are *our* way. They articulate with specific historic conditions, specific times and places.

Our experience of the world will never be identical with other peoples. It depends on who *we* are. Also it changes with different times in our lives, and even at a given moment it may be contradictory and conflicted. There is never *a* landscape, always many landscapes. And landscapes are not passive, not 'out there', because people create their sense of identity – whether self, or group, or nation state – through engaging and re-engaging, appropriating and contesting the sedimented pasts that make up the landscape (Bender 1993).

---

1. This chapter and the next first appeared in *Man* vol. 27, 1992, but have been tampered with.

In the context of a contemporary obsession with preserving and commodifying the past, it becomes particularly urgent that we take the measure[2] of landscape, both theoretically and in practice. More often than not, those involved in the conservation, preservation and mummification of landscape create normative landscapes, as though there was only one way of telling or experiencing. They attempt to 'freeze' the landscape as a palimpsest of past activity. But, of course, the very act of freezing is itself a way of reappropriating the land.[3] For the Heritage people freezing time and space allows the landscape or monuments in it to be packaged, presented, and turned into museum exhibits. We need to recognise that this is just one way of handling the past. We need to work against the grain of this passive, nostalgic, *heavy*-with-history notion of landscape.

This book is all about different experiences of landscape. But, first, in this chapter, I want to consider different ways of theorising an understanding of landscape. I begin by looking at the work of two landscape pioneers, W.G. Hoskins and Raymond Williams (Figures 3a/b). I want to show how, on the one hand, Hoskins's writings can be used to legitimate the idea of an apolitical past, one that is over and done with, whilst, on the other, Williams provides a politicised theoretical framework that is less open to such abuse and serves to enlarge our understanding of how landscape 'works'. However Williams does not address the *materiality* of the landscape, or the way in which it plays back into social relations and perceptions. As Inglis (1977, my italics) puts it:

> A landscape is the most solid appearance in which a history can declare itself. *It is not background, nor is it stage* . . . There it is, the past in the present, constantly changing and renewing itself as the present rewrites the past.

In the last part of the chapter I suggest that by meshing Williams's 'structure of feeling' with more phenomenological approaches to

2. 'Take the measure' – note again how our way of talking is loaded with particular landscape metaphors, ones that often invoke control.

3. Munn (1992) makes a similar point about clock time: 'An analytical perspective that views clock time as a "lifeless time", "a chronological series of points on a string" is misleading. Considered in the context of daily activity, clock time is quite alive, embodied in purposeful activity and experience . . . Endowed with potency and affect, the clock may be "hated, endured . . . [and] manipulated", or taken as a "moral time-piece".'

Figure 3a W.G. Hoskins: 'One could write a book about every square inch of the Ordnance Survey map'
(photo: W. G. Hoskins)

Above: Pandy signal box, Gwent (photograph: Mike Dibb)

Below: Saffron Walden 1986 (photograph: Mark Gerson)

Figure 3b Raymond Williams. Tensioned identity: working-class/Welsh/childhood/inarticulate understanding (photo Mike Dibb); middle-class/Cambridge/adult/abstract knowledge (photo Mark Gerson)

landscape we can move beyond descriptions of land-use, or legitimising and homogenising myths of origin, to explorations of tensioned and contradictory processes and experiences – both past and present.

W.G. Hoskins

I start with W.G. Hoskins who, in *The Making of the English Landscape*, lovingly describes the way in which the countryside has been reworked over and over again (Hoskins 1985 [1955]). He reads off the history of land occupation and land use from the shape of a hedge, the angle of a road, the size of a field, the layout of a village. He has said of the Ordnance Survey map that 'One could write a book about every few square inches of such a canvas. It is like a painting by Brueghel or a major symphony' (Hoskins 1985: 3). *The Making of the English Landscape* is evocative, observant and meticulously researched. It is also angst-ridden, conservative (with a small c), anti-modernist, post-Imperial, and Little Englander. I suggest that it risks being appropriated by the Heritage industry as part of their effort to commodify and mummify the English countryside.

Several recent books on contemporary Britain have suggested that in a climate of unwanted change, there is a wish to turn back the clock to a mythologised and sanitised past (Hewison 1987; Wright 1985; Nairn 1977). Moreover, in an era of flexi-capital, imaging the past is good business. There is little doubt that the sorts of pasts invoked by the Heritage industry, with their emphasis on the great and the powerful (men), or on bucolic villages or soft-glow Victorian back-to-backs, would have horrified Hoskins. He would have reiterated the significance of historical context, of daily life, of change and adaptation. And yet there is also little doubt that, if called upon, those in the Heritage trade would claim Hoskins as the intellectual inspiration for their mummification of the countryside.

One reason for this is that he cuts off the past from the present and creates a sense of nostalgia. His last chapter begins:

> Since the last years of the nineteenth century... and especially since the year 1914, every single change in the English landscape has either uglified it or destroyed its meaning, or both.

He goes on:

> It is a distasteful subject but it must be faced for a few seconds.

Bravely, he faces it:

> England of the arterial by-pass, treeless and stinking of diesel oil,
> murderous with lorries . . . Barbaric England of the scientists, the military
> men, and the politicians: let us turn away and contemplate the past before
> all is lost to the vandals (Hoskins 1985: 298).

In his horror at the dislocation and changes, he never pauses to note
that *his* palimpsest is also a landscape of dislocation and change.[4]
   Hoskins invokes a 'golden age' related directly to his own ancestry.
Writing long before the debate on the subjectivity of text, he
contextualises himself:

> My ancestors were men and women of no particular eminence even in
> local history, farmers nearly all of them, until the collapse of local
> communities all over England in the early nineteenth century drove them
> off the land and into the towns and across the water to the American
> continent (Hoskins 1954: xix).

Hoskins's sense of the up-slope and down-slope of history is coloured
by the fate of his ancestors. Unlike the Heritage people, he despises
the eighteenth-century landed gentry with their great mansions and
landscaped gardens who 'needed (or thought they needed) more square
miles of conspicuous waste to set them off' (Hoskins 1985: 170). His
'golden age' – what he calls the 'flowering of rural England' – was earlier,
1570 to 1700: the apogee of prosperity for the yeoman farmer. Transport
was improving, markets were expanding, prices for corn and cattle were
high. There was a burst of building activity, farmhouses were refurbished
and enlarged. They were unpretentious and solid, used local materials,
created regional styles.
   Hoskins called it the 'golden age', but it was very selectively golden.
Reading on, we find Hoskins remarking upon 'the savagery of the law
and the cheapness of human life in the late sixteenth century' (Hoskins
1954: 250). People were hung, branded, flogged for pick-pocketing or
sheep-stealing. In Devon in 1598 every woman who had a bastard child
was to be whipped. In the later seventeenth century there was trans-
portation for any infringement of property rights.

4. V.S. Naipaul in his wonderful evocation of landscapes, *The Enigma of Arrival*, has
exactly the same gut reaction. Change in the past is necessary and 'good', change in the
present is to be feared and rejected (Bender 1993).

The sorts of fears and nostalgias voiced by Hoskins can all too easily be hijacked by less scrupulous people. The focus on ancestors and rootedness can be misappropriated so that those who do not happen to have the *right* ancestors or the requisite roots are excluded. Only those who 'belong' can truly understand. As Sartre once said, it is not enough to have been in the woods a few times, 'one must have made notches in the trees in childhood' so that one can go back and find them 'enlarged in old age' (cited in Wright 1985: 85).

Hoskins is open to appropriation because he does not analyse his own position. Moreover, he describes patterns, rather than explaining them. He documents the landscape as the objective by-product of human action, charting the consequences of human intercession (Rowntree 1996). He takes feudalism, for example, and describes the material effects of the infield-outfield system and land clearance. But he explains neither the particular social and economic relations involved, nor the cultural subjectivities. He describes the effects of the Industrial Revolution in graphic detail, and in so doing falls, as Raymond Williams puts it, 'for the last protecting illusion of our time: that it is not capitalism which is injuring us, but the more isolable, more evident system of urban industrialisation' (Williams 1973: 96).

Hoskins's forebears were forced off the land and into the city, but why, how and what were the processes at work, and what effect did these processes have on them, how were they experienced and understood? And what effect did they have on Hoskins? Perhaps it is because he fails to understand his own sense of alienation that his landscapes risk being turned into panegyrics on the past, on permanence and rootedness, and risk being robbed of their historical graininess.

Raymond Williams

Turning to Raymond Williams, I want to concentrate on one book, *The Country and the City* (1973). It is not directly about landscape. It is about landscape filtered through literature: about changing socio-economic relations and changing cultural perceptions.

Politically a socialist, Williams works and reworks a seam of cultural materialism, and seems, as Eagleton (1989) points out, to be consistently one jump ahead of mainstream West European marxism. In the sixties and seventies, the heyday of structural marxism, he abandoned the base/superstructure dichotomy and insisted on the interlocking and interleaving of cultural understanding and socio-political structures. He focused, too, on 'history active and continuous: the relations not

only of ideas and experiences, but of rent and interest, of situation
and power; a wider system' (Williams 1973: 7). The fit that he perceives
between social relations and cultural perceptions is nuanced and fine-
tuned. He understands the political colouring that informs a pastoral
poem or a novel, its tones of regionality, patronage, and so on.

Take two examples: one the writings of the labourer-poet John Clare,
the other the great improver, Arthur Young. They both lived at the
end of the eighteenth, beginning of the nineteenth century. Clare lived
at Helpston in Cambridgeshire. His life, sensibility and writings were
deeply affected by the enclosures that occurred around his village in
1809:

> There once were lanes in nature's freedom dropt
> There once were paths that every valley wound –
> Inclosure came, and every path was stopt;
> Each tyrant fix'd his sign where paths were found . . .
> – Inclosure, thou'rt a curse upon the land,
> And tasteless was the wretch who thy existence plann'd . . .
> (cited in Williams 1973: 136).

There was in Clare's writings a direct sense of the humiliation within
the new order: 'When the prosperity of one class was founded on the
adversity and distress of the other, the haughty demand by the master
to his labourer was "work for the little I choose to allow you and go to
the parish for the rest – or starve"' (a letter quoted in Barrell 1972:
194). There was also the emotive response to the changes wrought on
an intimate childhood landscape and the landscape of his maturity.
There is a sense of social unease. Existing precariously within his village,
labouring and writing, Clare despises his untutored fellow villagers,
and is in turn despised and feared by them.[5] And then again he takes,
perforce, his literary cues from a polite contemporary and earlier
pastoral mode of writing. Such writing embodies notions of landscape
'prospect' and perspective in which the eye is supposed to sweep to
the horizon and then circle back more slowly to the foreground. The
overall impression, the total design, is supposed to take precedence
over detail, so that the landscape becomes a vehicle for meditation.

---

5. Perhaps Williams has a certain empathy with Clare. For Williams, as he spells out
both in the Introduction to *The Country and the City* and in many of his novels, was also
a 'border-man': working-class Welsh, Cambridge academic, international communicator,
straddling uneasily different landscapes, different identities.

But Clare comes unstuck because his landscape is all detail, his passion is for the small territory that is, as he puts it, 'in his knowledge'. He is untravelled, has little sense of the comparative. He cannot create distance because his instinct is to describe 'what it is like to be in each place'. For a while he is patronised by the London elite, but his publisher is forever trying to edit out the particular and the vernacular, and his patron, Lord Radstock, is disturbed by the political overtones of his poetry – his 'radical slang'.

In contrast to Clare, Arthur Young was gentry. He was a great agricultural innovator (he wrote on his wife's tomb: 'the grand-daughter of John Allen Esq. . . . the first person to use marl'), and a passionate believer in enclosure. He wrote the *Annals of Agriculture* in 46 volumes. Unlike John Clare, he travelled widely. He was discomforted by the open field system, he disliked the circulating cattle ways and the paths that petered out in fields, hated the lack of markers and signposts and yearned for roads that would take agricultural produce out and away and open up the villages (Williams 1973: 66). Young, the improver, lingering over a fine crop of waving corn, or a well kept farmyard, highlighted the production and labour that the great landowners in their perambulations, their gardens and paintings, sought to dismiss. But again, like Clare, Young is caught up in contemporary aesthetics. He knew that he should admire 'wild' mountain scapes, and there is a fine uneasiness between his modulated response to a mountain scape and his much more heartfelt enthusiasm for a fertile stretch of upland cultivation. But a person's experience of landscape can change, and towards the end of his life Young became sickened by the effects of the enclosures. He began to doubt the benefits of his 'improvements', began indeed to *re-view* his landscape: 'I had rather all the commons in England were sunk to the sea, than that the poor should in future be treated on enclosing as they have been hitherto' (cited in Williams 1973: 66).

In his analysis of the writings of Young and Clare, Williams allows us to recognise the complexity, the contradictions, and the change-ability, of people's engagement with the land. What he also explores is the historical development of attitudes to, and engagements with landscapes that colour our own understanding, and about which we need to be clear if we want to explore other ways of being and perceiving. The drive behind *The Country and the City* is to expose the nexus between town and country from the sixteenth century to the present. Williams is concerned with the linkage between mercantile and later forms of capital and changing sensibilities, what he calls 'structure of feeling'. He begins by discussing the desire to create a golden age, always in the past, and notes how it is always referenced on country matters and country modes. The countryside is 'timeless' and 'wholesome', the city is dynamic, but also sinful and superficial. Williams is concerned to show, in a way that Hoskins never could, that this division serves to disguise the interpenetration of country and city. The changing social relations in the countryside generate much of the wealth underwriting the mercantile ventures in the city. Indeed, often the same people are involved in both places. The enclosure movement of the seventeenth and eighteenth centuries, which Clare repudiated so fiercely, was part of these changing relations. It permitted a huge aggrandisement of estates, a more effective exploitation of labour and of land. These 'improvements' were, of course, at the expense of the small landowner, the tenant farmer and the labourer. Williams is not suggesting that there was ever, for the commoner or smallholder, a 'golden age', but he does suggest that as long as there existed open fields, a system of inheritance by subdivision, and rights to grazing and collecting on common land, the smallholder retained 'a marginal independence . . . a protection against the exposure of total hire' (Williams 1973: 99). The enclosures were not new, they had occurred, differentially and piecemeal, across the country from the fifteenth century, but in the eighteenth century the extent and pace accelerated enormously.

Williams documents the way in which, at this time, words change and take on extra baggage: labourers lose substance and become 'hands'. Words like 'prospect', 'elevation' and 'improvement' become ambiguous (Williams 1973: 121). He explores the way in which philosophy, painting and writing move away from earlier notions of a mutual relationship between nature and culture, to one in which culture dominates nature. And more specifically, he shows how this sense of 'control' works in the arena of the perception and creation of landscape: starting in the seventeenth century with 'landskip' paintings, then moving off the canvas into an 'appreciation' of landscape, and then to the actual creation of landscape. The linear, perspectival apprehension of the land employs the same geometry as merchant trading and accounting, as navigation, land surveying, mapping and artillery. As Gold (1984) suggests, the world becomes 'male, mercantile and mathematical'.

This is the world that we are heirs to. Williams's historical analysis permits us to understand the roots of our own engagement with the land – our sense, as I suggested at the beginning of this chapter, of the land as surface which we survey from our ego-centred viewpoint. But we have to be wary of homogenising 'our' ways of relating and thinking. As Williams shows, even among the gentry in the hey-day of landscape aesthetics and gardening there were very considerable differences. Daniels and Cosgrove (taking their cue from Williams) discuss the tensions within the circumscribed universe of Jane Austen's *Mansfield Park*: the landscape of the absentee landlord, of the nouveau riche, of a modest country gentleman, and of a woman of limited means.[6] They also show how attitudes change: with revolution in the air the more overweening statements of power expressed in the grand formal parks give way to something more modest and less obvious (Daniels and Cosgrove 1993).[7]

Raymond Williams's approach to landscape has enormous potential. His 'structure of feeling' works at the intersection between people's interests, actions and perceptions and historically given structures and institutions. He allows us to understand how relative and changing landscape is; how, at any given moment, landscapes – even as experienced by a single person – are multiple and contradictory; how they may work on different scales; and how they are reconstituted and reappropriated over and over again.

We can learn much from Williams about our own and other people's engagement with the world. But there are limitations to his work. He restricts himself to 'high' literature. He could have used other written sources – diaries, court-proceedings and so on – and created a larger canvas. We might have heard more women's voices, children, and a range of less literate people.

He is good on class relations, less good on gender. He is good on multivocality, and on the way in which people hold many and contradictory understandings of the world. One feels that he would have been interested in some of the recent feminist writing on identity.

6. Said (1989) muses on the unmentioned slave plantations that underwrite the fortunes of the 'good' absentee landlord.

7. This is a nice example of Bakhtin's notion of 'positive shape' and 'negative space' – the way in which the 'voiceless' can be heard through the actions and discourses of those with power (Bakhtin cited in Foch-Serra 1990). Thus Daniels (1988) notes how the smell of revolution in the air provided part of the impetus behind the move from more formal and exclusive forms of landscaping to ones where the boundaries were softened. As Uvedale Price, landscape gardener, carefully explained, 'although the separation of different ranks and their gradations, like those of visible objects, is known and ascertained, yet from the beneficial mix, the frequent intercommunication of high and low, that separation is happily disguised and does not sensibly operate on the general mind' (Daniels 1988).

The recognition, for example, that people's sense of identity is often woven around a sense of *difference,* of (unequal) oppositions (us:them; man:women; black:white and other more subtle, overlapping, often contradictory oppositions), and that, therefore, identities are always *relational,* and also *contingent* in the sense that the construction of difference is always in process (Jones & Moss 1995).[8] And Williams would probably have approved of Mouffe's comment that:

> for an appropriate definition of identity, we need to take account of both the multiplicity of discourses and the power structure which affects it, as well as the complex dynamic of complicity and resistance which underlines the practices in which this identity is implicated (Mouffe 1995).

And then, moving into areas that Williams hardly (except perhaps in his novels) touched on, we have to consider more closely the *context* of this social relationality, the articulation of identity with place and space (Massey 1995). And, Thomas would add, with 'things': 'the broad relational network which encompasses people, objects and living things' (Thomas 1997). Williams does not really work with the *physicality* – and spatiality – of landscape. He does not spend much time considering the ways in which topography and other elements of landscape form part of human sociality, or how space (and time) are involved in the processes of socialisation and empowerment (Bender, Edmonds, Hamilton & Tilley in press; Bender 1997a).

We need, therefore, to mesh Williams's 'structure of feeling' with a more phenomenological approach. With, first of all, Bourdieu's *habitus*: the routinised social practices through which, within which, people experience and understand the world, often in ways that are completely inarticulate (Bourdieu 1977). *Habitus* is knowledge learned through the encounter with the world – by copying . . . watching . . . listening . . . by attentive involvement.

> Through time-space routines of movement a person knows where she or he is in relation to familiar places and objects and 'how to go on' in the world (Tilley 1994: 16).

8. J. Thomas makes the same point about relationality in the context of communities (Thomas 1997).

Habitus is about:

> The preoccupied active presence in the world, through which the world
> imposes its presence, with its urgencies, its things to be done and said,
> things made to be said, which directly govern words and deeds without
> ever unfolding as a spectacle (Bourdieu 1990: 52).

Bourdieu's *habitus* explains wonderfully well both the historicity and
the reproduction of social relations. But, whilst there is full acknowledgement of the way in which people negotiate their worlds, the
emphasis is on the way in which such negotiations, or potential
resistances and subversions, occur within the confines of what *habitus*
makes possible and thinkable. In contrast, Giddens's *structuration* theory
more emphatically engages with people's *active* involvement. With
structuration we recognise that though we are caught up in a world
not of our own making (a world that tells us where to be, what to do
and what to say), we also create that world through our own actions
and thoughts. People are agents; their agency creates the structures;
the structures constrain and enable agency. No one-way causal arrow,
no beginning or ending (Giddens 1981: ch. 1). Munn says the same
thing slightly differently: 'we and our productions are in some sense
always "in" time (the socioculturally/historically informed time of our
activity and our wider world) and yet we make, through our acts, the
time we are in' (Munn 1992). Life is always in process of *becoming* (Soja
1989: ch.6).

Giddens also charts in some detail how our movements are constrained and constraining, and how movement through space always
involves time, and how there are many sorts of time – personal time,
clock time, gendered time, cyclical time and so on. He talks of locales,
of front stage and backstage, of formal and informal spaces (Giddens
1985). However, as in so many accounts of landscape, Giddens fails to
remark on 'the role of gendered spaces in the ordering of social
experience, . . . the power relations that physically separate male and
female practical (time-)spaces, [and] the power relations that are
reproduced by men and women practicing in separate (time-)spaces'
(Pred 1990: 25/26). Rose goes some way towards rectifying these over-
sights (Rose 1993: ch.2).

Most of these more phenomenological approaches are indebted to
Heidegger who emphasised that human beings are *beings-in-the-world*
and stressed the importance of *dwelling* in the world (Heidegger
1962;Thomas 1996: 39–54; Tilley 1994: 11–14). Heidegger's recognition

of an embodied experience of the world, and his challenge to the Cartesian split of mind from body, or culture from nature, is hugely important. Nonetheless there is a danger in some of his writing, and in that of people following in his footsteps, of creating a romantic, almost ahistorical sense of a being-in-the-world rooted in rural activities and past-times. Perhaps it is because we know something of Heidegger's personal history and of his flirtation with Nazism that – for me at least – his famous invocation of a Black Forest farm-house with its stress on the 'simple oneness' of the peasants' self-sufficient lives smells slightly of *blut and boden* – of the Nazi hymn to an Aryan peasantry grounded, rooted through kin and 'blood', in the German soil (Heidegger 1972: 338[9]). You are left wondering what happens to those not rooted, not *dwelling*, perhaps not 'authentic'?

Ingold's *taskscapes*, although this time trailing a more innocent romanticism, are also deeply ahistorical (Ingold 1993). His description of Brueghel's The Harvesters (1565) as a peasant taskscape of sweat, toil, pleasure, of seasonal rhythm, of track and tree and church, is wonderfully evocative, and is surely an important recognition of part of what is involved in people's experience of the world, but in his determination to think of landscape as something created out of people's activities rather than through their representations he loses any sense of historical particularity.[10] Ingold rightly emphasises the sociality embodied in the 'multiple rhythms of which the taskscape is constituted' whereby people 'attend to one another'. But this sociality is also born out of quite specific social, economic and political conditions. He mentions that the sixteenth century – the time of Brueghel's painting – was a prosperous time, a prosperity shared by all 'to some degree', but this (unequally) shared prosperity is historically specific and forms an important part of the engagement with the land. In Ingold's account, Brueghel's peasants become *ur*-peasants rather than precisely located sixteenth-century peasants, and just as Hoskins

9. Bourdieu, in his book *The Political Ontology of Martin Heidegger*, insists that 'Heidegger's philosophy is political from beginning to end' (Bourdieu 1991: 96). He notes the 'regressive yearning for a reassuring reintegration in the organic totality of an autarchic agrarian (or feudal) society' (p. 26), and an underlying anti-semitism whereby 'the oversophisticated refinement of urban, Jewish 'modernity' [is set] against the archaic, rural, pre-industrial simplicity of the peasant . . .' (p. 49).

10. 'It seems unhelpful to polarize, as Ingold appears to, perception and interpretation, practical activity and the cultural world of explication and discourse . . . The cultural construction of the environment is both "prelude" *and* "epilogue"' (Tilley 1994: 23).

divorces changing technologies from larger socio-cultural transformations and thus allows Heritage purveyors to follow suite, so Ingold
permits an ahistorical (golden) evocation of labour practices at the
expense of embedded social, cultural and political relations.[11] 'It is',
Ingold concludes, 'within the attentive involvement in the landscape
that the human imagination gets to work to fashion ideas about it'.
Nice, but not sufficient. Harvey puts it succinctly: 'Representations of
space and time arise out of the world of social practices but then become
a form of regulation of those practices' (Harvey 1996: 212; Harvey &
Haraway 1995). And so does Massey: 'place is the reproduction of
a particular set, a particular articulation of . . . power-filled social
relations . . . There is always a history that is brought to each situation
of political practice' (Massey 1995).[12]

So I return to the need to mesh an understanding of *embodied*
landscapes with a *political* landscape of unequal power relations, the
need to mesh Williams's 'structure of feeling' with a phenomenological
approach. In the next chapter I try to do something along these lines
in the context of the prehistoric landscapes of Stonehenge.

11. In the context of Heidegger's work, Harvey says something rather similar: 'It is
not hard to see how the crass and commercial side of postmodernism could play upon
these sentiments and market the vernacular, simulate the authentic and invent heritage,
tradition, and even commercialized roots' (Harvey 1996: 315).

12. Pred, less succinctly, continues the argument: 'Production, distribution and
consumption practices . . . interwoven by human movement along the ground and
through seconds, minutes . . . To conduct one's daily routines, to be caught in the
constraining and enabling web of local power relations, to be swept down the maelstrom
of the social, [is] repeatedly to get from one here and now to another, . . . to trace one's
daily path, to construct one's own geography, to negotiate and navigate . . .' (Pred 1990:
184).

Prehistoric Stonehenge Landscapes[1]

Ten thousand years is long
and so a morning and an evening count.

Mao Tse-Tung (from 'To Kuo Mo-Jo') 1972

I came across a dry rose, its petals scattered, behind a row of books as I was
tidying up my library.
I smiled. The depths of the remote past gave way to a fleeting light.

Naguib Mahfouz 1997: 10

Archaeologists used to think that it was reasonable to start the story of
Stonehenge at around 3500 BC because that was when prehistoric people
started 'altering the earth' (Bradley 1993) in ways unknown before.
But now we find that already some *five thousand* years earlier gatherer-
hunters had marked the Stonehenge site. Equally we used to end the
story at around 1600 BC when the last hole was dug, but that too is an
arbitrary cut-off point, for not just the stones, but the burial mounds,
enclosures, remnant banks and ditches of avenue and cursus remained
(and remain) sedimented in the landscape, sometimes totally ignored,
sometimes invested with new meanings (see Chapter 4). There is no
beginning or end, but one has to start and end the story somewhere
and so this chapter is mainly concerned with the time between 3000
BC and 1600 BC, while Chapter 4 continues the story . . .

1. This chapter (and the last) first appeared in *Man* vol. 27, 1992. This chapter has
been quite heavily reworked, not least because the twentieth-century excavations have
finally been published and the new carbon-14 dates rather dramatically alter our ideas
about who was doing what, and when (Cleal et al. 1995).

In this chapter, however, I have chosen not to proceed in an orderly – sequential – fashion, but rather to comb through the prehistoric sequence several times over, in order to pick up on different elements of landscape. For those who prefer a more sequence-orientated approach, the summary presented in Figure 4 may be useful. Figure 5 is a map of Stonehenge and its environs.

In relation to the prehistoric landscape I want to touch on the following themes: (1) the indivisibility of nature and culture; (2) conceptual boundaries within the landscape; (3) the possibility that, sometimes, the act may be more important than the material result; (4) differential experience of the landscape; (5) contested landscapes; and (6) the appropriation, over and over again, of past landscapes.

Indivisibility of Nature and Culture

I mentioned, in the first chapter, that we (all of us, including archaeologists) tend to focus on the surface of the land, and to talk of things done to the land, of culture dominating nature. In his book *The Earth, the Temple and the Gods*, Scully argues passionately for an alternative approach. He is concerned to understand, in the context of prehistoric Greece, the depth of the relationship between, on the one hand, the temples and processual ways (movement within a place, movement along a path), and on the other, the surrounding topography – a topography which is anthropomorphised and mythologised:

> not only were certain landscapes . . . regarded by the Greeks as holy and as expressive of specific gods, or rather as embodiment of their presence, but also . . . the temples and the subsidiary buildings of their sanctuaries were so formed in themselves and so placed in relation to the landscape and to each other as to enhance, develop, complement, and sometimes even to contradict, the basic meaning that was felt in the land (Scully 1962: 3).

Nature and culture, in this account, are not separated.

It is hard for the archaeologist to understand how prehistoric people might have conceptualised their relationship to the land, hard to understand the 'world views' of a people without written history. There *is* evidence, but the imaginative leap in interpretation that Scully's thesis demands is alien to archaeological training. In this section, which is both longer and more tentative than those that follow, I begin with some ethnographic and historic conceptualisations that may help towards an understanding of prehistoric Stonehenge.

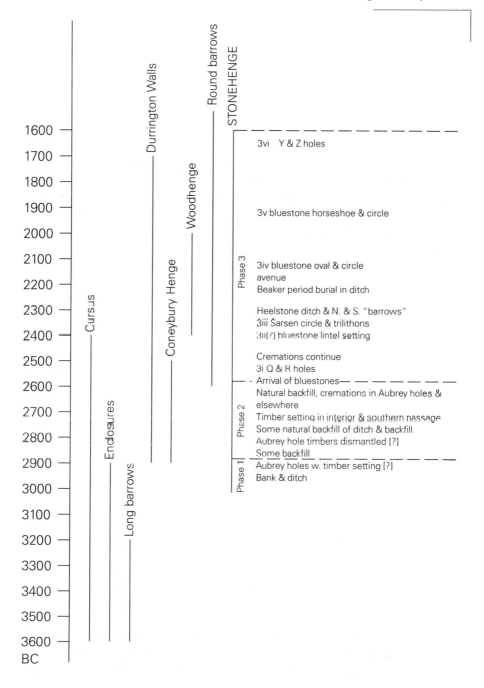

Figure 4 Calibrated dates for some of the Neolithic and Early Bronze Age developments in the Stonehenge landscape
(after Cleal, R. et. al. 1995: 467 and Darvill, T. 1997)

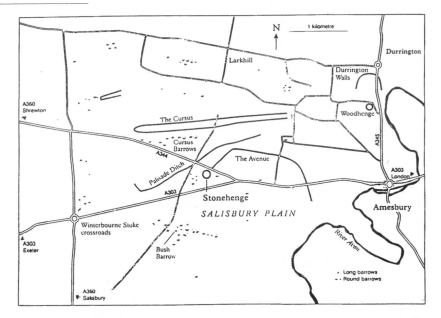

Figure 5 Map of the Stonehenge Area. Auto-critique: no contours so no feeling for the lie of the land

Taçon, talking of Arnhem Land, Australia, discusses the way in which not only the topography, but also the substance of the landscape, empowers. He talks about the way in which the aesthetic or symbolic values influencing the manufacture of stone tools relate to ideas of power. These ideas include:

> the power of the Ancestral Beings that created the landscapes, including rocky outcrops used as quarries; the power and properties of stone as a substance, and especially quartz and quartzite; the power of initiated males who made, used and controlled access to certain stone tools . . . Some of this power was harnessed during the manufacture and later was heightened through ritual, story-telling and other practices (Taçon 1991) (Figure 6).

This resonates with Thomas's comment that objects embody many associations,

> the raw material and its symbolic connotations, the place from which the thing originates, the history of manufacture, the marks of use and traces of wear are all together responsible for the way in which an artefact manifests itself, and the way in which it is understood socially (Thomas 1997).

Figure 6 Stone quarry with contemporary painting of a kangaroo near Mangalod on the Mann river in Central Arnhem Land, northern Australia, 1975 (photo H. Morphy)

And it resonates, too, with Jackson's comment, in the quite different context of early church-building, that 'the early church fathers interpreted the quarrying, the shaping and polishing and putting into place of the stones used in building the churches in theological terms' (Jackson 1984). There is a further parallel between Taçon's observation, in the Aboriginal context, that objects exhibiting brightness (fat, blood, quartz, quartzite, cross-hatched white pigment) are both aesthetically pleasing and spiritually charged, and Sedlmayr's perception that the stained glass and stone of an early medieval cathedral act on one another to: '"shine", "sparkle", "glitter", "dazzle" . . . It would be false to say the cathedral denies its stone character. It keeps it throughout, only it idealizes it by giving it a gemlike, transfigured, vibrant, cryst-alline aspect' (cited in Jackson 1984).[2]

Taçon, in his conclusion, notes that in many societies, bone and stone are symbols of persistence and immortality, and that 'the earth is a symbol of fertility and femaleness because of the plant life it nurtures and supports. As a counterpart to the earth's more fragile produce, hard stone was perceived as a male phenomenon' (Taçon 1991). Eliade suggests a more complex interplay between male and female substance:

> The stone parentage of the first men is a theme that occurs in a large number of myths. Deucalion threw 'the bones of his mother' behind his back to repopulate the world. These 'bones' of the earth-mother were stones; they represent the *Urgrund*, indestructible reality, life and holiness, the matrix whence a new mankind would emerge (Eliade 1962: 43).

In this account, as in many others, we find one of those ritual elisions through which processes of social reproduction (the *male* 'stone') come to encompass – to make possible – biological reproduction (*female* 'earth').

We can ponder an empowering and often gendered landscape, while recognising that the gendering of the elements will surely vary across cultures, and meanings will shift and change depending on context,

---

2. Howard Morphy (1989) explores in fine detail, in the context of the Yolngu of northern Australia, the brightness of a cross-hatched picture, of fat, blood, red ochre and feathers, the lightness and joy these engender, the way they connect with song and ritual, and how, as part of the sacred law of the ancestors, they empower both ownership of the land and those that take part in the ritual.

and on people's variable knowledge.[3] We shall also have to acknowledge that more fragile elements will be less visible in the archaeological record. Things that grow, that are fertile, may have formed an important counterpart to hard rock and white chalk. Though we have relatively few prehistoric timbers, we have the evidence of post-holes to show the importance of wood. Taken from trees that link the earth and the sky, used for fire and in building, wood (different woods) will have carried many meanings. Among the Zafimaniry of Madagascar, wood is metaphorically associated with the development of people, bones of ancestors and other social transformations. 'What fascinates the Zafimaniry about wood', Bloch suggests,

> ... is that it originates as a living thing which, nonetheless, ultimately gains far greater permanence than human beings. It is because of this fact that they use hard wood to make the houses and villages into which the living become transformed . . . It would seem however that, because it originates in a living thing, it is, although very hard and permanent, not eternal. Stone is seen as eternal but, on the other hand, it is not, nor ever has been, in any way alive (Bloch 1995).

Bearing these general points in mind, what of prehistoric Stonehenge? I want to consider briefly the changing relationship of monuments to the land – to forces within or above the surface of the land, and to the power of particular 'natural' substances such as wood, chalk, sarsen, bluestone and water. I also offer the tentative suggestion that, as part of the layered meanings that people gave to their world, there may have been a gendering of monuments, artefacts, and landscape.

We can start with an origin myth. There are three white spots in the Stonehenge carpark. They mark three large post-holes that once held three great pine timbers. On the same alignment is a pit that the excavators thought might have been a tree-hole. Recent carbon-14 dates from the post-holes show that they are extraordinarily old. They fall within the eighth millennium BC.[4] It would seem that gatherer-hunters, moving around the landscape, attached meaning to certain places and features, and returned to them over and over again (Bender 1985). From these bits of information, Tim Darvill creates a Stonehenge origin myth: it was the tree that gave significance to the place (Darvill 1997). The

3. The varied ethnographic accounts assembled in Carmichael et al. (1994) all emphasise the sacredness of natural features – of trees, cliffs, lakes, caves, rock fissures and so on.

4. 8820–7730 and 7480–6590 cal BC (Cleal et al. 1995: 43).

ur-tree. Gatherer-hunters came to this place and put up three great timbers in line with the tree. The timbers stood for centuries, until they finally rotted away. The place was a place of remembering and myth . . .

Could myths and memories attach to a place for millennia? There is no evidence for any further marking of the place for several thousand years (although in the welter of post-holes in the centre of the enclosure, it would be very hard to distinguish more fugitive early wooden settings). And even around 3500 BC, in the Early Neolithic, when people began to build more durable monuments, nothing has been remarked at Stonehenge.

Earth and Chalk. Elsewhere in the landscape, in the Early Neolithic, in a world of open woodland, shrub and temporary clearances, where wild resources still formed a major part of subsistence, and people still moved with the seasons, long mounds and causewayed enclosures made of earth and chalk were built close to each other on higher ground (Bradley 1991; Cleal et al. 1995: 56; Richards 1990) (Figure 7). Barrett has suggested that within a long fallow economy with much seasonal movement, these were seasonal and communal 'places' in a landscape of paths, returned to over and over again (Barrett 1991; 1994: 144). Often, it seems, the long mounds were to be approached from lower ground, for, as Stukeley already noted in the mid-eighteenth century, walking up towards the mounds, their tops false-crest the sky-line

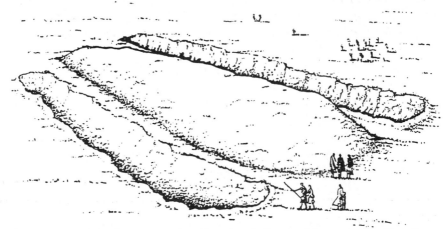

Figure 7 Neolithic long mound: taking the chalk *out of* the ground, piling the chalk *onto* the land
(drawing by Jane Brayne)

(Piggott 1985: 68). Thus they were placed in relation to the hills behind them (just as Silbury Hill, near the Avebury henge, related to the hills to either side).

As Thomas has noticed, it is not just that the white chalk is used to create features *on* the land, but that it is dug *out of* – it opens up – the land. Digging out, creating ditches, placing offerings, creates 'a set of relations of reciprocity with the earth itself' (Thomas 1997).

The dramatic chalk whiteness of the long mound and of the ditches and banks of the causewayed enclosures were reiterated on a larger scale later in the Early Neolithic. First, around 3100 BC,[5] in the parallel banks and ditches of the cursus and then, around 2900–2950 BC, in the circular bank and ditch enclosure at Stonehenge (Figure 8a). Moreover, the shapes of the earlier constructions – the *long* mound, the *circular* enclosure – were repeated and magnified in cursus and circle.[6] There was continuity in substance, shape, and – perhaps – in

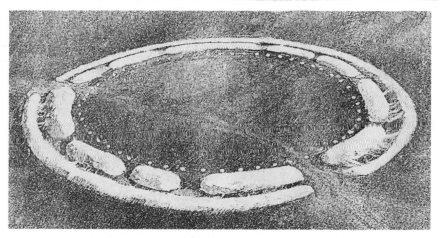

Figure 8a Stonehenge I, c. 3050–2900 BC. *White* chalk bank and ditch, circle of Aubrey Holes perhaps with timbers.
(from Anderson, C., P. Planel, P. Stone 1996: 4. Kind permission English Heritage)

5. The lesser cursus has dates of 3630–2920 cal BC (first phase), 3640–3040 cal BC (second phase), and 2890–2140 cal BC (destruction phase) (Cleal et al. 1995: 8). The greater cursus has a much later date which is either regarded as an anomaly, or is woven into the later Neolithic Stonehenge story (Darvill 1997).

6. In an interesting paper on the Breton Neolithic, Thomas and Tilley (1992) suggest symbolic links between different material expressions, from megalithic structure to axe and pottery. Many of these, including a strong link between long mound, menhir and stone axe, may hold for the Stonehenge area.

orientation: both the long mounds and the northeast entrance to the Stonehenge circle may have been aligned on the moon (Burl 1987: 65; Bradley 1991).

There was another very significant orientation within the landscape. The double chalk-banked Stonehenge cursus ran from Fargo ridge to King Barrow ridge for nearly 3 km across hill and valley (see p. 42). This line – perhaps a processual way, perhaps part of a song-line or an ancestral pathway – is referenced by other monuments. Sometime after the cursus had been constructed, the white circular bank and ditch at Stonehenge were built directly to the south of the centre point of the cursus. After several more centuries had passed, the Cuckoo Stone was placed on the line of the cursus 900m further to the east. And around 2500 BC Woodhenge was constructed on the same line, about 420m beyond the Cuckoo Stone.

Earth, chalk and *wood*. Although the evidence is somewhat tenuous (Whittle 1996), the Aubrey holes are now thought to date to the same period as the bank and ditch and to have held wooden posts (Figure 8a).[7] And then, between 2900 and 2400 BC, in the Late Neolithic, a proliferation of timbers went up – first at Stonehenge, and then, around 2500 BC, to the east at Durrington Walls and Woodhenge (Figure 8b). The timber settings within the Stonehenge enclosure are off-centre, and the plethora of timbers that cram the northeast entrance are concentrated towards the eastern end of the entrance, extending over the back-filled terminal of the ditch. Only a narrow passage is left, close to the western ditch terminal. It may be that the entrance is being re-orientated. It may even be that this re-orientation is radical, marking a move from a lunar to a solar alignment (but see Cleal et al. 1995: 145 and Darvill 1997 for other interpretations). Perhaps the earlier lunar orientation had been associated with the placing of cremations within the henge (though the dating is less than secure, see p. 56), and the solar orientation may mark a refocusing of rituals and ceremonies away from cremation and death towards affirmations of life and renewal.

By the time of the timber settings, the cursus had probably gone out of use, but now (or probably now – there are no firm dates) a great

---

7. Whittle (1996) notes that some of the new interpretations are rather tenuous. The Aubrey Holes could have pre-dated the bank and ditch, or followed them. And they may not have held posts. The timber structures may be the same age as the bank and ditch, or later.

Figure 8b Stonehenge II, c. 2900–2600 BC. The ditch and bank are no longer so white. A mass of timber settings has been put up inside the henge and within and just outside the northeast entrance.
(from Anderson C., P. Planel, P. Stone 1996: 5. Kind permission English Heritage)

trench was cut in the chalk and a close-set timber palisade was set within it (see Figure 5. Cleal et al. 1995: 161).[8]

Earth, chalk, wood, then *stone*. In the later Neolithic, starting around 2550 BC, and into the Early Bronze Age, through to about 1600 BC, stone replaces wood at Stonehenge (Figure 9a/b). Or, perhaps, for a while they worked alongside each other. Sarsen and bluestone complement white chalk. With the new earlier carbon-14 dates, stone-built Stonehenge overlaps in time with the massive timber henge to the east at Durrington Walls, and with the great stone-girt henge monument to the north at Avebury.[9] The people from Stonehenge and from

8. There are no carbon-14 dates for the palisade but the closest parallels are with the West Kennet palisaded enclosure which dates to the second half of the third millennium (Cleal et al. 1995: 161).

9. The interpretation of the new dates puts the first stone setting at about 2550 BC. This is phase 3i in which the bluestones are set up in the Q and R holes and then dismantled. Phase ii involves the construction of the sarsen circle and trilithons, perhaps coeval with another bluestone setting including the bluestone trilithons (phase 3iii). Phase iv has the rearranged bluestones set in a circle and an oval, and phase v has them set in a horse-shoe. Finally, in phase vi, which takes us to c. 1600 BC, the Y and Z holes are dug, presumably for the bluestones, but the stones are not erected.

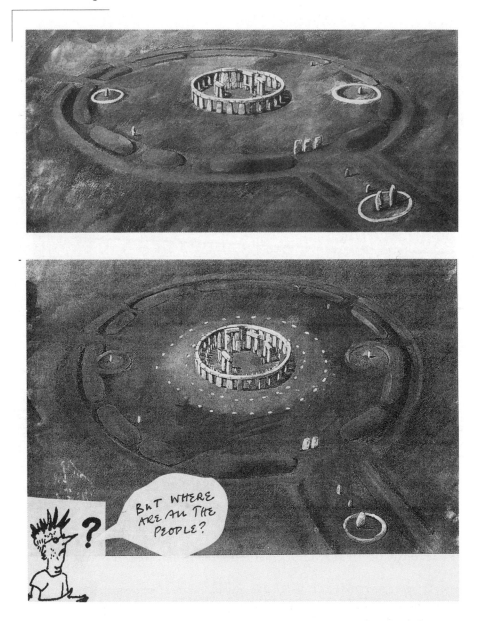

Figure 9a/b Two phases of Stonehenge III, c. 2600–1600 BC. Note the renewal of chalk: the small circular bank and ditch around the two Station Stones and around the two stones outside the northeast entrance. Later, one of the entrance stones is removed and a new bank and ditch surround the remaining Heel Stone. In the final phase the Z and Y holes were left unfilled.
(from Anderson, C, P. Planel & P. Stone 1996: 5/6. Kind permission English Heritage)

Avebury extract their sarsen stones from the same valley close to Avebury. The people from Stonehenge schlepp theirs for 30 km across relatively open downlands (Figure 10a/b). The people at Avebury leave their stones unworked though they may well choose them and place them carefully by size and shape. Perhaps the chosen stones were gendered: along the Avenue at Avebury long thin stones alternate with low wide ones.[10] At Stonehenge they work the stone, shaping, smoothing, perhaps pairing rough, pitted stone with smooth (Whittle 1997).

It is possible that at Stonehenge and Avebury (and also at other henges) there was a still more grandiose symbolic gendering. Where before the *long* mound complemented, but was separate from, the *circular* enclosure, so now, in the later Neolithic and Early Bronze Age,

Figure 10a Pulling a sarsen across the downs – 1995
(photo J. Richards)

10. Among the Madagascan Zafimaniry, megalithic stone monuments are set up to commemorate a parent: 'If the person commemorated is a woman, the monument takes the form of three stones, like a hearth, covered by a large flat stone by way of a cooking pot. If the person is a man, the monument recalls the central post of the houses and looks a little like a menhir' (Bloch 1995).

So interesting!

Figure 10b Pulling a sarsen across the downs – 1995
(photo J. Richards)

first the *upright* timbers and then the stone settings complement – and
are contained within – the *circular* ditch and bank.

At Stonehenge, the smaller bluestones come by river and across land
either from the Preseli mountains over 385 km away in southern Wales,
or from a dismantled monument en route. They too are worked and
reworked. This bluestone was clearly highly valued and very powerful:
two groups of stone axes are made from it and circulate widely, and at
Stonehenge bluestone chips are placed in graves and below mounds.[11]
Alongside the sarsen and bluestone, the chalk maintains its potency.
Interestingly, Whittle has suggested that the stepped verticality of the
bluestone and sarsen at Stonehenge might be conceptually linked to
the great tiered white mound of Silbury Hill close to Avebury (Whittle
1996).[12] And there are, or were, other great artificial white hills, one to

11. Some of these powerful bluestone chips may have circulated in Wessex long before
the bluestones were brought to Stonehenge. There are chips below Boles Barrow, 35 km
from Stonehenge, which considerably predate the first bluestone setting (Anderson,
Planel & Stone 1996).

12. The very earliest description of Stonehenge, by Henry of Huntingdon in 1130,
curiously suggests this tiered effect: 'Stageges (sic), where stones of wonderful size have
been erected in the manner of doorways, so that doorway appears to have been raised
on doorway; but no one can conceive how such great stones have been raised aloft, or
why they were built there' (cited in Anderson, Planel & Stone 1996: 14).

the east of Avebury in the grounds of what is now Marlborough College, another southward at Marden on the route between Avebury and Stonehenge, and perhaps another at Silk Hill, 5 km northeast of Stonehenge.

Often-times the *whiteness* of the chalk was re-emphasised. Thus the ditches at Stonehenge were, at different times, back-filled with clean white chalk. The white chalk was not only used in monumental constructions but was also carved into small objects such as axes, balls, and phalli which were carefully placed, 'particular combinations of material items and substances appear to have been appropriate for distinct types of locations' (Thomas 1997). Occasionally, among the many cultural juxtapositions, the gendering of objects becomes visible, like the placement, in the ditch at Stonehenge, of two chalk balls with a horncore.

There were also potent symbolic representations of artefacts: numerous axes, a dagger, perhaps an anthropomorph, were pecked on the sarsens. These symbols may also have been gendered, though not necessarily along the most obvious lines. There are, for example, carvings at the entrances to the more or less contemporary rock-cut chalk tombs in the Paris Basin of a female. She has breasts and a necklace and a fine *axe* slung round her waist. Interestingly, metal axes and daggers were rarely found together, the former were placed in votive offerings, the latter in graves (Bradley 1991). But on the sarsens, the dagger is placed close to two axes (Cleal et al. 1995, Figure 20) .

Earth, chalk, stone, *sky.* As part of the stone remodelling of Stonehenge, a pair of stones was placed beyond the northeast entrance (Figure 9a). One was soon removed, the other – the Heel Stone – was encircled with a ditch (Figure 9b). From the centre of the stone-setting, viewing between the pair of trilithons, the sun rose over the Heelstone at the Summer Solstice, and, turning round, it set between the two great trilithons at the Winter Solstice (Richards 1991: 128). 'Always over the shoulder . . . the opposed alignment of the midwinter sun' (Whittle 1996). Somewhat later the Avenue was built coming up to the northeast entrance: a bank and ditch with, perhaps, stones set at intervals along it.[13] On the last stretch, coming up to the henge, with the stones on the skyline, the Avenue follows the Solstice orientation.

Earth, chalk, stone, air, *water.* The Avenue swings round, over King Barrow Ridge and down to the river Avon – processional route, route

13. Suggested by small geophysical anomalies (Cleal et al. 1995: 506).

for the bluestones to be hauled from the river, and link between the elements. As Avebury was linked to the river Kennet, and the huge wood henge at Durrington Walls opened towards the river Avon, so the Avenue linked the stones to the water. It was also at this time, or perhaps earlier, that the one hundred foot deep Wilsford Down shaft was dug, and offerings were thrown down into the water.

Chalk again. The white chalk retained its symbolic potency through the millennia, reworked in different ways. In the Early Bronze Age period there was a final extraordinary reworking. Where the old long mounds had false-crested the hilltops, the linear cemeteries of small mounds constructed in the Early Bronze Age often silhouetted the sky-line surrounding Stonehenge. They hug the near horizon within what Cleal et al. have called 'the visual envelope' of Stonehenge (Cleal et al. 1995: 34) (Figure 11). Not only would the white mounds have stood

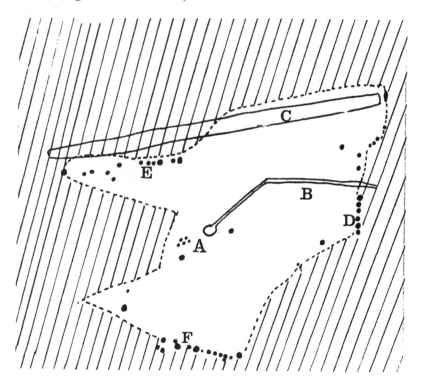

Figure 11 Stonehenge visual envelope. A = Stonehenge; B = Avenue; C = Cursus; D = New King Barrows; E = Cursus barrows; F = Normanton Down barrows
(simplified version of Cleal, R. et al. 1995: 36)

out, but, it would seem, stretches of chalk were stripped of their turf. For, when the great gales of 1990 upended the beech trees that capped the mounds along the King Barrow Ridge, the tops of the mounds were ripped open and it was possible to look down inside them. Some of the mounds had been capped and recapped with chalk. Others were built entirely of turf. These are very large mounds, and the surrounding soil is very thin. The removal of the turf to create the mounds would have exposed sheets of white bedrock.

EARTH – CHALK – WOOD – STONE – AIR – WATER

(reproduced by kind permission of Merrily Harpur)

Conceptual Boundaries within the Landscape

In their contemporary National Trust/English Heritage setting, the prehistoric monuments are grassed over, roped off, set apart. Although we know little about the Neolithic settlement, because so much of it was fluid and impermanent, it is clear the monuments were not segregated within the landscape. In the Earlier Neolithic the major area of settlement was probably along the King Barrow Ridge to the east of Stonehenge, and the long barrows and the causewayed enclosure were on the edge of more sparsely occupied territory (Harding 1991; Richards 1991: 21). Even so, the long mounds, causewayed enclosures, cursus, and the first bank and ditch at Stonehenge were all contained *within* the area of settlement and everyday land use (Richards 1984; 1991: 78). Clearance, flint working, planting and grazing washed up to the very edges of the monument.

Because settlements were so impermanent, we cannot easily get a sense of the ritual of everyday coming and going, but the evidence from the causewayed enclosures again suggests that things we hold apart, they combined. The enclosures were used for exchanges, for feasting and for burial. For at least some people, the funerary processes were long drawn out: after primary inhumation (perhaps in mortuary enclosures, like the one at Normanton Down), the skeletons were disarticulated and some of the bones, often the skulls and the long-bones, were placed in the ditches of the enclosures, others eventually came to rest in mortuary houses below the long mounds. Equally, the bones of animals used in ritual contexts, particularly oxen in the earlier Neolithic, were sometimes placed in the enclosure ditches, sometimes – specifically the skulls – in the mortuary houses, and sometimes, a little later, in the ditches associated with the henges. At Stonehenge large ox bones were placed in the ditch terminal close to the northeast entrance, and ox skulls brought in from elsewhere were placed in other sections of the ditch (Burl 1987; Cleal et al. 1995: 109; Thorpe 1984). Thus the rituals of life and death were not anchored in one particular context: they moved between contexts. There was, Thomas suggests, an homologous movement 'of people from place to place, of artefacts from hand to hand, of cattle between pastures, and of human bones between resting places' (Thomas 1997).

In the later Neolithic there seems to be the beginning of a drawing apart of the public and the domestic, and of the rituals of life and death. At Durrington Walls and Woodhenge, artefacts were absent from the area directly around the henges, even though they lay within a general area of quite intensive occupation (Harding 1991). Within the wood henges there was evidence of intensive exchanges, feastings and depositions, but, unlike the earlier enclosures, there were almost no human bones (Richards & Thomas 1984).

At Stonehenge, in contrast, probably at about the same time (though there is not a lot of dating evidence), there was little evidence of feasting, and very little pottery deposition. Instead, the Aubrey holes, with their timbers removed, were used for cremations, and other cremations were placed in the upper ditch and around the circumference of the monument, on and just inside the bank (Cleal et al. 1995: 145).[14] It seems to have become a cemetery. Perhaps it was the deathly counterpart to Woodhenge.

14. Despite the lack of C-14 dates, Cleal et al. (1995: 154) suggest that the cremations began around 2500 BC when the timber structures were in place, and probably carried on for some time after the stones began to be erected.

And again, at Stonehenge as at Durrington Walls, as the stones begin to replace the timbers, ordinary everyday life seems increasingly to hold its distance from the site. Where, in the earlier Neolithic, the settlement debris and activity areas had came right up to the circle, now, at around 2500 BC, the area around the monument is left empty, or at most is used only for grazing. Though the small field systems, more permanent and bounded, and the droveways and corrals, date mainly to the later Bronze Age, this more defined landscape may have begun to be established in the Early Bronze Age – but only at some distance, and out of sight of, the stones (Richards 1990: 263).[15] On the other hand, the Early Bronze Age round barrow cemeteries both hold their distance *and* reference themselves on the monument. There are at least ten cemeteries within a 6 km radius of Stonehenge (and more than a hundred isolated mounds), but very few are within 2 km of the stone circle. Many of the barrow cemeteries, particularly the fine Wessex ones, both claim the high skyline around the stones *and* look down towards them (Cleal et al. 1995: 489).

The Act and the Material Result

It may often have been the case, and there are good ethnographic analogies for this, that it was the process of *ritually working* the landscape, the acts of *making* and *depositing*, rather than the creation of an enduring end result, that was significant. It may well have been important to destroy the result, or to allow it to decay, because then it could be recreated in memory (Kuchler 1993). Rowlands notes that we often ignore the memory work involved in such actions because we tend to think in terms of linear time: *we* observe/perceive/learn and then recollect, and we need material markers to act as memory pegs. In contrast, unmarked practices – where something is buried or

15. Within the new Stonehenge volume there seems to be an agreement to differ between Allen who suggests that there were perhaps fields in the Early Bronze Age, and Cleal who believes that people were still quite mobile (Cleal et al. 1995: 169 & 166). Anderson, Planel & Stone (1996: 19) follow Allen and suggest that not only were there permanent boundaries, paths, tracks and fields at this time, but that manure was being used, and that this more intensive agricultural regime provided the necessary surplus that underwrote the labour-intensive monumental constructions. On the other hand, Whittle (1997) follows Cleal: 'built constructions [still] anchored collective allegiance to place against the tide of individual or small-group settlement mobility', and Richards (pers. comm.) is also adamant that this was still mainly a pastoral economy, and that there is no evidence of agriculture until 1000 BC.

destroyed – do not *embody* memories of past events but rather become *embodied* memories which are then reproduced or transformed as part of the negotiation of future relationships (Rowlands 1993).

Precisely because such acts leave no mark upon the land, they are not easy to find. Nonetheless there are examples. During the Earlier Neolithic, when the long cursus was being constructed close to Stonehenge, another smaller one was built to the northeast. It was built in two stages. In the second stage, the ditches were dug, the chalk flung up onto the banks, stone and antler tools were placed in the ditches – and then the banks were shovelled back (Richards 1991: 83). It seems that it was the act of digging and of deposition which was significant, not the creation of a feature. There would be memories, but the memories would play over something no longer visible. So too, in the ditches at Stonehenge. Stories would have wound themselves around activities that occurred within the ditches but which were swiftly covered over: the burning of substances in the segment close to the northeast entrance, the placement of antlers and large ox bones (Cleal et al. 1995: 109).

Alternative Landscapes

At the beginning of the Neolithic, the long mounds were relatively small, and they housed a number of disarticulated inhumations, female and male, old and young. In the context of a landscape that was still extensively rather than intensively cultivated, where boundaries were fluid, and where there was seasonal movement with pastoral herds or in pursuit of wild resources, these mounds and their disarticulated contents may have been 'a fixed place and an architectural context' (Barrett 1994: 117) in which – through which – communal ownership of the land, mediated by the ancestors, was affirmed.

Several hundred years later, towards the end of the fourth millennium, long mounds were still being built. They were larger, but they only covered a single, usually male, articulated inhumation, or no burial at all. Some part of the acknowledgment of communality has disappeared. There seems to be a greater acknowledgement of individuals, and an exclusion of many 'categories' of people, most obviously women.

Already in the form and construction of the long mounds and causewayed enclosures, and more so with the cursus and early bank, ditch and wooden structures at Stonehenge, people's experiences were 'orchestrated' (Bradley 1993: 48), and there was the potential for social differentiation. Who went where? Who did what? Who saw what? The spaces and the entrances work to define and differentiate people's respective places in the world (Barrett 1994: 107; Thomas 1991). If, as recently suggested, the Aubrey holes originally held timbers, they would have encircled and to some extent enclosed the interior (Cleal et al. 1995: 112). Later, between 2900 and 2500 BC, when the Aubrey timbers came down, parts of the interior were perhaps more visible, but other parts, with their dense settings of timber, became more secret. Whilst the mass of timber settings within the enclosure are not easy to decipher, it seems as though a timber passageway led from the southern entrance towards the interior circular timber settings and had a blocking facade at both ends (Cleal et al. 1995: 483). At the same time, a crush of timbers went up in the northeast entrance leaving only a narrow passageway; whilst, outside this entrance, beyond a timber-setting across the Avenue, a massive close-set timber palisade blocked the view from (or to) the west (Cleal et al. 1995: 482).

Who, in this circumscribed world, walked through the narrow entrance and the passageway? Who moved around within the circular settings? Who placed the cremations? Who knew in intimate detail where to go and what to say and do? People's abilities to do things, to be in certain places, would have changed through their life-time as they became initiated. But were there some people who always stayed at a distance?

Putting up the timbers at Stonehenge would have required a great deal of communal labour, and, later, putting up the stones would have required much more. It has been estimated that placing the southern timber circle at Durrington Walls would have required 11,000 work hours, digging the ditch would have taken another 500,000 hours. To the north, near Avebury, Silbury Hill would have taken 35 million basket loads of chalk and soil, or 18 million work hours to build (Burl 1979:133; Startin & Bradley 1981).

Did the monuments created by this labour increasingly serve to exclude most of the labourers? The great henge at Durrington Walls had a massive external bank, then a great ditch, and then small tight circular settings of post-holes. Within the henge there was 'an area of rigidly defined settlement activity, constructed and used in a manner embodying equally rigid ideological codes' (Richards 1990: 269). There were also tight concentric timber settings at the neighbouring smaller Woodhenge and Coneybury. At all these henges there is a suggestion of intense, circumscribed activity, and of a division between those outside on the great bank, and those half hidden within the tight inner circles (Richards & Thomas 1984). As Burl put it: 'One could look, but one could not see' (Burl 1979). Barrett has explored in some detail the way in which movement and orientation is part of the way in which authority – or lack of authority – can be defined, refined, sometimes even contested: 'At certain places, in front of certain backdrops and behind certain screens, words are spoken and others left unsaid, creating the discourse of a social practice' (Barrett 1994: 14). He points out that, through time, from the early Stonehenge bank and ditch, through the steady embellishment and the increased density of the concentric timber structures at Stonehenge and at Durrington Walls, and back to the rebuilding in stone of Stonehenge (which now seems at least in part to be contemporary with Durrington Walls), movement, operation and observation were increasingly restricted. The sense of exclusion at the reconstructed stone Stonehenge seems palpable (Figure 12). Already in 1655, Inigo Jones suggested that the henge was a barrier 'into which it was unlawful for any profane Person to enter', whilst, outside, 'the promiscuous common Multitude' attended 'the ceremonies of their solemn though superstitious Sacrifices' (cited in Burl 1987: 209). And Burl notes that the carved axes, daggers, and the (disputed) anthropomorph are in the most obscure part of the inner stone ring (Burl 1987: 205).

In our accounts of Stonehenge we have tended to think in terms of increasing hierarchy, and of leaders (see Figure 22). But perhaps these chiefs-and-followers scenarios are overly simple and we are imposing our own ideas of social order onto the past (see p. 90). Julian Thomas has recently suggested that, rather than a hard and fast hierarchy, there was a series of ritual contexts in which different people with different knowledges performed different activities:

> It seems far more likely that the social groupings involved in these spatially segregated practices were defined by a series of cross-cutting criteria. Thus some activities may have been restricted on the basis of age sets, some according to gender . . . some by membership of kin groups, some by agnation, and some by other sodalities such as hunting societies, sorcerers' lodges and so on . . . This is not to suggest that the later Neolithic should be characterised as egalitarian. Rather it may have been a period in which power and authority were relative to the context in which they were exercised (Thomas 1996: 178–9).

If this were so then, although there would have been social distinctions, people's sense of who they were and what they had to do would

Figure 12 In the nineteen-eighties *everyone* joined in the celebrations within the sacred stones. Was it like that in the third millennium BC – or did most people watch from outside like the tourists in the nineteen-nineties? (photo Alan Lodge)

fluctuate depending on the time and place and circumstances, as well as their life-histories.

People, differently placed, with different knowledges, would also have had more or less extensive and comparative landscapes. Today we see Stonehenge as a 'fixed' and bounded landscape, but, in reality, the landscape would have concertina-ed inwards and outwards, depending not only on the particularities of people's biographies, but also when, in the long prehistoric time range that we are talking of, you lived. Already at the earlier causewayed camps there had been exotic pottery and stone axes, mainly from southwest England, suggesting that some people had knowledge of distant places. But by the later Neolithic, in the time of the timber, and then with the sarsen and bluestone settings at Stonehenge, these stone axe exchanges were on a greater scale and the axes came from further afield. So some people must have known, even if at fourth or fifth hand, of Cornwall, Wales and the Lake District. Many of the ritual deposits of fine grooved ware, or the occasional engraved chalk plaques, have motifs – lozenges, spirals, meanders, dots and lines – almost identical to those used in the Boyne valley in Ireland and Skara Brae in Scotland (Burl 1987: 93). And again, for some people, there was not just the knowledge of a larger world 'out there', but also more intimate contacts, negotiations, meetings and ritual and feastings, with people in the Avebury area 30 km to the north, and with people along the route to the Welsh bluestones. It is hard for us to imagine this journeying and the encounters over three hundred km of wild terrain and a multitude of clanscapes – the rituals, the gifts, the stories, the fictive kin relations that must have been enacted. And did the people from the bluestone area, and from places along the route, then come to Stonehenge and see the stones set in place?

By 2100 BC, while the stones were still going up, some of the Stonehenge communities were beginning to use copper and bronze, and *some* of the people, within some of the communities, were meshed into extensive West European exchange networks. It would seem that the exchange and display of prestigious items was part of the way in which some people signalled and confirmed their status. Now, as never before, there was less masking of status, and certain people – in the first instance mainly male, but later both male and female – were individually buried, their bodies intact and surrounded by fine funerary paraphernalia, in flat graves or below round mounds. As Thomas points out, in the Early Neolithic the long mound had been the dominant element in the symbolic order and was associated with protracted communal rituals, while the human bodies were broken down into

[handwritten: shift from communal to individual]

constituent bones to be redeployed and rearranged (Thomas 1991). But now, in the Early Bronze Age, there was a single funerary ceremony that focused tightly on the individual, and, through the careful place-ment of mounds or secondary interments, on the individual's place within a descent line (Barrett 1994: 120). If authority, as suggested above, was still to some degree context- and activity-specific, the great variability in mound morphology and the increasingly formalised and differentiated grave assemblages found through the Early Bronze Age may mark subtle distinctions between people during life, or after death. It is also likely that these tighter statements about people's affiliations and descent go hand in hand with tighter control of the land, more land-intensive subsistence practices and increasingly physical bounded-ness within the landscape (Barrett 1991).

By the Early Bronze Age, people's experience of place and space would have been very varied. Some would have travelled widely and known many comparative landscapes. Others may not have moved far afield but, nonetheless, at certain times of year, would have met up with distant kins-people who came to celebrate at the great ritual centre of Stonehenge, perhaps accompanying the funerary corteges of their own people of renown.

Contested Landscapes

Human agency is often discussed in terms of 'negotiation' – a contemp-orary word that rather neutralises potential confrontation, resistance, or subversion. But these too are contemporary words that are perhaps inappropriate for societies that lack the heterogeneity, alienation, secularity and restlessness of our own. Some archaeologists opt for the more neutral word 'transformation', but that says little about how change occurs. At least sometimes, in any society, because people are differently located, have different conceptions of the world and make different demands, there will be tension and contestation. Thus while I have talked about the way in which movement through the landscape was increasingly controlled in the later Neolithic and Early Bronze Age, it is worth remembering that, to misquote Marx, people 'make paths as well as being made by them'. As Pred puts it,

[handwritten margin note: how do we know they do?]

> In following the steering rules generated by the particular alignments of physical barriers, in trudging a well trodden path, in creating short cuts and detours to interrupt the humdrum and the accustomed, in self-imposing obstacles and intentionally avoiding accessible pathways, in

making .. marks that are immediately eradicated . . . [a person makes] a
statement (Pred 1990: 185).

It seems reasonable to suggest that the move towards using the site
for cremations, or the back-filling of the ditch terminal, the screening
of the entrance way, perhaps the move from lunar to solar orientation
and so on, are not necessarily smooth transformations, and there may
well have been elements within the population that felt reluctant about
the changes. Indeed, until very recently, it seemed to be the case that
Stonehenge was semi-abandoned for several hundred years during the
later Neolithic, that the ditches silted, the cursus went out of use, the
long mounds were blocked up, and the main concentrations of settlement and ritual arenas moved to the easterly ridges and to the river
beyond. All of which might well signal antagonisms, and a rejection
of at least some part of an internalised, as well as an external, landscape.
With the more detailed excavation evidence and the new dates that
push the sarsen construction further back and suggest that there might
have been an overlap between timber and stone settings, this hiatus
has been questioned, and it is suggested that the abandonment was
short-lived (Cleal et al. 1995: 163). Nonetheless, there is evidence that
scrub had to be cleared from the bank and ditch, and that there were
changes. Cremations were, for the first time, placed in some of the
Aubrey holes and in the bank and ditch. It seems unlikely that such
changes were always comfortable.
We might also suggest that during the long period in which the stones
– sarsens and bluestones – were erected and dismantled, re-erected, re-
mantled, some of the re-setting may have played a part in the active
constitution and reconstitution of a less community-orientated, more
lineage-orientated society with potentially greater competition between
lineages. Around 1600 BC the last set of holes was dug (the Y and Z
holes), but the stones were never put in place.

Appropriating the Past

People use the past as part of the way in which they create a sense of
identity or identities, and they create links through myth and legend
with established places in the landscape. They may also use the past to
legitimate the present, or to mask change by stressing continuity. Thus
in the Early Neolithic, the radical shift from communal, disarticulated
burials towards individual, articulated burials was muffled by the
retention of the long mound, while the recutting and recleaning of

the ditches of the causewayed camps, and the addition of new circuits of ditches, created a link to earlier labour and construction (Bradley 1984; Edmonds 1993). Equally, the building of the great cursus was perhaps 'legitimised' by the construction of a very large but empty (at least of human beings) long mound at the east end. A little later, the first bank and ditch at Stonehenge echoed elements of the causewayed camps, including the digging of ditch segments, the creation of multiple entrances, and the deposition of ox jaws and skulls. But the activities carried out in this new place were different, there was no feasting, no placing of human remains, and the deposition of far fewer artefacts (Bradley 1991).

Later again, the stones brought on site to replace the timbers came empowered by earlier histories in far off places. The bluestones either came direct from the Preseli mountains from quarries long used for the manufacture of highly valued polished stone axes, or perhaps from a ritual site en route from Wales.[16] The sarsens come from the Avebury region, from a valley source that had already been used a thousand years earlier in the construction of the megalithic tombs, and then used again as elements of a powerful local ritual landscape within which the old wooden Sanctuary was reworked in stone and linked by the Avenue to the great henge at Avebury and to important places in the landscape en route.

At Avebury the stones were used in their natural state, at Stonehenge the stones were shaped using wood working techniques. At Stonehenge some of the stone settings seem to perpetuate the earlier (or perhaps in part contemporary) wooden settings (Cleal et al. 1995: 485).

Meanwhile, the carving of motifs on the inner faces of some of the sarsens 'borrows' from a tradition usually associated with megalithic tombs, and the repertoire of axes, dagger and, perhaps, female anthropomorph, span the Late Neolithic and Early Bronze Age.[17]

16. The bluestones show signs of tenons that have been battered away, and of mortice holes, suggesting that originally the bluestones were part of a lintelled construction (Richards pers. comm.)

17. The closest parallels for the carved 'anthropomorph' – if such it be – comes from the Breton Neolithic tombs. Such tombs, though they date to the Middle Neolithic, were frequently re-used for Early Bronze Age Bell Beaker burials, and there were certainly strong connections between Brittany and Wessex. The daggers and axes are similar to those that were in circulation as part of the prestige exchange network of the Early Bronze Age.

Up on the higher ground around Stonehenge, the Early Bronze Age cemeteries sometimes seeded themselves around long mounds, the last of which had probably been constructed a thousand years earlier.

Thus, in the Early Bronze Age, there is an imaginative and vigorous reworking of places, artefacts, and substances, of histories, stories, and memories from a sedimented past that spans at least two thousand years.

Conclusion

In the later Bronze Age, Stonehenge seems to have been more or less abandoned, or perhaps avoided. The Late Bronze Age settlements seem to hold their distance, and the field systems to the west are out of sight of the monument (Cleal et al. 1995: 339). There is very little Iron Age material and no evidence of Roman settlement in the vicinity. The Stonehenge monuments have lost their official power – they are no longer an arena in which power is legitimated by being linked with the ancestors or the gods. But perhaps the stark abandonment speaks to an unofficial, unofficiated, power. When the record re-opens we find that the Anglo-Saxons, who rarely bothered to rename natural landscape features, feel the need to lay claim to the Celtic Gôr y Cewri (Court of the Giants). It has become Stan Hencg (Jones 1990).

Discussing Raymond Williams's work in Chapter 1, it became apparent that our notions of landscape have to be historically contextualised, and that people's sense of place, their engagement and understanding of the world, depend upon cultural, socio-economic and political particularities. In this chapter, I have tried to move beyond the taken-for-granteds of our own experience and engagement with the land to explore utterly different prehistoric landscapes. The chapter was written somewhat across the grain of historical narrative in order to provide a more multi-faceted understanding of how people's experience of the land is shaped and changed, and the way in which the land engages with experience, rather than simply reflecting it. Though I do not mind forgoing a stronger sense of linear change, I am concerned that, in holding the facets apart, I risk losing their interrelationships. There is a danger, which I hope the reader will have circumvented, that 'feeling' (as in the section on the indivisibility of nature and culture) and 'structure' (as in the more politically and socially orientated sections) have been pulled too far apart. On the one hand, talking about 'appropriation' and 'contestation' only begins to make sense if we have some small understanding of the symbolic universe that is being appropriated. On the other, the empowering of the stones, or other elements in nature, is dependent upon the particularities of the social, economic and political relations, and is part of the process through which people are both created by, and creators of, the world in which they live.

Dialogues 1: Prehistoric Stonehenge Landscapes

Dialogue with Mark Edmonds

Mark Edmonds's most recent book is Stone Tools and Society *(1995). He is particularly good at not losing sight of how people make a living – the practice, the rituals and mythologies that surround day-to-day existence. I knew that Chapter 2 had been thin on day-to-day subsistence activities, so I wanted to talk about that. But as you'll see, we also talked about a lot of other things . . .*

It's mid August and we're walking up the Avenue towards Stonehenge. Looking up towards the Stones and the adjoining visitors' centre, it looks like some great festival. The car park and the over-flow field are full to bursting, there's a marquee and, stretched across the horizon on both sides of the fence, are throngs of people. But where we are there's no one. And yet this was the way that, at least on feast-days and ceremonies, people would have approached the stones.

Mark: This is how to see the place isn't it? From here you can see the Heel Stone – it was one of a pair. Lying outside the circle, these were the only two stones that weren't shaped. These stones, like the banks of the Avenue, guide your movement and orchestrate your view. They direct your attention through to the middle of the inner circle and frame what would have been a focal point for many of the ceremonies. And this is really almost the only approach where the monument is properly sky-lined . . . (Figure 13).

Figure 13 Moving up the Avenue, the stones sky-lined on the horizon (photo P. Basu)

BB: *Coming up this way makes you realise that the views we usually get, driving down the A303 or walking from the visitors' centre give a completely wrong impression. The stones look small, set in a huge shallow basin, rather than sky-lined . . .*

Mark: That's why people often think the stones are smaller than they expected. It makes it hard to grasp that, at one level, the monument's very simple: approached along the Avenue, it links the earth and the heavens, and at the Solstice the sun itself moves along the same path that people would have walked.

BB: *But of course, earlier on, the timber constructions and the pathway would have angled differently . . .*

Mark: True, but the main thing is to let visitors recognise that there were conventions that shaped how people could approach, walk in procession and move into the interior of the monument . . .

BB: *With the new dates, much of this more circumscribed landscape is being pushed back into the later Neolithic (Cleal et al. 1995).*

Mark: Yes, I guess so, and the revised phasing is obviously important. But we've hardly even begun to interpret the new findings.

BB: *Meaning?*

Mark: We think in such gross terms. This harking on about 'phases' makes it hard to realise that this place was being visited, worked and reworked at the timescale of people's lives. Sure, there were times when the site was proscribed and choreographed. That's why all the new evidence of the timber settings is so exciting. But there would have been other times when encounters were less formal and involved a different roll call.

       Part of the problem is the legacy of socio-evolutionary models. We still tend to assume that the creation and use of these monuments relates to political authority at a regional level – at the level of paramount chiefs if you like. But maybe something like that only lasted a generation or two. Probably, more often than not, structures of political authority oscillated around something more akin to Big Man systems. And also, the use of the site would have been keyed into a much wider range of discourses than we allow for. Think about the earlier causewayed camps (which may even have been an inspiration for the first phase). The way they work at different levels of social integration – local, regional, and so on – and the way they form a context for any number of different activities which probably don't always involve the same people.

BB: *Despite reading the* Stonehenge Environs Project[1] *and the recent* Stonehenge in its Landscape[2] *I still don't have a strong sense of the lived landscape, of people going about their business – what Ingold called 'task-scapes'[3]* . . .

Mark: Well, again, one of the problems is that we tend to look at the settlement patterns in abstract terms and contrast broad phases of settlement – earlier Neolithic, later Neolithic and so on – without taking them apart more locally.

If you look at the Environs Project, which is an incredible piece of work in many ways, there are all these dots on the maps. We assume that the varying densities of worked flint or whatever correlate with settlement. But what does it mean? Some of the scatters may be about small kin groups going about their business on a regular basis, returning to places over and over again. Others are about seasonal gatherings, different kin groups with their cattle and everything else, camped out around the monument for some great ceremony.[4] There were probably times when local groups came to celebrate, and other times when a more extensive company – distant kin and relative strangers – massed around the timbers and then the stones. You get a sense of the same thing with some of the barrows; maybe quite a small kin group was involved in the original burial, and then, after an interval of time, neighbouring groups got together, and the turf mound was erected, and maybe there'd be more burials.

We need to try and write a biography of the landscape. Dots on the map, contours on the page don't establish a sense of inhabited landscapes or lived topography. All the lithics picked up during the survey could tell us plenty about different sorts of stone-working activities undertaken in different places. There are some places, like over at Wilsford Down, where you've got lots of tool production and evidence for people getting hold

1. Richards (1990).
2. Cleal et al. (1995).
3. Ingold (1993).
4. Thrift & Pred (1981) talk about the way in which 'the project-based ties of people to a locality and to other people in the locality are strong and interwoven and are continually reinforced by the everyday activity-experiences of living', and of 'the biographies of not only people and families, but also animals, institutions, and all other man-made and natural objects . . .'

of stone. Other places the activities are more varied . . . What are the biographies of these places? [5] How do their associations with certain practices change, or stay the same, over time? We need half a dozen PhDs trying to do more taskscape- orientated work using the waste material. Julian starts to do this in his Batsford book.[6] There he allows himself to say more about a landscape that he knows well . . .

BB: *It's a problem though – a taskscape when you've still got very few clues as to where the paths were, or the temporary settlements and woodland clearances. Obviously if you can begin to say: 'ah, this is where they were knapping – this is the sort of tools they were making'; 'this is a place that they came back to again and again' you begin to get a sense of intimacy . . .*

Mark: It's a start . . . But again, I don't think the problem lies with the data. I think the problem is that we look for settlement or the absence of settlement and that's it. We don't think about the complexity of routine life. Routines carry people between different places at different times and in different combinations. And, over time, the routines get renewed and reworked in various ways. As archaeologists we should begin to take these taskscape routines apart. It's frustrating that we don't do more, because it's the routines that provide the structures through which people understand themselves and their place in the world. And the routines create at least part of the context in which ceremonial times and contexts are encountered. Look at Chris Tilley's *Phenomenology of Landscape*.[7] His summary of the ethnography of several small-scale societies is a wonderful evocation of how the social is caught up in the tasks that people undertake. Think of the activities of the dreamtime beings in Australia – the formation of the land itself is often all about their labour. This binding of the economic and the social is brought out very clearly in the first half of Chris's book. The trouble is, he doesn't follow it through as much as he might in the case-studies. Take the discussion of the Dorset Cursus.

5. Mark worked with Richard Bradley on the prehistoric Langdale stone quarries. The particular form of the mountain was identifiable from miles away. They discovered that the most intensive areas of activity were in very inacessible, difficult places. They also had stupendous views (Bradley 1996).

6. Richards (1991).

7. Tilley (1994).

What are people doing when they encounter these monuments? How and why are they moving and in what company? I don't know if it's because we're desperate to avoid any form of economic determinism, but recent phenomenological work doesn't pay enough attention to the physical experience of practical life itself – the character and tempo of tasks, and the people they're undertaken with. We don't even say much about the physical experience of building the monuments. We talk about *dwelling*, but we don't ask what it's like to move with cattle, to open up new clearings or return to old ones . . . seasonality, meeting up with people (Figure 14).

Again, take the Dorset Cursus. It cuts a landscape across which small groups travelled on a seasonal basis between the lowlands, the pockets of pasture on the higher ground, and patches of clay with flints. These rhythms brought groups together at certain places and times long before the Cursus got started. Along the transitional zone, over the generations, as

Figure 14 Coppiced woodland
(photo M. Edmonds)

grazing and pasture became more important, they built the mounds – the ancestral houses. That's the context in which the Cursus is established and brings with it massive gatherings and new patterns of residence and movement.

BB: *That's nice. Trying to map the intricacy of movement.*

Mark: Yep ... I think technology like GIS (Geographic Information System) will help when it's more powerful, and cheaper and easier to use! You could navigate terrain maps, and then you could cross-cut these with various forms of multi-media. It's not a panacea for all our analytical problems, but for teaching and for the public it'd be brilliant. At the visitors' centre you could navigate the monument at a human scale at different times. And you could do the same with Callanish or the Stone of Stenness. You'd come to monuments from different directions, change the scale as you enter, appreciate how sites or people fall in or out of view, and how monuments look under different environmental conditions ... Stonehenge in a clearing, or in open grassland, or surrounded by fields ...

BB: *And then you have to build in the dialogue between present and past – us to them, and them to their real and imagined ancestors.*

Mark: That's right. One thing that struck me looking at the sequence of maps in the Environs Project: when you reach the so-called after-life of the monument, you get the lattice pattern field-systems of the later Bronze Age and they're *still* respecting the monument. They don't encroach. The monument may not be actively used in rituals, but it still occupies a place in myth and oral tradition. A place where ghosts live – they're no longer your ancestors, but they're still very powerful. You get it with barrows too, albeit on a different scale. Some of the Early Bronze Age cemeteries are sky-lined from Stonehenge. The genealogies of these places were grounded in references to a monument established a thousand years before. When you look at the medieval map, the cultivation comes in much closer. Mind you, not all places retain the same sacred or mythic qualities – there's a barrow at Durrington that's capped with flint-nodules that get re-used as a flint source later on in the Bronze Age.

BB: *That ties in with something that both Ronald Hutton and Peter Ucko commented on (p. 136 and 139) – that medieval people, or most medieval people, often had no interest in the stones, and also, that it's not just that places accrete new meanings, but that there are times when they drop out of people's consciousness ...*

Mark: That's right. At Knowlton, there's an early church in the middle of the henge, so maybe there are strong references to local myth and invented traditions – drawing on them, changing them. Whereas at Long Meg in Cumbria there's a wonderful ridge-and-furrow system that runs straight through the monument . . .

BB: *One of the interesting things about the new chronology is that it suggests that instead of the stone version of Stonehenge following after the timber henges at Durrington Walls and so on, it's actually partly contemporary with them. And it had its own timbered history before, or alongside, the appearance of the first stones. Somehow it makes that use of wood technology – tenon and mortice, tongue and groove – more immediate, and highlights that moving from wood to stone must have had huge significance . . .*

Mark: The working in stone – which is so much more resilient – has to be about making a statement about a more distant future. You're projecting the thing much further. It'll stand or endure for a lot longer, and so will all the relationships that are bound up in it.

BB: *I like Alisdair's comment: 'the contemporary made eternal in stone'.*[8]

Mark: There must be plenty of other dimensions to the symbolism of using stone rather than wood, not least where (and who) it comes from. One of the things that's nice about the new Stonehenge volume is that it confirms the density of varied timber arrangements – facades, screens, and other settings which control movement and vision. So there are connections between what's going on at Stonehenge and at other henges in the area.

BB: *It's interesting, too, that the new dates seem to suggest that the sarsens coming from the Avebury region, are coming from close by another thriving, ceremonial centre. They're being moved from a source that's close to one large living ceremonial centre to another, equally living, ceremonial centre, but they're using the stones in very different ways. It seems now that the differences between the two centres aren't so much about changes through time but about cultural preferences and decisions . . .*

Mark: Yes, the importance of the local tradition. I keep thinking of that book by Barthes, *Cosmologies in the Making*,[9] in which he

8. Whittle (1996).
9. Barthes (1987).

shows how communities linked by what we might regard as a shared cosmology actually interpret that order in lots of different ways. Things that we might assume would be absolutely solid and fundamental are actually quite flexible from one side of the hill to the other. In the space between Stonehenge and Avebury you've got people bound by close kinship, and others linked by more disparate ties. You've probably got raids and rustling and maybe even blood feuds.

BB: *And yet these people would know about each other, maybe even attend ceremonies together . . .*

Mark: That's right, and through acts of building and elaborating these monuments they'd create new connections between people – close kin, distant kin, relative strangers. That's what I mean about the problems that come from concentrating on political authority. These places are as much about the reproduction of horizontal ties between communities as they are about the prestige and renown of individuals. Imagine a 13-year-old girl living a few miles to the east of where Amesbury is now. Think of the drama attached to the occasion of coming to a place like Stonehenge for the first time. All those people, hundreds certainly, thousands maybe. If you've spent most of your life seeing no more than a hundred people or so, that sheer press of people would be incredible . . . People with dialects that were unfamiliar, dressed or decorated in different ways . . . You'd be constantly finding ways to make connections – real or fictive – not just with living people, but with past generations, through the ancient monuments all around you . . .

BB: *Sounds just like Hilary's account of coming to her first Free Festival! (p. 199). Just imagine the provisioning of those meetings . . .*

Mark: The giving of food to others on these occasions would be so important . . . one lot of people camped here, one there, the cattle getting mixed up . . . All these things would have powerful metaphoric qualities for the way people understood a social world that went beyond the horizons of close kinship. These were the formal and informal exchanges that went hand in hand with the stories that were heard by some within the stones . . .

Dialogue with Chris Tilley

Chris Tilley wrote A Phenomenology of Landscape (1994), *a book that has greatly influenced recent rethinking on prehistoric landscapes. We have been working, together with Sue Hamilton, on the Early Bronze Age settlements of Leskernick on Bodmin Moor.*

Chris has hardly ever visited Stonehenge, so perhaps it was a bit unreasonable to ask him to produce a phenomenological scenario. But we thought we would see what happened if we walked the landscape. It was a fine day in February, and he brought his small twins along. Walking with one each strapped to our backs we got to know the contours of the land! (Figure 15)

Although they were unaware of it, there was a dialogue going on between Chris and Mark Edmonds (p. 73).

Figure 15 Chris Tilley with Alice and Benjamin
(photo B. Bender)

We're standing in the Stonehenge car-park (Figure 16, point I).

BB: *I know you don't much like Stonehenge, but why?*
CT: One of the reasons is because Stonehenge has lost its aura of the past, it's much more a contemporary monument. That's because of the car-park, the thousands of people there, all the information signs, and the guards and the fencing. Also all the struggles over it. It's a site that's peopled, and a site that's contested. I find it really distracting – the mêlée and circus. In all these respects Stonehenge is as contemporary, say, as Canary Wharf. But, of course, for all the same reasons Stonehenge is incredibly interesting, the way in which it spawns more and more and more discourses – including your book! In a sense it interests me more on paper than being here, seeing its material reality.

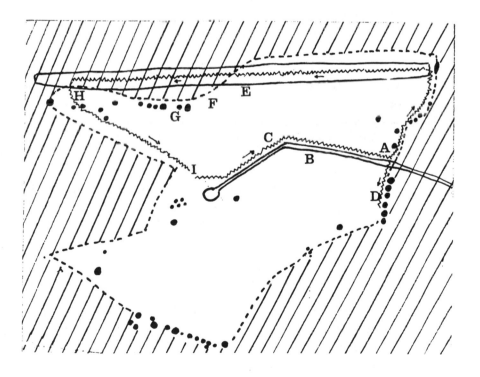

Figure 16 Walking the Stonehenge landscape. Points A to H are stopping places en route

BB: *So it's nothing to do with the fact that you find it over-bearing or over-weaning in itself?*

CT: Well, another thing about it is that it's totally unique, and in some sense I don't react to the scale and the size of it in the way that I would to a much more modest stone circle. On the other hand I can't say I find it a very impressive site. It's always much larger in the imagination than it is on the ground. I'm always a bit disappointed. I feel, which is contradictory, that it ought to be *more* impressive. But part of my reaction is because I've only actually been round the stones like all the visitors, I've never actually walked the landscape around Stonehenge.

So we start walking from the north-east entrance, following the Avenue first on its north-east axis and then as it swings sharply East up onto the King Barrow Ridge (Figure 16, point A). We stop and look back from the ridge and try to reconstruct what people would have seen if they'd walked in the opposite direction from us – moving down from the ridge along the Avenue and then swinging up towards the stones.

CT: From here the monument is very visible, but at first, as you walk down from the ridge, it's cradled within the landscape. Then, as you descend into the Stonehenge Bottom valley (Figure 16, point B), it becomes more and more sky-lined. The landscape beyond disappears, so you become more focused on the monument until, in the dip, it goes out of sight for about 50 metres. Then, as you turn up the Avenue towards the monument it becomes sky-lined again (Figure 16, point C), and it's only when you reach the monument that you again see the wider landscape. It's as if your attention becomes more and more focused on stones themselves, particularly when you reach the last section on the solar axis.

BB: *It's an extraordinary trick of perspective: when there is landscape behind the stones they immediately seem much smaller. Twenty metres on, with the sky behind them, they increase dramatically in size.*

CT: Another thing that strikes me, particularly in comparison with other areas in which I've worked on the landscape – southern Sweden, Wales, Cornwall and Dorset – is the wide open landscape of the setting and the absence of hills. In other stone circles I've looked at, the hills near to them are obviously important. They form a visual backdrop, an integral part of the power and theatricality of the monument. Stonehenge is in many respects the reverse of this. The absence of hills means you become much more focused on the stones themselves. There isn't the same dialectic between the monument and the local topography which is much more mute and recessive.

We sit on one of the large King Barrow mounds, feeding the babies (Figure 16, point D).

BB: *If you wanted to work with this landscape, how would you approach it, what sort of questions would you ask?*

CT: First thing, I'd be interested in the stones in relation to their entire landscape. I'd walk up and down the Avenue, up and down the cursus, around the barrows. I'd try to build up an intimate knowledge of the landscape-setting through walking from one place to another, looking at views, the intervisibility between features, what things go out of sight, or come into sight at various points. This all takes an incredible amount of time. When I first come here, I wouldn't actually be recording anything, I'd be walking around. And then I'd go back, walking and stopping every couple of hundred metres to make very detailed notes. I'd use a video and cameras. That's how I worked on the Dorset Cursus. When I finally started making notes it all came out very fast, but it required weeks of preparation. Over time, your perception and cognition of the landscape gradually change and deepen. It's nothing that you can force – you keep on finding more and more things. I think that if I spent two weeks walking round here I'd probably find Stonehenge an incredibly interesting place.

Doing a phenomenology of the landscape involves the intimacy of the body in all its senses. What I mean is that it's synesthetic, an affair of the whole body moving and sensing – a visionscape but also a soundscape, a touchscape, even a smellscape, a multi-sensory experience. GIS has become very popular lately, everyone seems to want to do it, but basically it can only produce an abstract knowledge. It can't reproduce a sense of place acquired through being *in* place.

BB: *One of the problems, though, with a phenomenological approach, is that a landscape is always cumulative and reworked. This is a contemporary landscape. We're sitting on one of the mounds on the King Barrow Ridge. For a lot of the time that people were using the monument the barrows weren't here. When the stones were being put up the banks of the cursus had already grassed over, and the cursus had become a place of memory . . .*

CT: I think you have to start off with what you can see around you today. Pretend that everything was contemporary. Then as you build up an intimate familiarity you can start imagining it without the barrows or whatever. For the time before the timber or stone settings you'd think more about the topography, the lie of the land, and then you'd superimpose elements like these barrows to get a changing perspective on the monument itself.

BB: *But then there are the invisible activities. We've just walked over dozens of large fresh mole-hills with bits of flint tumbling out of them. A lot of those flints are about people being in the landscape.*

CT: This isn't an answer to your question – but looking over towards Stonehenge now, there are all those people wandering round it. In one sense that is how you should see it.

BB: *The same ones you hated when you saw them in the car-park!*

CT: It's better to see them at a distance than to be amongst them and see all the cameras being taken out. But there is a very real problem with envisaging the land being tilled and people moving around doing everyday things. I think that we can relate much more to the symbolic ritual and social power of the monuments for the people, than to them moving around on a day-to-day basis. Thinking about the people must entirely be a work of the imagination, without the tangible visual clues that the monuments provide today. Even if you can't see the cursus you can follow its course and see where it goes and what it does, how it relates to a wider landscape and monuments that would or would not have been there at the time of its construction and use.

BB: *A different sort of question. You're writing a book on metaphor. In this book I only rarely use the word. How would you want to use it in the context of thinking about the stones?*

CT: If you look at the discourse around Stonehenge you'll find that it's fundamentally metaphorical, in that one understands Stonehenge in relation to other types of stone circles and monuments. The essence of metaphor is basically a mapping from one domain with which you're familiar onto another, unfamiliar, domain. Part of our understanding of the significance of Stonehenge is its difference from other types of stone circles that are broadly contemporary. It's a process of analogical reasoning. Stonehenge is obviously a metaphor for power in the past, and is now a metaphor for power relations in the present with the guards and the fences. We're not so much making literal statements about Stonehenge, as poetic statements. Stonehenge becomes a trope by which we understand the past, and by which we understand our relationships in the present. It lives through its relationship to ourselves and others. We don't have to foreground metaphor, it's just a constant basis of our work.

One thing that interests me about metaphor as a form of interpretation and explanation of things is the way it brings forth new ways of understanding, illuminates things. It provides – to use a metaphor – our doorway to the past. Understanding the ways in which we constantly use metaphors enables us to understand archaeological discourse in a different way and provides a way of making fresh constellations of connections and linkages that enable us to produce different, perhaps more relevant, and certainly more self-reflexive pasts.

We move off, walking the cursus, moving westwards. We get half way along (Figure 16, point E).

CT: Both ends of the cursus end on high land and are intervisible. About a third of the way along (from the east end) it dips down into this watery valley. A transition point where you cross water. Looking south, the Avenue crosses this same valley, and then turns abruptly towards the stones. The Avenue, after it turns, almost reiterates the line of the valley, the line of transition. In the first section of the cursus – the easterly section – the cursus is sky-lined with dramatic views to both sides. When its banks were built they'd have blocked out these views. It seems to be sited very strategically.

BB: *Looking up towards it from the north or south would also have been very dramatic – a long sky-line of white chalk. When I was thinking about the cursus I didn't think about it in terms of these immediate visual, tactile encounters, I thought of it more as marking a significant pathway, perhaps an ancestral pathway, because of the way the orientation continues on, marked by the Cuckoo Stone and then by Woodhenge.*

Moving West beyond the watery valley (Figure 16, point F):

CT: In the section beyond the watery bottom, it's almost as though you've become inward focused rather than outward focused, in that there's higher land both to the north and the south and the cursus seems to be running along a sort of gulley, mimicking the lie of the land.

BB: *And now there's the line of round barrows which follow the line of the cursus (Figure 16, point G).*

CT: It appears as if these barrows presence the cursus. They're presence-ing the past, the cursus, in relation to Stonehenge and making the cursus, which would otherwise not be visible, visible in a Bronze Age form. The eastern end of the barrow line more or less marks the point where Stonehenge goes out of view.

BB: *You could turn that round. It's always said – and I've said it too – that Stonehenge lies south of the cursus at the midpoint. But actually Stonehenge lies south of the cursus at the point at which the cursus comes into view.*

CT: Now we're in the last section towards Fargo Plantation (Figure 16, point H). We're getting much more extensive views to the north and south. It is curious how – on the plan – the cursus narrows at both the east and west end, and there's a change in orientation towards the east end. It's not just a linear monument, it may be keyed into the landscape.

BB: *Yes, Tim Darvill[10] noted that the cursus is in three sections – it would be important to see exactly where the changes in orientation occur. It again emphasises the way in which archaeologists' surveys and maps always present a bird's eye – a God's eye – view of the land.[11] Sometimes that may correspond to people's conceptualisations of the land – a lot of Australian Aboriginal bark paintings have a bird's eye perspective – but what it can't do is give an intimate sense of an experienced landscape. The slight changes in orientation might well be linked to subtle topographical changes. The visibility envelope that Cleal uses in the new Stonehenge volume goes some way towards an experienced landscape (Figures 11 & 17, pp. 54, 85). It works because it records a landscape of distant views, of panoramas.[12] But it misses out, for example, that the stones go in and out of view along the Avenue. It can't record the visual impact of walking or moving around the land.*

Five hours, and two baby-feeds later, back in the car-park (Figure 16, point I).

10. Darvill (1997).
11. Barrett (1994: 9–12).
12. Cleal et al. (1995: 36).

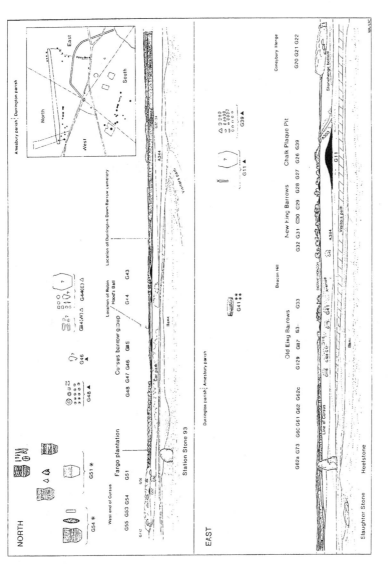

Figure 17 The view from Stonehenge looking a. north and b. east, showing grave goods from barrows on and within the near horizon

(kind permission of Wessex Archaeology)

CT: The view that the visitors who come to this dire car-park, and go through the tunnel, have is a totally degraded view of the stones. As one walks around the landscape the stones get lifted up; they become, paradoxically, much more impressive when you see them from further away. It's given me a totally different impression of Stonehenge – I like it a lot more now than I did before I came here today! But even in the landscape around Stonehenge there are the long linear fences that serve in part to control movement and access to the monuments, imposing a contemporary impediment to the way people would have moved between them and experienced them in the past. It would be nice if they were all removed in any new plan for the monument and its environs.

People came to me and said they had decided to stand still until they discovered the meaning of life. I said to them, 'Move about without delay, for the meaning is concealed in movement'.

Naguib Mahfouz 1997: 114

Dialogue with Ruth Tringham

Ruth Tringham, Professor of Anthropology at Berkeley, California, writes on gendered prehistory. In one particularly innovative paper she focused on a small Late Neolithic settlement called Opovo in northeast Jugoslavia. Within that settlement she looked at a house that had burnt to the ground, she set it in its wider context, and then briefly, as the flames caught hold, let the woman talk (Tringham 1991; see also 1994).

BB: *When I was writing Chapter 2, I felt that, although I began to talk about a gendered cosmos – gendered topographies, substances, elements – and about social differentiation, at the end of the day I couldn't, to any great extent, talk about* gendered *social relations. In contrast, in your work on the Late Neolithic site of Opovo, you really did try to focus on a gendered household . . .*

RT: There's no question – it's really difficult to gain knowledge about gendered activities . . . the important thing is that you should be *willing* to talk about gendered social relations. This means being willing to consider *multivocality*, which means microscale – or multi-scale – interpretation.

BB: *Even if you could work out who does what, the more important question is what meaning and importance are ascribed to these gendered activities.*

RT: Lewis Binford[13] used to say that if you couldn't prove something, the question wasn't relevant and shouldn't be asked. What the feminists are saying is that maybe we can't 'prove' gender, but we *must* ask questions because we know that gender, and tensions and conflicts around gender, are, and always have been, important.[14] We have to develop a theoretical framework through using our imagination in order to understand how and why gender might have been important, and then apply this understanding in the interpretation of the archaeological data. Alison [Wylie] has said that we're not just struggling with a feminist critique of archaeology which deconstructs, but with the construction of a feminist prehistory.[15]

So then the question is, what's distinctive about a feminist construction? Well, your emphasis on multivocality is feminist, but you do tend to concentrate on contemporary rather than prehistoric multivocality. Breaking the authoritative voice down, creating or imagining many voices and perspectives, and recognising that archaeologists also have different perspectives because of their different life histories, are all crucial.

The other thing that you have caught, both in this chapter and when you talk about Raymond Williams's work, is the idea of multiple scales of analysis – the importance of holding different scales of interpretation in your head at the same time, and weaving them together dialectically.

BB: *That's what you were trying to do at Opovo: moving backwards and forwards between a regional social geography, the story of a big settlement and a small daughter community, the biography of a house, the moment when it's burnt down, and the woman's story as she watches it go up in flames . . .*

RT: Yes. I had had some ideas, at a macro, more inclusive, scale, about the deliberate destruction of houses and the role of burning, and how that fitted in with periods in European prehistory of decentralisation, of dispersal of settlement, followed by aggregation. I

13. Lewis Binford was an early and very vocal spokesperson for processual archaeology. He espoused logical positivism.

14. Gero & Conkey 1991.

15. Wylie (1992a).

wanted her voice to be heard within that context, within that larger scale interpretation . . .

BB: *It's both a question of scale and of structure and agency. The woman acts out her story and, in the process, makes history . . .*

RT: I need to tell other stories – the man's story, the older woman . . .

BB: *One event: multiple ways of being part of it . . .*

RT: And, of course, I'm in the story too. Living and working in the Balkans I've seen the importance of individuals within the larger households. It's those people who are inside the house that are really making things happen.

BB: *You've created a narrative that's partly based on your understanding of the archaeological evidence, partly on a contemporary ethnography of the Balkans, and partly, maybe, on your own sense of what it's like to be a foreigner in a small village . . .*

RT: True! It is based on personal experience, as are all interpretations. If archaeologists would acknowledge that, it would enrich their interpretations. We need to accept that there's no definitive prehistory . . .we each construct different prehistories.

BB: *One of the things that bothers me is that in recent feminist writing there seems to be a stress on gender complementarity and a downplaying of gendered inequality. Maybe it's because we're worried about loading our sense of what constitutes inequality onto people who may have a very different understanding of their social relations. But it goes back to what I said at the beginning, the problem is not so much who does what, but how what they do is valued. You can show, as Meg Conkey did in the context of the Upper Palaeolithic Magdalenian, that an object may be used by a man but still contain a great deal of women's work.[16] That tells us something, but the question is, is the woman's input acknowledged? Is it valued? Rosemary Joyce talks about complementarity in the portrayal of men and women in Mayan iconography, and, yes, the women are portrayed, but most times they're kneeling to the man and making an offering![17] The women and their work are totally essential, but there's a power imbalance.*

RT: In a more recent paper, Rosemary [Joyce] does bring in hierarchy.[18] But I agree. What's also important is that inequality, for example in terms of how labour is valued, is not just along gendered lines, but is cross-cut by age and so on.

16. Conkey (1991).
17. Joyce (1992; 1993).
18. Joyce (1996).

BB: *Your narrative of the burning house does acknowledge gendered imbalances . . .*

RT: That's because I'd worked out a macro-scale model about how this imbalance was crucial to the fissioning and dispersal of settlements. But I need to create other scenarios. There should be one about someone who's in charge, but also not in charge, or someone else who thinks they're not in charge but in reality has quite a lot of power – the young woman sees herself as junior to the older wife, and yet she is in charge of her own life, she'll return to her old home . . .

BB: *That's it! Like everything else, power is ambiguous – in one context you have it, in another you don't! And that ties in with ideas of identity as something more relational and contingent (p. 35). And with the idea that, perhaps, at Stonehenge, there was more of a horizontal than a vertical hierarchy – people were empowered in one context but not necessarily another (p. 60).[19] Greber suggested something like that years ago in the context of the Hopewell Indians – that there were lots of different, and often temporary, leadership niches.[20] Trouble is, it still seems easier to nuance empowerment and authority than to gender it!*

RT: But see how important thinking at the micro-scale is! One thing you could have done more of is not just acknowledge the ambiguity of the evidence, but *celebrate* it . . . it would make the last sections of the prehistoric chapter, on appropriation and contestation, more comfortable.

BB: *It's true that I'm beginning to feel less comfortable about using that sort of language – 'appropriation', 'contestation'. It's aggressive. I used them because I wanted to create a thread that runs through the book (and through the Stonehenge exhibition) – that right from the start people would have different and complex understandings of both past and present, and they would use – appropriate – the past in many different ways, and they wouldn't always agree . . .*

RT: You could play with all the ambiguities: the past and the present. This is *your* interpretation, maybe you should link these ideas back to your intellectual autobiography . . . why do you care about these things? The Brits think that talking about oneself is narcissistic and uncool. Playing with the ambiguities permits your model to have resonance.

19. See Thomas (1996: 178–9).
20. Greber (1979).

BB: *A more fluid interweaving . . . multiple levels . . .*

RT: That's why you need hyper-texts! You get round the linearity of the written word, move between levels, press the button for Power, or Ambiguity, or Autobiography, not just dialogues but multi-logues! (see pp. 210–11).

Dialogue with Hilary, Wes, and Paul

Hilary Jones, Wes Burrage, and Paul Aitken are the three free festivalers who helped me put together the Stonehenge Belongs to You and Me *exhibition (see Chapter 6). Whilst we were discussing the exhibition (pp. 198–208), they also started to talk about the prehistoric chapter. Their comments seemed very worth recording . . .*

BB: *. . . What you're saying is that the way that I've interpreted social relations in prehistoric times mirrors contemporary political conditions?*

PA: Yes, and political fashion. In the 1980s there was a reinterpretation of everything, in particular around Stonehenge, as symbols of power and prestige. And then, when you move into the corporate nineties with multinationals that seem to have more influence than politicians themselves, there's an emphasis on large groups having appropriated things. The idea that things could have been done co-operatively, with enthusiasm, is completely missing. But there's no evidence at Stonehenge of fortified hide-outs, of haves and have-nots and all the rest of it . . .

BB: *I know what you're saying. And it's true that in the work we're doing at Leskernick on Bodmin moor, on a small hillside settlement which probably also dates to the later Neolithic and Early Bronze Age, everything suggests an intense relationship between people and stones, and everything also suggests a strong communal ethos. The passion for the stones and the ritual permeates every moment of their waking life, it's not just about feastdays and Sundays . . .[21] So in one sense I feel much more comfortable thinking about communal activity, but on the other hand Leskernick is on a completely different scale to Stonehenge. It's a wonderfully modest engagement with the stones, rather than the rather immodest display at Stonehenge.*

---

21. Bender, Hamilton & Tilley (1997).

WB: There's absolutely no evidence that Stonehenge is contested . . . one bloke in a ditch with axe wounds in his skull and the archaeologists assume that there's a fair bit of fighting going on . . .

BB: *Maybe it's not so much a contestation over place, but over meaning. Why do the bluestones keep getting shifted around?*

PA: I'd say that the crux of the whole Stonehenge phenomenon is that it had been going on for a long time *in the mind*, before anything appeared on the site; and that there were enough people with enough influence – whatever kind of influence – to enthuse people to actually create it; and that it was not an answer, it was a *searching* for an answer over a long time. It was a continuous process. In terms of the observations of the heavens, you can see very well that this could go on for centuries before they'd decide whether or not what they did last time actually fitted with their ideas of what was going on in the heavens, and that they'd keep on rethinking. And, if you think that the setting has a function, as opposed to a passive existence, perhaps they're also wondering how the thing actually works. They'd go on experimenting over generations, all the way through until the final phase. You don't have to have – as a symbol of the nineties – competing groups of property developers, where one wins over another and builds their idea of whatever needs to be there. That's what happens now . . . but there's no need to transfer it back into the past.

BB: *How would you interpret the shift from wood to stone, and maybe from a lunar to a solar orientation? Are they trying to make a more permanent mark – a statement for the future?*

PA: Well, there are two ways of putting that. Either they're building for the future in order to impress people; or they're building it to last because they believed that its function, or its use, or its message, was going to be useful for as long as that way of building in stone was going to last . . .

I don't think they are replacing one orientation by another. Once you've got the Avenue everything that comes after unifies the solar base-line with whatever else concerns them, particularly the moon . . .

BB: *I like the idea that you're accreting complexity: maybe they're trying to find a way of expressing both lunar and solar, wood and stone, maybe female and male . . .*

PA: It's the same thing as grasping for the unified field theory in physics.

They have the sun and the moon which seem to rule their lives, but they can't understand the connection. They can follow one or follow the other, but they don't seem to be related. And if they actually believe that the relationship between the sun and the moon has some effect on their life and the fertility of their crops and so on, then they'd want to understand it so that they could in some way influence it in their favour . . .

BB: *So that would be your main criticism about this chapter, that it's too much about power and manipulation and not enough about a communal spirituality or a communal way of understanding the world?*

PA: The big problem with Stonehenge for archaeologists, is that it doesn't fit. They can dig all over the place but there's nothing in what they find or, more particularly, in their interpretation, that logically explains why these people would have built something like Stonehenge . . .

WB: It's as though archaeologists are looking for a rudimentary version of their own life-style . . .

BB: *O.K. But we are becoming more aware that we write ourselves into our stories!*

PA: In the sixties when all those non-archaeologists were putting out theories about the significance of the alignments, the archaeological establishment poo-pooed everything. I think it was Newham (who got there before Hawkins) who thought that the three post-holes in the car-park were interesting – he suggested they formed an alignment with the Heel Stone.[22] Eventually the

22. Newham (1964); Hawkins (1965).

archaeological establishment announced with great glee that the post-holes were Mesolithic, and therefore had nothing to do with the Heel Stone, and that, therefore, all these astronomical theories were bunkum . . . And that's all they said, just negative, there was nothing about what these uprights could be. But now, because ideas have moved on, they're being commented on, and people are suggesting that they might be totem poles – that maybe they were the focus for rituals and that people danced around them . . . Someone in our lot got really excited, they dragged us across the car-park, 'Look, this used to be the totem pole'!

BB: *Sure, we have got excited at the idea that there may have been large Mesolithic timbers or totem poles because it ties in with ideas that we're working on now about the way in which particular places and pathways used by gatherer-hunters gradually accumulated meanings and ritual significance and eventually become marked in some way . . .*

But going back to the sixties' interpretations of alignments and so on by people like Thom[23] and Hawkins. I was always turned off their ideas because they made it sound as though there was this elite that spent all their time scanning the heavens. It always seemed a very twentieth-century scenario to me . . . There didn't seem to be much concern to link these celestial calendars with seasonal rhythms or life events . . .

PA: That's unfair – Thom was a mathematician and he was just looking at the mathematics, he was using his skills to see what he could see. The thing about the stones is that they are multivalent – that's *your* word, isn't it! – a temple, an observatory, a meeting place . . . But it's still legitimate for a person to focus on a particular angle, and to look at it very carefully and say 'wow!' if they do discover something . . .

If you accept a co-operative scenario then you have to accept that people in general were actually knowledgeable, not about the high technicalities of astronomy but about the importance of numbers and shape. Some people would, of course, be more knowledgeable, but it's the difference between a government ministry that says: 'We've got the knowledge, we're going to take this action, we know best', or something that's more diffused throughout the society, a gradation of knowledge . . .

BB: *Given that archaeologists are beginning to recognise that their views of the past are subjective, that they write themselves into their histories,*

23. Thom (1967).

and that they need to think much more about how prehistoric people felt about their world, you could say that some of you have been thinking along these lines for quite a while . . .

WB: I still think that archaeologists are very hostile to people outside their own closed groups . . .

HJ: Look at what happened when I talked at the Cerne Abbas Conference.[24] I was labelled 'The orange-haired lady who seemed to have dropped in while en-route from the Newbury bypass' [the Road Protest occupation]. If I couldn't be pinned down to a university I must come from Newbury!

WB: If archaeologists open the debate up to everybody it wouldn't belong to them any more, would it, and they still want to retain control of their work . . .

PA: Archaeologists would have to venture into speculation which – obviously – they don't like . . .

BB: *I think we're beginning to recognise that we are speculating . . . But obviously we remain interested in the evidence, otherwise there's no point in being an archaeologist . . .*

HJ: There's always a suppression of evidence, a tinkering and manipulating to fit the current theory, and stuff gets cast aside into some dark cupboard . . . an intellectual as well as physical cupboard. It's the lack of broadness of view; the blowing with archaeological fashion . . .

BB: *Don't the alternative theories coming from people outside of archaeology also reflect fashion? You're anti-authority, you want communal social relations. And that affects your interpretations. So, just as archaeologists, working within the establishment, get hung up on questions of social differentiation, 'alternative' people, trying to break free of contemporary social hierarchies, construct a past that is full of communality . . .*

PA: I don't agree. It's not a question of constructing a communal past, but of looking at those parts of the past that seem to represent it. Alternative people have no difficulty at all in seeing no communality in Roman rule . . . There are times when there was authoritarian rule, and times which you might call the 'golden ages' – times that are really interesting and you can ask, 'Why is it that things seem to be working here, where are all the armies and forts and everything else that's supposed to go with highly advanced society?'

24. Bender (1998b).

BB: *Is there any consensus amongst alternative viewpoints?*

PA: No way: people often believe quite erroneous things, but you don't feel the need to correct them. People will associate Celtic art with Stonehenge. We do it ourselves in the Stonehenge Campaign Newsletters, we put Celtic art and Stonehenge together and we know that's erroneous, but we don't feel unhappy about it because it's part of the presentation. The art takes people back – not far enough – but it takes people back in a way that they understand, and it's up to them to make the further jump if they want . . . There's no attempt to maintain a correct consensus . . .

HJ: Archaeologists and academics are looking for a definitive truth, whilst what we're looking at is life-styles, evolving traditions, things like that. We're not looking for 'truth', we're looking for usable bits, and relevant bits, and personal bits, and taste . . . It's more of an overview than this endless search to be the one that finds the truth. We don't need to be correct every time we talk, we don't need the people we're talking to to be correct, because we're re-using, not re-finding . . .

BB: *You want the past as something that is usable . . .*

HJ: Whereas archaeologists want it as a career move. It's a different agenda.

Contested Landscapes: Medieval to Present Day[1]

The Cumbales, who live in the Bolivian Andes, say:
Although events occurred in the past, we live their consequences today and
must act upon them now. What has already occurred is in front of us, because
that is where it can be corrected.

J. Rappaport 1988

Introduction

On a small, heavily populated, down-at-heel, off-shore island, with illusions about its position in the world, the past can become oppressive. Fay Weldon, in her *Letter to Laura* (1984), describes what it is like to live in a country with too much past, too little present:

> Every acre of this tiny, densely populated land of ours has been observed, considered, valued, reckoned, pondered over, owned, bought, sold, hedged – and there's a dead man buried under every hedge, you know. He died of starvation, and his children too, because the common land was enclosed, hedged, taken from him . . . The past . . . is *serious*.

She is describing an English, rather than a Scottish or Welsh landscape, one in which, at least from medieval times, armed interventions were short-lived, where appropriations – and contestations – were somewhat more subtly negotiated. She gets the sense of the 'terrible beauty' to be found in many such landscapes, the tension between the pleasure gained from a worked-over, lived-in landscape and the uneasy know-

---

1. This chapter and Chapter 6 first appeared in *Landscape, Politics and Perspectives* (1993) which I edited.

ledge of what the working and living often involved; the way the 'historical rootedness' of the English landscape, the seeming slow evolution, has served to disguise a proprietorial palimpsest, the working out of a long history of class relations.

Not just the land, but the very word 'landscape' has often been used as though it 'belongs' to a particular class. Recently British Rail put up two Intercity posters for First Class travel. One of them began with the words: 'The only Constable you'll see at a hundred miles an hour . . .' The assumption was clear: those who matter know who Constable is, those who might be confused by a seemingly obscure reference to the forces of law and order will not get the joke and do not matter. The other poster, reproduced in Figure 18, shows a quiet landscape, monotone, almost monotonous, acceptable to those who know how (and can afford) to appreciate the understatement – and those desirous of joining their ranks. It is a view from a window. You are the observer. It is not your land but it is certainly *someone's* land. The fields are cultivated, but the cultivators and their machinery are not visible. You could perhaps view it as an 'old' landscape with the tree and the hedge standing for something stable and unchanging. Or you might view it as a 'new' landscape in which, in fact, most of the hedges have been grubbed up to make way for 'economies of scale' and agribusiness. There is perhaps, for those in the First Class, a satisfactory elision between old and new so that the changes associated with a monetarist climate are referenced on symbols of stability and the old order – the old tree – and thereby gain legitimacy.

In this chapter, working with one small (albeit heavily symbolic) corner of the English landscape, I want to explore not only the different ways in which, over a period of several hundred years, those with economic and political power and the necessary cultural capital have attempted, physically and aesthetically, to appropriate the landscape, but also how these appropriations have been contested by those engaging with the land in quite different ways. In the first chapter I suggested that people's experience of the land is based on their everyday attentiveness to the tasks in hand, the routines, their relations to each other, to their animals and crops, and to the world around them, but that that engagement is also shaped by the particularity of the historical moment. The decoupling of 'the cultural' from the political, and the individual from the larger historical structures, found in recent postmodern writings, has to be resisted (Thrift 1991; Jackson 1991). We need to retain the coupling while recognising the complexity of interactions, and eschewing any one way causality. We may also, I

Figure 18 Intercity travel poster

believe, retain the notion of hegemonic discourse. There is, in fact far less difference between Gramsci and Foucault than people seem to think, and for the purposes of this chapter it is important to stress that those with power will attempt to impose particular ways of doing and seeing which serve to disguise the labour process. However, those with power, and the strategies they invoke, are not only riven by internal factions and tensions, but are dependent upon some degree of acceptance by those 'without' power, and must perforce take on board their reactions, contestations and subversions (Harvey 1996: 44; Keesing 1994;Thompson 1974; Williams 1994). But see Chapter 6 for more on this.

Having stressed that one can only understand the contestations and appropriations of a landscape by careful historical contextualisation, it goes against the grain to attempt to sketch the history of the Stonehenge landscape over a period of several hundred years in one chapter. What follows can be no more than an outline and is piecemeal. I concentrate on the medieval (and in one of the Dialogues Ronald Hutton questions part of my interpretation), the landscapes of the seventeenth and eighteenth century, and, finally, in somewhat more detail, the present-day landscape.

For each period the evidence is very different. For the medieval period one can draw on both archaeological and literary evidence. But the latter is primarily derived from the work of clerics (but see p. 135 for other sources now being tapped). There are references to the commoners, but only as the (despised) 'other'. As we move on in time, the description thickens, the voices quicken, but always, even in the present, there is unevenness in the way in which different people can be heard.

Medieval Stonehenge[2]

You will remember (perhaps) that at the end of Chapter 2 the Anglo-Saxons had laid claim to the Celtic *Choir Gaur* and it had become Stan

---

2. In this medieval section, there are many allusions to Avebury, the other great stone circle that lies 30 km. to the north. Avebury is less well known than Stonehenge, though for some, like John Aubrey, it 'did as much excell *Stoneheng*, as a cathedral does a Parish church' (cited in Hunter 1975: 158). A medieval village straddled part of the Avebury circle, and the church, built sometime after 900 AD was located just beyond the bank and ditch. Because of the proximity of the church and village to the stones, there is often more detailed information about Avebury than about Stonehenge. Obviously there were differences between these medieval landscapes, but also much that was similar.

Hencg. Since the Saxons did not bother, on the whole, to rename natural features, this suggests that the site still carried meaning. Most probably the stones had been incorporated into folk culture, syncretic, changing, but possibly enduring over the millennia, or perhaps their significance had ebbed and flowed within people's consciousness (see the Dialogue with Hutton, p. 136) (Piggott (1941).

We have the renaming, and then a long silence. The next mention of Stonehenge is in the later medieval period, in the middle of the twelfth century. And now the stones express the conflict between Church and commoner.

For most of the medieval period the Stonehenge downlands were marginal land, probably used for common grazing. To the east, the open fields belonging to the villages of Amesbury Countess in the north, and Amesbury West in the south straggled the valley bottom and lower hill-slopes of the river Avon. The stones lay on the edge of the familiar world; beyond lay the 'wilderness' (Anglo-Saxon *Wylder ness*, nest or lair of a wild beast) (Stilgoe 1982: 10). For the medieval commoner, the landscape, both familiar and unfamiliar, was imbued with magic – half-pagan, half-Christian. The stones in their liminal setting were revered and believed to have curative and procreative powers. In the villages, houses had to be protected from witches. Sometimes a carved rowen post would be set to one side of the hearth. Sometimes the post, carved with St Andrew crosses, was set in place by the local priest who, rarely a man of letters, trod a fine line between the old and the new religion (Stilgoe 1982). The higher echelons of the Church could protest. As early as the eighth century, King Canute exclaimed that:

> It is heathen practice if one worships idols, namely if one worships heathen gods and the sun, or the moon, fire or flood, wells or stones or any kind of forest tree, or if one practices witchcraft (cited in Burl 1979: 36).

But, as Le Goff makes clear, the Church authorities, faced with the power of passive resistance, negotiated, trimmed, and adapted their doctrines (Gurevich 1988: 5; Le Goff 1980: 160–88). The commoner did likewise.

In many ways the positions of Church and commoner were not so far apart. For both, 'the material world was scarcely more than a sort of mask, behind which took place all the really important things . . . Nature . . . in the infinite detail of its illusory manifestations . . . was conceived above all as the work of hidden wills' (Bloch 1962: 83). Both imbued the landscape with magic, and there was no dearth of 'magical' Christian sites and relics. The problem was simply how to interpret the magic. Where the Church saw the hand of God, the commoners, in their fearful encounter with the wilderness, confused Satan with Pan, and continued to relate hoary tales of the wild hunt when, '. . . on moonless nights, and especially Walpurgis-nacht (May Day eve), Satan and his hounds coursed through the forest, pursuing with a terrible roaring and baying all the wild creatures and any humans unlucky enough to stumble in their way' (Stilgoe 1982: 8).

The Church, heir to the Graeco-Roman tradition, was more prone to define good and evil, true and false, black and white magic. The old religion – which was part old, part new – was more equivocal, more ambiguous: forces were good *and* bad, natural forces were to be propitiated and thereby rendered beneficial (Le Goff 1980: 159–88).

The Church, embedded in the hierarchical relations of a feudal society, preached of a 'natural order' homologous to feudalism; the pyramidal social relations were reiterated in the hierarchy of heavenly relations and in material representations. Demarcations – social, material, ritual – were to a large extent played out within a single body of space rather than, as later on, between distinctive, class-differentiated, spaces. The inside of a church, of a manor, even a poor man's house, was physically 'open', but socially and mentally heavily demarcated (Johnson 1993). In this world of interdependencies, the commoners, the worshippers of stones, were represented as 'the other' – their labour necessary, their visage hideous. They also acted as a foil for the qualities of wealthy men and saints, as 'fodder' for the redemption of the upper classes (Le Goff 1980: 95). There is little that is positive about the commoners in the writings of the clerics, and much that is passed over in silence. Our sense of their world is filtered through the contortions, concessions, and suppressions of the Church.

The Church physically 'appropriated' the stones. Amesbury, close to Stonehenge, housed a religious order,[3] and 'the presence of a religious house nearby may have been influential in bringing about the destruction of parts of the monument' (Cleal et al. 1995: 343). At Avebury the Anglo-Saxon church was built alongside the great bank and ditch (but see p. 139). The stones and mounds were also 'intellectually' appropriated and adulterated. They became a malignant part of a Christian iconography, the work of the Devil – Devil's Den, Devil's

---

3. There is some suggestion of an early minster church, superceded by an abbey in 979 AD, and in turn replaced by a priory of nuns in 1177 (Cleal et al. 1995: 343).

Quoit, Devil's Chair. The great cone of Silbury Hill, near Avebury, became the place where the Devil had dropped a spadeful of earth. The Heel Stone at Stonehenge compounded a diabolical and Arthurian etymology. It bore, supposedly, the impression of a holy father's heel. The heel had been struck by a stone thrown by the Devil angered by Merlin, King Arthur's magician, magicking the stones into place (Burl 1979: 36).

The medieval Church vacillated between attempting to appropriate the stones, and destroying them. One of the earliest accounts of Stonehenge, c.1136, by the Welsh cleric Geoffrey of Monmouth, embedded in his *History of the Kings of Britain*, combines 'pure legend and a sense of the marvellous that is sometimes still completely pagan' (Bloch 1962: 100).

In Monmouth's account, Aeneas, arriving from Troy, conquered the giants that inhabited 'Albion'. Later, a Celtic King, Emrys (Ambrosius), brother to Ythr (Uther Pendragon, father of Arthur), intent on establishing a memorial to kinsmen killed at Amesbury by Saxon treachery, enlisted Merlin's help in transporting the great stones from Ireland and erecting them at Stonehenge (Figure 19). According to Monmouth,

Figure 19 Merlin hefting the stones into place
(Egerton 3028 fl40v; kind permission of the British Library)

these stones had originally been brought by giants from Africa to Ireland.[4] In a matter-of-fact way, he cites Merlin's description of the magical power of the stones:

> Whenever they felt ill, baths [w]ould be prepared at the foot of the stones; for they used to pour water over them and to run this water into baths in which their sick were cured. What is more, they mixed the water with herbal concoctions and so healed their wounds. There is not a single stone among them which hasn't some medicinal virtue (Geoffrey of Monmouth 1966: 196).

In later medieval times such benign empowering of the stones was forbidden and the Church moved to obliterate their magic.[5] At Avebury, in the early fourteenth century, the Church authorities made the local inhabitants destroy the stones. Nevertheless, the destruction was done with caution. The stones were not broken up; instead the villagers dug large holes and tumbled the stones into them, 'handled with reverence, covered without hurt to the sarsen, doing God's work without upsetting the Devil' (Burl 1979: 37). Compare this with the late seventeenth century, when the local farmers broke up the stones, partly for purely utilitarian reasons, partly, as we shall see, as part of the Protestant backlash against paganism and popery. Now they were broken with fire and water, and were incorporated into local buildings (Figure 20).

The Seventeenth and Eighteenth Centuries

Ucko et al.(1991: 163) suggest that by the end of the seventeenth century the commoners no longer worshipped the stones, and broke them with impunity. But perhaps this is too simple a reading. There remains a tension, right through the seventeenth and into the eighteenth century, between the stones seen as something utilitarian, a

---

4. Piggott (1941), much impressed by this part of Monmouth's saga, suggests that it indicates that Monmouth was heir to the Welsh bardic tradition that, in faint outline, resonated with millennia-old traditions recounting the movement of the bluestones from Wales to Wessex.

5. In a contemporary setting, Herzfeld comments on the need to destroy the past. In Crete, during the militantly nationalist regime of 1967–74, 'one official had even wanted to demolish the proud minaret at the mosque of *gazi* Huseyin Pasa ... As long as it stood, he reasoned, the Turks could use this monument to make territorial claims on Crete. History had to be remodeled to make the present safe' (Herzfeld 1991: 57).

An Abury take 20 fo. May 20. 1724

Figure 20 Breaking up the stones at Avebury
(Gough Maps 231, fol. 5r; kind permission of the Bodleian Library, Oxford)

source of building material, an encumbrance to be got rid of by farmers 'chiefly out of covetousness of the little *area* of ground each stood on' (Stukeley, cited in Ucko *et al.* 1991: 249), and the stones invested, however vestigially, with supernatural power. The Nonconformist preacher, harnessing all the populist rhetoric at his disposal to force a disassociation between 'pagan' ritual and festival and true Christian piety, not only succeeded in repudiating the 'emotional calendar of the poor', but also drove a wedge between the teachings of the Church and everyday life, between 'polite' and 'plebeian' culture. In attempting to destroy the 'bonds of idolatry and superstition – the wayside shrines, the gaudy church, the local miracle and cults' (Thompson 1974), he undermined traditional remedies against the devil and his agencies, and made witchcraft and pagan practices appear both more powerful and more menacing (Hill 1982). Added to which, by the end of the seventeenth century, with the acceleration of the enclosure movement, many a member of a church congregation had been cut loose not only from the land, but also – a negative freedom – from traditional forms of obligation and service (Thompson 1974). There was, thus, not only a degree of political anarchy, but also a considerable residue of super-stition. Indeed it was not unknown, in the late seventeenth century, for preachers to attempt to 'tame' their congregations by threats of 'petrification' for those who danced on the Sabbath, and several stone circles were attributed to just such divine intervention (Grinsell 1976). *Fools Bolt*, an anonymous diatribe also from the late seventeenth century, both threatens, and remains threatened by the power of the stones at Stonehenge:

> These forlorne Pillers of Stone are left to be our remembrancers, dis-suading us from looking back in our hearts upon anything of Idolatry, and persuading us . . . so to . . . deride, it in it's uglie Coullers, that none of us . . . may returne, with Doggs, to such Vomit, or Sows to wallowing in such mire' (cited in Legg 1986: 4).[6]

There are many mentions of the magical properties of the stones in the seventeenth and eighteenth centuries. John Aubrey, in the 1660s, notes, in the context of Stonehenge, that 'it is generally averred . . . that pieces of powder of these stones, putt into their wells, doe drive away the toades . . .' (cited in Olivier 1951: 157); while the Rev. James Brome noted in 1707: 'if the stones be rubbed, or scraped, and water thrown upon the scrapings, they will (some say) heal any green wound or old sore' (shades of Geoffrey of Monmouth nearly 400 years earlier) (cited in Burl 1987: 220).

In the 1740s Stukeley records that people chipped off bits of bluestone because they were thought to have medicinal properties. And when John Wood, also in 1740, attempted to survey the stones and a violent storm blew up, the locals reckoned he had raised the devil (Burl 1987: 182).

In the longer term, the old ways, the old superstitions, the last vestiges of a 'deification of nature' were undermined by what Marx called 'the great civilizing influence of capital' (quoted in K. Thomas 1983: 23). The change in people's attitudes towards the natural world occurred

---

6. Various guesses at the authorship had been made: J. Gibbons perhaps (Piggott 1985: 86), or Robert Gay, a Parliamentarian rector (Legg 1986). Whoever he was, the author was exceedingly scornful of Inigo Jones – 'Out-I-goe Jones' – and of his Romano-British origin for Stonehenge.

in piecemeal fashion, depending upon who they were and where –
economically, politically, socially – they were located. An illiterate
peasantry (slowly being commodified into farm-*hands*) abandoned
more slowly the notion of 'a natural world redolent with human
analogy and symbolic meaning, and sensitive to man's behaviour'
(Thomas 1983: 89). It was the literate classes that embraced the concept
of nature as something detached, 'to be viewed and studied by the
observer from the outside, as if by peering through a window . . . a
separate realm, offering no omens or signs, without human meaning
and significance' (Thomas 1983: 89). And – more sinisterly – as something 'to be put to the question' (Bacon), racked for its secrets and
treasures (Gold 1984).

The more pronounced attempts by the Church, in the seventeenth
and eighteenth centuries, to impose Christian teachings and Christian
marriage upon the vestigial paganism and easier-going sexual mores
of the countryside, were only part of the greater intervention in the
lives of ordinary people by both Church and State. Having followed
through the contestation between Church and commoner, I have now
to backtrack in order to discuss the way in which the State interceded,
and to consider the importance of Stonehenge in the context of an
emerging national, and then regional, sense of identity.

Already in the fifteenth century, the Church had begun to lose its
exclusive hold on the past – history was no longer a matter of
ecclesiastical precedent. 'Time' ceased to be the gift of God and became
'the property of man' (Le Goff 1980: 51), and 'Time's arrow' began to
replace the repetitive cycles – the endless chain of cause and effect – of
earlier history. Instead, historical precedents and 'genealogies' became
part of the process of internal pacification and nation-state consolid-
ation.

As early as the fourteenth century, Stonehenge begins to be drawn
into a nationalist diatribe. Langtoft tells the story of 'the Wander Wit
of Wiltshire', who:

> rambling to Rome to gaze at Antiquities, and there skewing himself into
> the company of Antiquarians, they entreated him to illustrate unto them
> that famous monument in the contry called Stonage. His answer was
> that he had never seen, scarce ever heard of it, whereupon they kicked
> him out of doors and bad him goe home and see Stoneage. And I wish
> that all such Episcopal cocks as slight these admired stones and scrape
> for barley cornes of vanity out of foreigne dunghills, might be handled,
> or rather footed, as he was (cited in Olivier 1951: 156).

Under the Tudors, historical and archaeological precedents were used to formalise custom and tradition into instruments of government and a defined code of law (Piggott 1985). And at a time when the Act of Union (1536) extended the English law of the land to Wales and menacingly set out the need 'utterly to extirpe all and singular the senister usages and customes differinge from [the Realme of Englande]' (cited in Jones 1990), the myth was created that the inhabitants of England and Wales were one people with a common ancestry and shared history (Jones 1990; Piggott 1985: 16). Henry VIII, intent on breaking with Rome and siezing the Church lands, employed Leland to ride around the country, mapping, collating, and 'spying'. And Leland, professing himself 'totally enflammed with a love to see thoroughly all partes of your opulente and ample realme . . . thereby to expose . . . the craftily coloured doctrine rout of Roman bishops', rode around the land:

> By the space of these vi yeares paste that there is almost nother cape nor bay, haven, creke, or peere, river or confluence of rivers, breches, washes, lakes, mere, fenny water, montaynes, valleis, mores, hethes, forestes, woodes, cities, burges, castelles, principal manor places, but I have seen them (cited in Chamberlin 1986: 69).

Inter alia, he mapped and described Stonehenge, appending, without comment, Geoffrey of Monmouth's explanation.

Compilations, categorisations and a comprehensive mapping of Britain became increasingly important during the seventeenth and early eighteenth centuries. Refinements in surveying and mapping were part of a changing technology of power, integral to the development of mercantile capital, and the opening up of the New World. These new techniques allowed the redefinition of property: 'It created geometrical, divisible, and hence saleable space by making parcels of property out of lands that had previously been defined according to rights of custom and demarcated by landmarks and topographic features' (Olwig 1996).

Control of knowledge, of resources, and of nature. By the late seventeenth century, as the 'county naturalists picked their way through all the legends of prognosticatory springs, portentous birds and similar marvels', popular and learned views of nature significantly separated out (Thomas 1983: 78). James I demanded that Stonehenge be made to give up its secret and ordered his court architect, Inigo Jones, to map and explain it. Giants and Merlin were no longer considered sufficient. Inigo Jones, steeped in Italianate landscapes, claimed Stonehenge for the Romans. It was, he said, as he manipulated his plans, built c. AD 79 by British chieftains subject to Rome and was based on Vitruvian geometry. The king encouraged the Duke of Buckingham to dig the monument, causing – as, a little later, Aubrey laconically noted – the 'falling downe, or recumbancy of the great stone' (cartoon 3).

With the influx of capital into the countryside, with 'new' families competing with and marrying into the older aristocracy, and with both the old and new aristocracy hastening to enclose open field and common land in order to 'improve' their fortunes, the mapping and description of land-use, natural curiosities, and the genealogies of local families, helped both to create and legitimate the new class and property relations.

". . . So to make up for the disappointment we had to let him have a home computer."

Reproduced by kind permission of Merrily Harpur

More and more, chorographers [created] books where country gentlemen [could] find their manors, monuments, and pedigrees copiously set forth. In just a few decades chorography thus progressed from being an adjunct to the chronicle of kings to become a topographically ordered set of real-estate and family chronicles (Helgerson 1986).

Aubrey, the 'discoverer' in 1666 of Avebury (the commoners had, of course, been there a while!) and of the Aubrey holes at Stonehenge, was the first to propose that Stonehenge was not Roman or Danish but rather Celtic and (probably) associated with the Druid religion. He was also not reluctant to admit that he was recording with the explicit intent that the knowledge be made available to those who might find economic advantage (McVicar 1984). Walter Charleton, three years earlier, was in favour of a Danish origin and proposed it as '*a court royal*, or place for the *Election* and *Inauguration* of Kings', and, in the same vein, dedicated it to Charles II (Ucko *et al.* 1991: 15). And John Smith of Boscombe, in the later eighteenth century, noting that Stonehenge was built 'to show the steady, uniform and orderly motions of the heavenly bodies', dedicated it to the Duke of Queensbury at nearby Amesbury House, 'as a symbol of your Grace's steady, uniform and orderly conduct through life' (Olivier 1951: 36). Based in large measure on the formidable treatise on *Brittania* by Camden (first published in 1586, republished 1695 in an enlarged edition), antiquarians increasingly focused on regional, rather than national, coverage.

The economic advantages reaped by the antiquarians' patrons were real enough. The commoners were physically evicted as part of the seventeenth- and eighteenth-century enclosure movement. They were also evicted aesthetically. In 1726, the Duke of Queensbury, owner of Amesbury House near to Stonehenge, enclosed the open fields of West Amesbury and Amesbury Countess to the east of Stonehenge, and laid great parts of the estate down to park. He realigned the Amesbury-Market Lavington road, landscaped the Iron Age camp and built a 'Druidical' grotto. In passing, he 'preserved' Stonehenge from a plague of rabbit warrens planted by his predecessor.

The antiquarian, William Stukeley, though a churchman and a friend of the gentry, occasionally hints at a darker local experience of landscape enclosure. Writing, in 1740, of his survey of the Stonehenge area, he says, 'this . . . will . . . preserve the memory of it hereafter, when the traces of this mighty work are obliterated by the plough . . . that instrument gaining ground too much, upon the ancient and innocent pastoritial (sic) life . . . and by destructive inclosures beggars and depopulates the country' (Royal Commission 1979: iv). It is, of course, the technology that Stukeley blames, rather than the changing social relations.

Stukeley, apart from his threnody about enclosure, was an Establishment man. In his writings on Stonehenge and Avebury there is a tension between his desire to record in meticulous 'scientific' detail and his need to validate his theological interpretation. There has been a tendency to periodicise Stukeley's life, separating out an earlier 'scientific' fieldwork phase from a later 'druidic' phase, and lamenting his lapse into romantic fabulation (Piggott 1985: 15). More recent work suggests that, from the beginning, the two went hand-in-hand (Ucko et al. 1991: 53), and now that we all admit to the subjectivity that imbues our practice, we can more readily accept the contradictions in Stukeley's work. So, on the one hand, in the early 1720s, he meticulously maps the cultural landscape of his forebears, engaging Stonehenge as part of a larger landscape. On the other, having read (and rather under-acknowledged) Aubrey, he promulgates a Druidic origin and, more, attempts to place the Druids in a direct line from Moses and Abraham – finding in the Druidic religion the lineaments of the Christian Trinity. Avebury becomes 'a landscaped model of the Trinity' in which the great circle represents 'the ineffable deity, the avenues . . . his son . . . in the form of a serpent'. Stonehenge, he believes, is a temple erected in 460 bc by Egyptian 'refugees', aided by Wessex Druids (Piggott 1985).While he held these notions from the 1720s and had 'revised' some of his plans accordingly, they were given added urgency in the 1730s and 1740s. Having moved from being a medical man to taking holy orders, perhaps in part because his hopes of patronage were disappointed, he found that Tolund and the Deists were also promoting Stonehenge as a Druidical temple. Their intention was to relativise all religion and to suggest that 'Christianity was as old as the Creation'. In the face of this heretical intervention, Stukeley altered the title of his book from the original 'History of the Ancient Celts' to 'Patriarchal Christianity: or A Chronological History of the Origin and Progress of True Religion and Idolatry'.[7]

Stukeley appropriated the Druids in the service of the Church of England. Others, particularly the Welsh nationalists in the aftermath

7. The first entry to the Index of the volume, published in 1740, runs:

They were of the patriarchal religion Page 1, 2, 17

Which was the same as Christianity 2, 54

of the French Revolution, rediscovered them as early patriots, Celtic leaders of the opposition to the Romans, symbols of resistance and liberty (Jones 1990). In both Thomas's poem 'Liberty' and in Collins's 'Ode to Liberty' (1747) the Druids figure as the apostles of freedom (Piggott 1985).

Cleric, antiquarian, landed gentry, Welsh nationalist – the number of voices increases. Each appropriates Stonehenge in their own fashion, each creates a particular past. Some voices remain muted. The voice of the labourer, or of women of any class, most often come down to us at second-hand. Other people talk about them, or do not talk about them. Silences are important. And often the bitterness seeps through. The radical claim to the land that the Diggers and Levellers fought for in the seventeenth century was superseded, in the eighteenth century, by frustration and anger of the wholesale appropriation and enclosure of the land, as expressed, for example, in the writings of the poet-labourer John Clare (Chapter 1, p. 31).

In contemporary Britain, even with all the media available, it is still not easy to hear all the voices that contest the Stonehenge landscape. Moreover, while the stones remained 'open' right through to the beginning of this century and people could come to them with their different understandings, they are now 'closed' and Stonehenge has become a museum which attempts to 'sell', not always successfully, a particular sort of experience, a particular interpretation of the past. People with alternative views have to fight for the right of entry and the right to express their views.

Contemporary Landscapes

A Site for 'the Nation'

The first impulse to 'protect' Stonehenge emerged from late nineteenth-century radical protests at the effect of industrialisation on people and places alike. On the one hand, 'romantic' socialists like John Ruskin, appalled by the destruction wrought by the Industrial Revolution, proposed in 1854 that an inventory of 'buildings of interest' threatened by demolition be drawn up. On the other hand, the fierce intercession by working-class socialists demanding access to the countryside for the urban working class led to the creation of the Youth Hostelling Association and the Ramblers Association (Bommes & Wright 1982). In the late 1870s, John Lubbock attempted to introduce a National Monuments Preservation Bill. Three times the bill was furiously opposed by conservative members of the House of Commons who recognised that public amenity might come to override the rights of private ownership (Murray 1989).[8] There was, for example, a fine intercession by Francis Hervey, a Tory M.P: 'Are the absurd relics of our barbarian predecessors,' he clearly roared, 'who found time hanging heavily on their hands, and set about piling up great barrows and rings of stones, to be preserved at the cost of the infringement of property rights?' (Bommes & Wright 1982). Tennyson once wrote a poem in which father and son are trotting across their estate. The sound of the hooves merge with the father's opening credo – 'Property, property, property'.

Eventually, following the precedent set by the Commons Preservation Society in the 1880s, a wonderful British blurring of the distinction between 'private' and 'public' ownership was concocted and the politicians were won over. The National Trust (founded in 1895) holds the properties and land *privately* in the national and *public* interest.

In 1894 Sir Edmund Antrobus, owner of Stonehenge, refused to allow the Ancient Monuments Commission to fence Stonehenge. He still saw it as an important public space. If they tried to fence the stones, he said, 'an indignant public might act as the London public did in regards to the railings of Hyde Park, when the claim to hold meetings was interfered with' (Legg 1986: 162). His son, however, offered Stonehenge to the nation, at the excessively high price of £125,000 and with the proviso that he retain hunting and grazing rights. When this offer was turned down, he threatened to sell it to the Americans. In 1901, with the approval of the Society of Antiquaries, he erected a barbed-wire fence around the monument on the specious grounds that the new military camp on Salisbury Plain might result in damage. He put in two custodians and charged an entrance fee of a shilling a head (the equivalent of £5 today – obviously beyond the means of most people). Flinders Petrie and Lord Eversley (founder of the Commons Protection Society) took Antrobus to court, but as Eversley remarked,

> the judge appeared to regard with equanimity the exclusion from the monument of the great bulk of the public. He was evidently under the impression that the vulgar populace had, by their destructive propensities, disqualified themselves as visitors to a place of antiquarian interest (cited in Legg 1986: 166).

8. The political implications of celebrating a Celtic past at a time when the English were putting down the Irish was not lost on the House of Commons (Murray 1989).

Eversley surmised that the judge was much influenced by a line from Horace which, freely translated, runs: 'I hate the profane crowd and I exclude them.' Ninety years later things have not changed that much.

In 1915 Stonehenge was put up for auction, and a Mr Chubb (perhaps ironically of the lock-and-key family) bought it for his wife after she remarked over breakfast that 'she would like to own it'. Mr Chubb paid £6,600. In 1918 he gave Stonehenge to the nation, with the express wish that access should remain free. Unfortunately he added the proviso 'unless the Ministry of Works deemed otherwise' (Legg 1986). The Establishment 'deemed otherwise', and Stonehenge became a museum. Fenced in, available only to those who pay, it is no longer part of a living landscape (Lowenthal 1979, but see Dialogue with Ucko, p. 140).

Protecting the Site 'for the Nation'

Jacquetta Hawkes's archaeological writings are no longer in vogue, but one terse statement has been cited and re-cited: 'Every age', she said, 'has the Stonehenge it deserves – or desires' (Hawkes 1967: 174). At the time, she was reacting to the commercial development of the Stonehenge visitors' centre. Her comment was apposite then, and remains so now. Only, now, the Stonehenge that we have has not only become a tacky tourist trap, but also, once a year, at the approach of the Summer Solstice, becomes a gulag. The arc lights go up, the razor wire unrolls, and police and security men patrol with their dogs. For a brief moment the physical force that sustains the power of the ruling classes visibly flexes its muscles. In 1985 five hundred 'travellers' (a label that covers a great assortment of people who move around the countryside in old vans and buses) or 'free festivalers' were arrested and two hundred vehicles were impounded. In 1988 there was a repeat performance. In the last few years there has been an eerie silence: no one, except the police and selected journalists (and a few brave free festivalers crawling through the long grass), is there to watch the sun rise.

There is no doubt that the confrontational politics of the Thatcher years have thrown into high relief some of the conflicts that underwrite British society. It was not fortuitous that Wapping (the printers' strike), Orgreave (the miners' strike), and the Battle of the Beanfield at Stonehenge occurred within a year of each other. The same tactics, involving the deployment of non-local unidentifiable police, were used in each encounter. The same language defined and excommunicated 'the other'. For Mrs Thatcher the miners were 'the enemy within'.

JUST POINT OUT THE OFFICER WHO BEAT YOU UP AND SMASHED THE WIND-SCREEN OF YOUR PEACE VEHICLE...

Reproduced by kind permission of Hector Breeze

Assistant Chief Constable Clement admitted that he 'would not be the slightest bit troubled if . . . [the pickets] were trampled by horses'. As for the travellers, Douglas Hurd labelled them 'medieval brigands'; Mrs Thatcher brayed '[I will do] anything I can to make life difficult for such things as hippy convoys'; Sir John Cope, Tory MP, trumpeted 'we need a paramilitary police force'; and Robert Key, local Tory MP, gave away part of the reason for this anger and disquiet, 'two hundred nomads are squatting illegally on private land . . . there may be a sensible case for the use of troops.'

Media coverage reflected, and continues to reflect, similar prejudices. The *News of the World* headline read 'Sex-mad junkie outlaws make the Hell's Angels look like little Noddy' (Rosenberger 1991). In a post-Thatcher, less confrontational mode, damages against the police have been awarded to both travellers and miners.[9] There have been vaguely

9. The 'Battle of the Beanfield' took place in June 1985. Six years later, in June 1991, £23,000 was awarded to 24 plaintiffs for 'assault, damage to their vehicles and property, and for not being given the reasons for their arrest'. However, the judge managed to find the police not guilty of unlawful arrest and they therefore did not have to pay the costs of the trial. So the plaintiffs' awards were swallowed up in legal costs. The miners' confrontation with the police (or vice-versa) at Orgreave in Yorkshire occurred in June 1984. In July 1985 the case against the 95 pickets was dropped. In June 1991 39 (former) miners shared £425,000 out-of-court compensation from the South Yorkshire police for assault, wrongful arrest, malicious prosecution and false imprisonment (*Guardian*, 20 June 1991).

Reproduced by kind permission of Hector Breeze

conciliatory moves that never, however, materialise into anything solid. They muffle, rather than resolve, the underlying tensions.

The travellers, as an unpropertied, anarchic minority, enrage the Establishment. In particular, they enrage when they lay claim to Stonehenge. I shall return to them, but I want first to consider who attempts to call the tune. In an era of flexible capitalism, who are the power-brokers at Stonehenge? what are the economics of an imagined past? who writes the scripts? and who buys the product?

Who 'Owns' Stonehenge?

Who – officially – owns Stonehenge? English Heritage 'owns' the site 'for the nation'.[10] The National Trust 'owns' 1,500 acres around Stonehenge, also 'for the nation'. *Sotto voce*, the Ministry of Defence 'owns' vast stretches of Salisbury plain, presumably for the defence of the nation.[11] The new visitors' centre was scheduled to be built on the edge of their terrain, but this encroachment has been seen off (but see p. 183).

10. More accurately, the land on which Stonehenge stands is owned by the Department of the Environment, but its management is entrusted to English Heritage, a quango established by Act of Parliament in 1983 (Golding 1989).

11. Between 1897 and 1902 the War Office negotiated the purchase of 43,000 acres to the North of Stonehenge. Subsequent purchases have brought it up to 91,000 acres (36,400 ha) (Cleal et al. 1995: 346).

English Heritage and the National Trust act in the interests of the – heterogeneous and tensioned – Establishment. Through the 1970s, eighties and into the early nineties the radicalism that once informed attempts to protect and open up the countryside evaporated. Radicalism was replaced by populist rhetoric – doing *battle* for *our* heritage, maintaining *communal values* (apolitical, organic, stable, and deeply unequal), promoting *traditional* skills. A rhetoric that only thinly disguises both old and new class interests.[12]

The Stonehenge 'Honey-pot'

Contrary to a conservation rhetoric that emphasises a 'green' small business economy and the encouragement of specialised skills, the reality of preservation, conservation and public access is very 'big' business. In a climate of industrial uncertainty and in the computerised age of flexible capitalism, investment in industry and property becomes more problematic. And the tourist market, which requires less investment in fixed facilities, looks increasingly attractive.[13] Although the £15 million (and rising) ear-marked for the new Stonehenge visitors' centre seems a substantial amount, the returns will undoubtedly be equally substantial (p. 181).[14]

In 1983 government responsibility for the preservation of ancient monuments and for scientific research was handed over to English Heritage – a quango, autonomous but State-funded. Lord Montagu of Beaulieu (author of *How to Live in a Stately Home and Make Money*) took the chair and one of the stated aims became the heavy promotion of tourism (Hewison 1987: ch.4).

12. Jacobs (1994a; 1994b; 1996: 41, 43, 102) discusses this rhetoric in the context of the 'SAVE Britain's Heritage' campaign mounted in the mid-1970s in the face of threats by the then Labour government to impose a Wealth Tax detrimental to the propertied classes. The Victoria and Albert Museum put on an exhibition on the threat to country houses which seeded this campaign.

13. Although the figures are somewhat out of date, Lumley (1988) estimated the cost of creating a job in manufacturing at £32,000, in mechanical engineering at £300,000, and in tourism at £4000.

14. The takings from the Yorvik (Viking) shop at York were, per square foot, and prior to recession, more than every Marks and Spencers in the land except the Oxford Street branch (Baker 1988). The number of museums increased by over 50 per cent during the 1970s and 80s. Roughly one museum opened every three weeks and by the late 1980s there were over 2000 museums in Great Britain (Hewison 1987: ch.1). With the recession, some have proved short-lived.

Present-ing the Past

Stonehenge now has to make money. It also has to be preserved, conserved and presented. The visitors' centre – as everyone freely acknowledges – is a botched attempt to provide tourist facilities, keep people away from the archaeologically sensitive central part of the monument, and present information about the place and the landscape. It has been rightly berated for its neo-brutalist architecture, inadequate parking, and for its facile 'macho' historical presentation.

Until very recently, the tunnel that went under the road took one back through time via an Astronaut, Henry VIII, the Roman Empire, Egypt and the Pharaohs – not a woman in sight – to Stonehenge and the Beginning of Civilisation. The time-tunnel debouched onto the green sward surrounding the stones. There were (again until recently – they have now been moved to the car-park) three dioramas. The first depicts a sort of rural arcadia, a pastoral scene with early Stonehenge – the bank and ditch – just visible in the background (Figure 21a). In the second, a man stands poised between rural arcadia and civilisation (Figure 21b). In the third a chief – modelled on Kirk Douglas – brandishes his insignia of power as he talks to his male cronies (Figure 22). In the background the labour force beavers away. The emphasis is on power and on technology – building, construction, planning, control.

It is a very particular sort of history. One that goes hand in hand with the more general conservative version (vision?) of the past offered by English Heritage:

> The National Heritage is remarkably broad and rich . . . it is simult-aneously a representation of the development of aesthetic expression and a testimony to the role played by the nation in world history (The First Annual Report of the National Heritage Memorial Fund, cited in Hewison 1987).

See p. 180 for similar, more recent sentiments.

Apart from acting as the custodians and entrepreneurs of prehistoric monuments, English Heritage and the National Trust have focused on the landmarks of those with power and wealth, inscribed in an aesthetic that bypasses, as it has done for centuries, the labour that created the wealth. More recently the net has been cast wider, but, despite acquiring Victorian back-to-backs or derelict mills or mines, the presentation remains sanitised and romanticised, emphasing local colour rather than

Figure 21a English Heritage reconstruction of the first phase at Stonehenge
(photo: B. Bender)

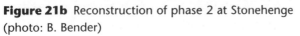

Figure 21b Reconstruction of phase 2 at Stonehenge
(photo: B. Bender)

Figure 22 Reconstruction of phase 3 at Stonehenge
(photo B. Bender)

the socio-economic conditions that generate both wealth and poverty, people's pain or their resistance.

Stonehenge is 'explained' in terms of roots, and of 'our' and 'deep' national past. It tells the story of those empowered to make decisions and to make claims on people's labour. It is a top-down past that ends when the last stone was put in place. It is a museum exhibit, a place to be looked at, caught on film, consumed on site and, via photographs and souvenirs (and memories), back home. Hence the incongruity of the marginalised travellers or Druids laying claim to the place and perceiving it as a 'living' space, a meeting-place, a ritual centre.

Stonehenge becomes 'our' national icon, exemplar of past glories, part of our national identity, part of our justification for remaining – against the odds – in the top league of world players. And yet, at the same time, and whilst being vigorously reworked as a commercial proposition, it exemplifies 'England's green and pleasant land', bulwark against the forces of modernity.

And the Role of the Archaeologists

The conservation and marketing lobby depend for their information and explanation of the past on the academic establishment – in the case of Stonehenge, the archaeologists. Archaeologists justify their monopoly on information in terms of the scientific rigour of their discipline. They have the artefacts, the dating materials and methods, that permit the rigorous reconstruction of the past. In reality the archaeological excavations at Stonehenge throughout this century have been piecemeal, often slip-shod, and, until recently, unpublished, and archaeologists still understand relatively little about the social and political conditions and the cultural perceptions of the people who built and used Stonehenge.[15] Nonetheless, as the 'official' interpreters, archaeologists, by and large, repudiate the 'alternative' theories of the New Agers, and side with the conservationists in limiting access to the stones and preventing celebrations on the grounds of potential damage. Only one academic book – edited by Chippindale – has been published that presents the attitudes and aspirations of a wider range of people, and even then there is no attempt to suggest possible compromises (Chippindale et al. 1990). When the police dug a trench 15 feet long and 6 feet wide across the entrance to the Free Festival field the archaeologists failed to protest, just as they have never protested at the despoliation of the landscape to the north of Stonehenge by the Ministry of Defence firing ranges and tank runs.

Archaeologists attempt to eschew politics. One of the archaeologists on the Commission that repudiated the Free Festival, washed his hands of the predictable confrontation that would occur. 'It is most important,' he said, 'to draw the distinction between the defensible decisions as such and their executive consequences, largely in the hands of others' (Fowler 1990). To the travellers the archaeologists are the 'unconscious

15. Ascherson (1988) remarked on two current renditions of the transition from Late Neolithic to Early Bronze Age. The first draws a contrast between those whose power derives from communal ritual expressed in collective architectural enterprises, and a new breed of thrusting individuals whose richly equipped single inhumations show a contempt both for traditional aristocratic ritual and for collective values. In the alternative reading, the Old Neolithic establishment were 'conservatives laden with gold and divine knowledge, scheming to defend their influence against local rebels and sceptics – who, in turn, chafed to get rid of the old frauds and run things in a modern way with Beaker pottery and metal tools'. Yet another version turns Stonehenge into an 'astronomical laboratory' – Fred Hoyle, Astronomer Royal, even suggested that the astronomers were, perhaps, a genetically distinct group (Chippindale 1983: 264). As Hilary, Wes and Paul (p. 90) point out, present-day social configurations often seem to weigh rather heavily in our interpretations of the past.

Reproduced by kind permission of Merrily Harpur

apologists for industrial civilisation', and the looters of graves (Thompson cited in Chippindale 1983: 248).[16]

Who Gets to Go?

For whom is the site preserved and the explanations offered? Mainly for the tourists who pay their money and are then corralled through the barriers and along the pathways roped off from the centre. Only those with academic credentials, or those in the advertising industry with enough money to pay for privileged access (Figure 23), cross the ropes and, under strict supervision, enter the stones. Those who do not have money, or are unwilling to pay, are kept out. By force, if necessary (Figure 24).

16. Sir Edmond Antrobus (who protested against the fencing of Stonehenge) grumbled in the House of Commons in 1874 that 'some of the ancient barrows, through having been first rifled by antiquarians, have been carted away and levelled by farmers. For himself, he believed it was the antiquarians who had done the most mischief in England' (cited in Murray 1989: 63). He wasn't far wrong: in the first decade of the nineteenth century William Cunnington and Sir Richard Colt Hoare 'ravaged' over three hundred barrows (Richards 1991: 33).

Figure 23 Consuming the stones

Bona fide tourists are the ones who have, since 1901, paid their entrance fee. In the 1920s there were 20,000 paying visitors; in 1955 184,000; in 1977 815,000; in 1982 530,000; in 1994 672,000. On a hot Summer's day in the peak year of 1977, 7000 people arrived in the course of a day and there were two thousand visitors in one hour. Nearly three-quarters come from overseas, and of those nearly half are from the United States. Only 18 per cent of the visitors thought Stonehenge was good value for money! (Golding 1989).

Tourism at Stonehenge as elsewhere, is an expression of the easefulness of long-distance communication and travel. 'Why', as Jencks put it, 'if one can afford to live in different ages and cultures, restrict oneself to the present, the local? Eclecticism is the natural evolution of a culture with choice' (cited in Harvey 1989: 87).

For many people 'sightseeing', as Bourdieu (1984) pointed out, is a form of symbolic capital: putting the emphasis on knowing where to go and what to see disguises both the surplus wealth required and the way in which symbolic capital translates into 'real' capital, increasing the 'value' of those who possess it. But 'sight-seeing' – connecting up with the past (multiple fragmented pasts), creating memories, reminiscing – is also part of the way in which people construct a sense of identity. And different sorts of tourists construct different sorts of identity (Urry 1990), and for some the significance of their experiences may well be 'deeper and be more complex than conventional studies and surveys of leisure and tourism . . . imply' (Clark et al. 1994). Those

Figure 24 'Protecting' the stones
(photo Alan Lodge)

"We decided to come
after all to see some of
your traditional hippy
convoys"

Reproduced by kind
permission of Hector Breeze

who come by car, bicycle or on foot distinguish themselves from the
'mass' tourists who arrive by tour-bus with a 'dwell-time' of twenty-
five minutes (more than half of which, it has been ascertained, is taken
up with buying souvenirs, food and going to the toilets). They may
prefer to see themselves as 'travellers' (hippy or high-class). Those who
come by bus will have equally diverse agendas, and diverse perceptions
of what they are doing and seeing. It is a mistake to assume that people
are the passive recipients or dupes of the heritage industry. Just as Hall
(1980) and others have shown with popular culture, so with heritage,
people mould and reconstruct their experiences. As Warren (1993) puts
it, 'Speaking the language of fantasy, [tourists] can remain sublimely
outside conventional structures of logic and always just beyond the
reach of the dominant hegemonic forces'. People's understandings of
the places they visit are wound around with memories, resonances,
and unpredictable connections. Reality, Lacan once suggested, is merely
a prop on which we lean our dreams (as cited in Crang 1994). And in
the 'epoch of juxtaposition, the epoch of the near and far, of the side-
by-side, of the dispersed' (Foucault 1986: 22), the 'views' of the 'foot-
loose' traveller/tourist will be impressionistic and comparative, and
resonate curiously and variably with the heritage packaging of a deep-
rooted and stable past.[17]

17. Urry suggests that with the increasing flows of capital and people across national
borders, people may lose a sense of a coherent national culture. They by-pass the national
to create a sense of local identity, whilst at the same time garnering a more global sense
of the past through fragmented t.v. presentations and tourist forays (Urry, workshop,
National Trust Centenary Conference, Manchester 1995).

Reproduced by kind permission of *London Evening Standard*

And Who Doesn't

So many different interest groups, so many different understandings of the Stonehenge landscapes. Finally we have the 'alternative' landscapes of both the eccentric but respectable Druids – people who often hold down perfectly good jobs but reject orthodox religion – and the travellers and free festivalers, who are often more sweeping in their rejection of Establishment orthodoxies.

The Druids take their cue from Stukeley. The ancient Order of Druids was founded in 1781, as part of the Romantic movement, happy to pick up where Stukeley had left off. A splinter group, the United Order of Druids, was founded in 1833. The Druids worship at the Summer Solstice but they only started coming to Stonehenge in 1905. Up to the 1970s the Druids were tolerated by the Establishment. They were 'exotic', and quite good for the tourist trade (Figure 25).

The unacceptable 'wierdos' are the New Age travellers and myriad other groupings (hippies, punks, bikers, musicians, clowns, jugglers, peace activists, Hell's Angels, Quakers, Hare Krishna devotees) who held their Free Festival in the field next to Stonehenge for a decade, from

Figure 25 Druidic celebration at Stonehenge (photo Alan Lodge)

the mid-1970s, culminating in the 1984 Festival which attracted over 50,000 people (Rosenberger 1991) (Figure 26). For many of them, Stonehenge is (was) an important meeting-place, a place for spiritual and other sorts of celebrations, weddings, exchanges, part of a seasonal circuit of summer festivals, winter park-ups on commons or derelict urban sites. Many of them, like the Druids, believe that there are psychic forces at Stonehenge – energy fields, leylines – or that it is a temple for the worship of the sun and the moon, for the renewal of seasons.[18] One free festivaler said:

> It's the main part of the earth energy system . . . It's like a *chakra* on the earth's energy. You've got your acupuncture – the system of the human body with all the meridians and all the burial mounds marking them. Then you've got the *chakras* of the human body which are the bigger ones like Old Jerusalem, Mecca, Egypt, Easter Island and Stonehenge . . . (Willie X: pers. comm.)

For several years the authorities remained tolerant. After 1978 the stones were roped off, and standpipes, temporary lavatories and rubbish collection points were installed in the Festival field (Golding 1989). There was very little vandalism, and there was considerable self-policing. But by the early 1980s government and media had turned against the travellers' self-named Peace Convoy, fearing them as anarchists and connecting them with the politically unpopular Peace Camps at Greenham Common, Molesworth, and elsewhere.[19] Despite the 1968 Caravan Sites Act which requires local authorities to provide sites for travellers, such places became fewer and fewer. In 1985 the National Trust and English Heritage took out an injunction and the police moved against them (Chippindale 1986). There were violent showdowns in 1985 and 1988.

18. On the other hand, the messages are not always so spiritual. In 1989 four great letters were grafittied onto the stone: L – I – V – E. They have been cleaned off, of course, but no doubt they will still be visible under X-ray. Were they a proclamation about the life-force, or a political credo, or – as rumoured – the unfinished logo of a certain football team?

19. V.S. Naipaul in *The Enigma of Arrival*, was not enthused by the travellers: 'not gypsies . . . but young city people, some of them criminals, who moved about Wiltshire and Somerset, in old cars and vans and caravans, looking for festivals, communities, camp sites . . . As a deterrent Mr Phillips had the round building wound about with barbed wire' (Naipaul 1987: 270).

FESTIVAL EYE   SUMMER 1989

Reproduced by kind permission of Pete Loveday

Figure 26 Free Festival at Stonehenge
(photo Alan Lodge)

The police have spent over £5 million policing Stonehenge. The government have passed a Public Order Act and a Criminal Justice Act. The police can now arrest two or more people 'unlawfully proceeding in a given direction', and can create 'exclusion zones' to prevent confrontation. The antagonism towards the traveller is not surprising. At the end of the day England's landscape is a proprietorial palimpsest. The travellers own no land or houses, and pay no direct taxes.

"When two or more are gathered together you're in breach of the Public Order Act".

Conclusion

What I have tried to do is to chart, and to begin to explain, a multitude of voices and landscapes through time, mobilising different histories, differentially empowered, fragmented, but explicable within the historical particularity of British social and economic relations, and a larger global economy. Marxist theory is not in fashion, but, as Harvey notes, re-negotiated it still resonates to our condition: 'What Marx depicts . . . are social processes at work under capitalism conducive to individualism, alienation, ephemerality, innovation, creative destruction, speculative development – a shifting experience of space and time, as well as a crisis-ridden dynamic of social change' (Harvey 1989: 111). Does that not begin to engage with the confrontations – emotive, intellectual, and physical – that surround contemporary Stonehenge? Marx's 'social processes' were of course focused along class lines. They must be widened and cross-cut by gender, age, ethnicity and so on (Deutsche 1991; Gilroy 1987; Massey 1991). And, too, the power of rhetoric, and the lived materiality of our existence – of which the time-tunnel, tarmac pathways and the ropes are only small indicators – must be recognised and included as integral to these social processes.

If this chapter is, towards the end, somewhat polemic, that is because it was, in part, spawned in anger at the efforts of English Heritage and parts of the Establishment to promote a socially empty view of the past in line with modern conservative sensibilities. I hope that it begins to justify the study of landscape, not as an aesthetic, not as grist for the First Class Intercity poster, but as something political, dynamic, and contested.

Reproduced by kind permission of Steve Bell

Dialogues 2: Contested Landscapes

The choice of pasts is negotiated in a shifting present

Herzfeld 1991: 257

Dialogue with Ronald Hutton

Ronald Hutton is Professor of History. He has written (among other things) Pagan Religions of the Ancient British Isles *(1991),* The Rise and Fall of Merry England *(1994), and* The Stations of the Sun: a History of the Ritual Year in Britain *(1996). He is particularly interested in the relationship between ancient pagan images and the modern British Imagination. I met him at a conference and he said that, although he liked Chapter 4, he was concerned with the rather repressive relationship I had sketched between the medieval Church and the commoners. I asked him to elaborate. I then discovered that he is working on contemporary paganism, and has some very interesting things to say about developments at Avebury. So I got into another dialogue with him, which comes later (p. 184).*

RH: The view we had of the medieval Church until the 1980s was that it was a rather repressive body that patrolled people's religion and existed on top of the cheerful semi-pagan populace who continued with a lot of the old superstitions – Green Men and whatever – on the sly and occasionally blended in with the Church practices. What we did in the 1980s was to actually go through the Visitation Records and the Parochial Records which people hadn't really used before and which have given us a rather

133

different picture of popular Christianity in the Middle Ages. What we're finding is a flourishing popular religion which is developing so fast that the Church authorities are not so much imposing it from above as trying to run as hard as they can to catch up and to retain any sort of monitoring. This popular religion makes paganism totally irrelevant, totally unnecessary, because it reproduces in parallel pretty well all its characteristics. You have polytheism in the sense that the most active centres of devotions are the saints, not Jesus. Christianity only becomes more Christo-centric at the end of the Middle Ages. And there are hundreds of saints to choose from – some of them are international, lots of them are local. And the relationship is, as in ancient paganism, totally ad hoc: if you've got a problem you choose your saint and go to him or her. What you don't have is a direct transfer from paganism – you don't find many pagan deities being turned into saints. And people choose how to use their religion according to their saint. And this is reflected in church building – by the fifteenth century the average parish church will have, cluttering up its nave, fifteen to twenty shrines built to particular saints with their own altars and often their own clergy. The parish guilds are associations of laity – often very poor laity – and they pay a penny a year, which suffices to pay a pittance to a priest who is there to worship at that particular little altar on behalf of that particular little body of thirty to forty people.

BB: *So how do you regard the work of the French historians – people like Le Goff and Bloch? There's a wonderful article by Le Goff about attitudes to dragons and the way in which the Church tended to see things in black and white, good and evil, whilst the ordinary people were more circumspect, they saw shades of grey and tended to want to propitiate the beast.[1] I was very taken with this sense of a hardening of attitudes – the Church calling the stones 'The Devil's Chair' or whatever. The way they're naming things in more oppositional ways.*

RH: The problem with the Le Goff picture is that it's part of a tendency amongst French intellectuals, in the 1970s in particular, to see an extraordinarily horizontal division in society with intellectuals on one side of it and the populace on the other, and the populace being 'acculturated' – the great buzz word of the seventies. British and American historians questioned this in the eighties, pointing out that when people like Le Goff talk about 'The Church' they

1. Le Goff (1980: 179).

usually mean three or four big-mouthed and rather eccentric Churchmen. Also France is almost destitute of the kind of local records we have in England. When you look at the English local documents you find that the village priest is talking the same language as the people. Every so often, perhaps once every fifty or sixty years, you get a local bishop who is an intellectual with a bee in his bonnet about rationalising everything, who generates huge amounts of paper-work and condemns people left, right and centre, usually among his own clergy. People like Le Goff have taken that as 'The Church'.

BB: *What you're saying is that the local populace used the saints in much the same way as they'd used pagan deities. Rather like, in Mexico, where the Indians seemed to accept the Christian iconography quite enthusiastically and created a sort of bricolage, something syncretic, that absorbed many of the qualities of their own indigenous figures . . .*

RH: It's a perfect parallel – in fact, I use Mexico as a parallel in one of my articles.[2] I was looking at the later period and showing ways in which key Catholic religious ceremonies which were banned, wiped out with painstaking care at the Reformation, left the Church, relocated in people's private homes and became folk ceremonies. So people were still getting the benefit. They were still getting their holy water and fire to protect them. This is in the sixteenth and seventeenth centuries and these things persist through into the nineteenth century when there's a general loss of faith in magic. And, for me, the most interesting thing was the silence – the Puritans sounded off against Catholicism and against maypoles but not against people blessing palm crosses and branches in their houses and making holy fires on Mid Summer's Eve and so on. They recognised that these things were fundamentally harmless . . .

BB: *Let's get back to Avebury. Some of the stones were taken down in the fourteenth century, and then again in the seventeenth century. In the first instance, Burl suggests that they're carefully buried: 'Doing God's work without offending the Devil' . . .*

RH: I don't believe Burl's idea that they were buried in the fourteenth century because they were regarded as satanic . . . or Michael Dames who looks at the figure of St Michael trampling the dragon on the font of Avebury church and says, 'This is the Church's attitude to paganism and the old stones'. This is the one thing I

2. Hutton (1995).

really disagreed with you about in your paper. And what influenced me was the new evidence assembled by Ucko and the others,[3] and particularly their work on the seventeen-century antiquarians which shows that the stones were still being taken down and carefully buried in the seventeenth century because they were in the way of people making gardens.

BB: *So you think that even in the fourteenth century people were getting rid of the stones for pragmatic reasons rather than because the Church thought that they posed a threat?*

RH: Yes, it's the same pattern – you want the stones out of the way so that you can build houses . . .

BB: *Even so, even if the Church was not directly involved and even if the commoners were getting rid of the stones for pragmatic reasons, there may still have been a residue of superstition, a need to go cautiously. Later, in the later seventeenth century, they're more callous in their treatment of the stones. They crack them open with fire and water . . .*

RH: That's because they want to use them to build roads. There was a huge improvement in the technology of road building from the 1680s onwards which burgeoned in the early eighteenth century with the turn-pikes, so big stones suddenly became real money . . .

BB: *Are you saying that through the medieval period and later the stones are not invested with any particular powers?*

RH: What I'm saying is that in the mid-seventeenth century the people at Avebury stunned antiquarians like Aubrey because although they thought the bank and ditch were an old Danish monument, they had no conception that the stones had been erected by people, they thought they were natural features – like those sarsens up on the downs. They didn't think they had been erected until the antiquarians told them they were.

BB: *True, and that's not just the local people. Ucko said that travellers going by coach on the road through the henge never noticed the stones. It is interesting, isn't it? Certain features (the bank and ditch) are invested with historical meaning, other features (the stones) become part of nature. It's not that the stones don't have meaning, but the meaning is not in terms of people or labour. They're not seen as monuments. Nonetheless, even if the stones were thought of as 'natural', and even if – as Ucko mentions – people sat in the shade of the stones and had picnics, they could still have been invested with meaning and power. The meaning and usages might have been reworked over and*

3. Ucko et al. (1991).

over to suit on-going needs. After all, in Brittany there are a good many
standing stones that have been christianised. They have crosses placed
on top, or sculpted onto them. And apparently, right through to this
century, people would go to church to be married and then hurry off
and hold hands around a standing stone to ensure fertility. Isn't it
likely that that went on at many places, whether it's Avebury,
Stonehenge, Carnac, or solitary stones close to some remote hamlet?
Grinsell noted that in the late sixteenth century parish priests threatened
their parishioners with petrification if they danced on the Sabbath –
they'd become a stone circle . . .

RH: That's part of the great Sabbatarian campaign of the late sixteenth
and early seventeenth centuries. What you find is that there's a
much greater tendency from the late sixteenth century onwards
for stones and monuments to be named after the Devil . . .

BB: *. . . So why is the Church bringing the stones back into social relations?*
Why are they re-scripted into Church and religious affairs if they're
not part of folk memory or custom?

RH: The stone circles are brought back into folk memory for the so-
called Reformation of Manners which begins in the late sixteenth
century. You don't get sermons against dancing upon Sunday
before the Elizabethan period, because it's O.K. to dance on
Sunday. What I'm suggesting is that when the campaign against
Sunday sport got under way in the late sixteenth century and
reached its peak, especially among Methodists in Cornwall in the
eighteenth century, preachers would point to well-known local
landmarks, whether they're associated with the Devil, with nature,
or with dead human-beings, and produce this legend that they're
petrified human-beings who danced on a Sunday . . .

BB: *It sounds rather like the North American Apaches who wrap moral*
stories around particular landmarks so that every time someone who
has transgressed sees the place, the moral is reaffirmed. They call it
'stalking with stories'.[4]

RH: Exactly, you attach stories to landmarks . . .

BB: *O.K. I take your point about the Church and the commoners – that*
there was less antagonism than I suggested in the last chapter. But I
won't change what I wrote – it'll be good for people to see how
interpretations get reworked! I guess it also confirms something that
Peter Burke once said about the time-lags that often occur when

4. Basso (1983).

academics try to cross disciplinary boundaries.[5] *I'm still seduced by Le Goff's account of the dragons but I can see that it's only a part of the story . . . But I'm still bothered about the question of folk memory and custom. You say that the stones become moral landmarks as part of the Reformation of Manners and that 'they're brought back into folk memory'. So are you assuming that right through the medieval period and later the stones hadn't been part of folk memory?*

RH: No. My only point of disagreement with your original analysis was your acceptance of Burl's and Dames's idea of ecclesiastical hostility to megalithic monuments in the Middle Ages – there's not a single case in the whole of Europe of a prehistoric monument definitely being destroyed by the Church as pagan or devilish . . . As to folk-lore: we have a real problem of evidence. From the sixteenth and seventeenth centuries onwards we have accounts of popular folk-lore in quite large quantity, burgeoning into the nineteenth century, but for the Middle Ages we have almost none. We simply don't know what medieval commoners thought of their local standing stones. What we can say with some confidence is what their ecclesiastical superiors thought of standing stones and dolmens, and they appear to mostly ignore them, to regard them as essentially unimportant. You get these great bonfires of small Anglo-Saxon wooden shrines and images in the early medieval period but no destruction of the long defunct ritual monuments . . .

BB: *Geoffrey of Monmouth, in the twelfth century, said that the stones at Stonehenge had curative powers; Stukeley, in the eighteenth century, mentions people chipping bits off the bluestones for medicinal purposes; at Carnac in Brittany women rub themselves against the stones in order to conceive. These things went on, stories and actions were woven around certain places . . .*

RH: Yes, what strikes me is that the folk-lore is very heterogeneous, you don't find a consistent tradition of use even between a couple of parishes. What you have is ways in which striking features like megalithic monuments have been developed for different emotional uses. I think they're a tribute to the sheer versatility and creativity of the popular imagination.

BB: *Maybe that was always true: the meaning of places and features was always heterogeneous, always varied from region to region, group to group (see p. 77).*

5. Burke (1980: ch.1).

Dialogue with Peter Ucko

Peter Ucko is one of the authors of Avebury Reconsidered. From the 1660s to the 1990s (1991)*; he is also the general editor of the Routledge One World Archaeology series. Many of the volumes in this series are concerned with the politics of the past. Peter has worked extensively in Australia. I wanted to get him to comment on the chapter, but also to tell me about a comparative case study from Australia.*

Peter, like Ronald Hutton (p. 136), queried the idea that medieval commoners at Avebury still feared or revered the stones. He also questioned whether the Anglo-Saxon church had really been built in order to appropriate or destroy the power of the stones.

PU: We've been taught that the church is up against the henge, but actually its quite far away and there were water meadows on both sides. If you were trying to oppose the stones why put it that far away? I think you've over-stated the evidence from the medieval period. Your general point would be just as valid if you suggested that half the medieval population took no notice of the stones at all . . .

BB: *O.K!*

PU: There's another point that comes out of our work at Avebury. When you talk about Stukeley and concentrate on how he incorporates Druidic material that's fine. Where you go a bit wrong – following Piggott – is to accept that Stukeley was out there being accurate in the field. The subtle point is that Stukeley is incorporating the past into his own world (and I bet you that's just as true of us today when we do a piece of recording). He incorporates assumptions into his recording method which are anything but scientific. He walks around the stones and records them, and he *invents* his 100 stones. As he walks around he says, 'Ah, there's a hollow with nettles in it – must be a stone'. But that's only because he is expecting to find a hundred stones. Its not about falsification, it's about incorporating preconceptions.

BB: *Preconceived ideas get worked into the drawings . . .*

PU: Absolutely. But it's also more than that. Stukeley's published record of Avebury has his well-known frontispiece. But he also *experimented* with a verbal description, drawings, and all sorts of conventions and plans. He finally opted for the frontispiece because he *thought* it was the most effective way to represent what he considered to be 'the reality' of the site. And yes, there is also a bit of evidence – which is what Piggott said – that Stukeley actually changed the shape of the head to look more snake-like. Now *that's* fabrication. But the recording methods and decisions of any period represent the assumptions which we have at that time which are incorporated as the evidence of the past and then justified as the real record.

BB: *I like that, the way our subjectivities inform not just what we think and say, but all our practices . . .*

PU: The stuff from Avebury completely supports your general thesis about contestation and the marginalisation of some groups. There's been an endless protesting by the local Aveburians – farmers, peasants, and now people in the council flats just down the road. The recent protests are about the *lack* of development at Avebury which has meant less local employment, and an outcry against the plans by English Heritage to bring in story-tellers and dancers from outside the local area when the villagers were not allowed to dress up as Elizabethan wenches in the Manor House. There's a continuous over-ruling of the local people.

Where I think you fall into a trap, and I think it's David Lowenthal's trap,[6] is when you say, 'Stonehenge became a museum, fenced in . . . no longer a lived landscape'. I think it's more subtle than this: to fence something in doesn't remove it. It actually emphasises that feature. It may change the conditions, but to suddenly deny that it is a living landscape just because it's been fenced is a non-sequitur.

BB: *I suppose so . . . But you could say that until it was fenced it could be used in any number of ways – cricket match, have a picnic, make an offering – and in that sense it was open. Once you fence it off it becomes one thing only, a place to be visited under very particular and very highly organised conditions . . .*

PU: Ah – I didn't think you were particularly talking about Stone-henge, I thought you were talking more generally about fencing sites in . . .

BB: *I wanted to stress that the fencing makes it a far more disciplined experience – you're right, it* is *lived, but there's far less choice about what you do when you get there, and where you go.*

6. Lowenthal (1979).

PU: It's still a form of living – it's just a change of its function. And it can work quite differently. Tiwanakuin in Bolivia became fenced off, became a heritage site, and the local people suddenly had to pay to get at their own sacred sites. They did pay, those who could afford it, and they went on complaining. And then a whole range of rituals developed – a sort of modification of previous rituals – to counteract the fact that they couldn't get to this most important place. In no way was it killed off as a piece of living landscape . . .

BB: *That's an important point. Shall we move on to the Australian Aboriginal case-study that you mentioned? I like the idea of bringing in a case-study that is totally different from Stonehenge but which underlines the connection between the claims people make on the past, the ways in which they identify with the past, the different sorts of past they create, and the economic, social and political particularities of a given moment . . .*

PU: O.K. I want to talk about Laura, North Queensland. There's an endless range after range of mountains. It's in an area where a gold rush happened, an area where the Chinese were out getting gold. The rock art was found in the early 1960s by an Ansett pilot. The passengers kept writing in to complain to Reggie Ansett that they were being made completely sick by this crazy pilot. What he was doing was trying to spot the rock art – he flew his plane into the mountains and the poor passengers suddenly saw sheer rock on either side. So he got fired. But, being Australia, Mr Ansett bought him his own single-engine plane. And Percy Tresize flew over the mountains, and then went in with pack-horses to find and record the rock art.

There is a town, what you and I would call a petrol pump and a pub, called Laura. And Percy Tresize, to cut a long, long, unpleasant story short, bought the pub and took over the art. On one side of the road was the pub, on the other a row of Queensland State houses for Aborigines. Percy managed to declare the rock art dead – prehistoric – thus dispossessing the Aborigines completely. This was, I think, based on his having totally failed to understand the very, very poor English of the old Aborigines who were around in Laura.

BB: *Did the local Aborigines take him to the rock art?*

PU: No, he first found the art from his aeroplane. Then, when he got to Laura, I think some Aborigines took him out to galleries that he hadn't seen before. But he claims that, from his interviews with them, they knew nothing about the art – that they had come in from different areas. He then mounts a huge chronology of the rock art to prove that virtually all of it is prehistoric, and he even came up with a theory that the destruction of the Aborigines had led to the end of the rock art.

Ten years later, by which time the rock art was getting known through his work, he brought in an Aborigine from Mornington Island – a little island off the top of Queensland. Now everything we know says that this island was culturally and linguistically totally different from anything to do with the Laura area. He got the Aborigine – Dick Roughsey – to explain the art. Percy produced endless published works, for children as well as adults, so that, by the 1980s, children – both white children, and aboriginal children who had been taken away from their traditional homes – were learning about this huge complex of rock art through the eyes of a Mornington Island Aborigine . . .

BB: *Why did he think that Dick Roughsey would know, when the local people didn't?*

PU: He felt Dick Roughsey could get at the stories because they were common to Aborigines. So first it's cast into prehistory, and then it's reincorporated through a non-local Aboriginal eye. Then, stage three, Queensland State suddenly realised that Laura was a tourist asset. So the Aborigines' houses were painted, and the road was improved, and instead of taking six hours from Cairns on a dreadful road, access was easier. Then the battle began. The local Aborigines said, 'Hey, this is ours, and of course we know what it is, and we want to take the tourists round.' I got involved – because I was head of the Federal Institute. The Aborigines appealed and so did Tresize, and the State authorities wanted to make it into a park. And so, to simplify the story, we ended up having three official versions of what the rock art could be about – one, local Aborigine-based; two, Tresize and the Mornington Island Aborigine – who claimed he had got it from the old men but really got it from himself – and three, the park officials who were archaeologists or part-archaeology trained and talked about chronology . . .

BB: *Did the local Aborigines suggest that the art was more recent?*

PU: Not necessarily – they just 'knew' the meaning. Although there was one old Aborigine, called Henry Lee Chew, who took me up into a gallery, which he knew and nobody else knew, including Tresize, and which he then 'interpreted', painting by painting.

Tresize then made an alliance with the State government and attempted to get the whole area designated as a World Wilderness. The proposal was that the Aborigines would have the right to apply for traditional hunting and gathering and fishing – but that otherwise it was wilderness! But it didn't get through and the State government took it over and made it into a State park.

Finally, the most recent twist. Nine months ago (1995), to my amazement, under the Labour government, land rights were introduced for the first time into Queensland and a claim for Laura and its rock art was lodged by the local Aborigines. The claim was challenged from Hopevale which is on the coast, about six hours drive. An Aborigine ordained Lutheran from the Mission at Hopevale had seen a confidential report that I'd written in the seventies in which I said that no one had ever tried to follow up any of the Aborigines who had been dispossessed of their land and shoved all over the place, including Hopevale, to see whether there wasn't anyone who might know something about the paintings. This bloke from Hopevale got hold of this, and lodged a counter claim against the local Laura Aborigines. So sitting over in Hopevale are people claiming to be the descendants of the painters who had been thrown out of Laura and dumped over there!

BB: *The past being dragged into the present to be used by different groups, partly because money's involved, partly as a claim on place, a reiteration of identity, as resistance to something being taken from them by white people . . . all those things . . .*

PU: Yes, the art has gone in and out of the modern situation in at least three very different contexts – the same body of material . . .

BB: *How many local people are we talking about?*

PU: Very few, hundred and fifty maximum – probably much less. They're very nomadic. In the wet it was probably much less. From one day to the next the number at Laura would treble. There were about twenty houses. Some of the old people, like Henry Lee Chew didn't normally live in Laura. Those people who were not Laura-based only became interested when they could see that it could bring money in.

BB: *But Henry Lee Chew was adamant that they knew this art long before Tresize came through – that he'd been involved in rituals in which people would use the paintings in some way?*

PU: Yes, absolutely. And that fits in with Bob Layton's work in other parts of Australia. The Aborigines – for example, a very old

Aborigine called Bob Flinders – took him and other archaeologists and anthropologists to places and they'd reincorporate – reinterpret – rock art which we know was already there a hundred years earlier. They and their ancestors had been changing it and updating it all the time. Henry Lee Chew was so specific about these individual representations. It was quite difficult to recognise some of them but he'd say, 'No, you can see it'.

BB: *It's a great story . . . You managed to hear the voices of people who don't often get heard; but will their versions get lost once Laura becomes a State park and there are official interpretations?*

PU: I think that they have been heard because of the Land Rights Claim, but otherwise they might easily not have been heard.

BB: *One last question: is it only men that are doing the talking? There's not been a mention of a woman at any point in the story . . .*

PU: Certainly in my time only the men talked about any of this. Physically the women always sat back. I've no idea whether they got incorporated into the tourism.

Another Way of Telling

The times require new imagination

Robin Grove-White (*The Guardian* September 1995)

Figure 27 'Stonehenge Belongs to You and Me' – the exhibition on the move
(photo: Polly Farquharson)

145

Introduction

The other chapters that I've written in this book are 'academic'. They were written to be placed in respectable journals. This one is rather different. It is, in part, more anecdotal, more akin to a personal ethnography. Nonetheless it touches on matters that are important in theory and in practice.

Christmas 1991. The usual jamboree at the TAG (Theoretical Archaeology) conference.[1] I gave a presentation on contemporary Stonehenge. It was – as you might have suspected from the last part of Chapter 4 and the Dialogues in 5 – about contestation and appropriation, and about exclusionary politics. It was about a landscape that had become ossified and roped off. About the (attempted) regulation of space – the way in which entrances, exits, and footpaths corralled people – and the (attempted) regulation of perception and understanding. It was about the purveying of an elitist, masculine narrative. And about the exclusion of undesirable consumers: how some categories of person were acceptable, some not. And, finally, it was an acknowledgement that, as always in such matters, things, ideas, and relationships were discordant, contradictory, fractured, and volatile.

In the presentation I suggested that archaeologists risked becoming the apologists for intolerant and inflexible heritage policies, bolstering an image of time past as something over and done with, legitimising an obsession with origins, and playing a part in sustaining a management policy that rarely looked beyond the needs of preservation and commoditisation.[2] I suggested that the exclusionary politics of Stonehenge builds on and shelters behind a powerfully prevalent archaeological discourse (Smith 1994).

At this TAG conference some fellow archaeologists agreed that muttered *mea culpas* about the current Stonehenge confrontations were not enough: we should make some sort of stand. Mark Edmonds and I

---

1. TAG = Theoretical Archaeology Group. A place where postgraduates get to be heard.

2. As Clark et al. (1994) point out, in the more general context of leisure and tourism, such 'discourses of management are unable to take on board the full range of what's at stake: access and the right to roam, notions of "heritage", conflicts about animals, local distinctiveness and national uniformity, dilemmas over the car, new age travellers, politics of farm diversification . . .'

Rowlands suggests that in a climate of anxiety about national or regional integrity, and 'fears about the coca colonization of global culture, identity as something perduring and consistent has become a key value that archaeology, due to its access to the long term, is credited with being particularly well situated to exploit' (Rowlands 1994).

wrote a piece for *The Guardian* (Figure 28) in time for the Summer Solstice of 1992. It was picked up by the 'serious' media because it was seen as an example of 'the Establishment' breaking ranks. Not surprisingly, it was ignored by the popular press who were busy fulfilling their annual knee-jerk obligation to rubbish 'the dregs of society': exposing the Stonehenge hippies for what they really were – tax-dodging, giro-gypsies. At an interview for ITV, the cameraman told me I should express myself more forcefully, and then said, as he put the film in the can: 'They'll edit it, of course, they always do, they'll cut the radical bits ...' He went on to discuss the freemasonry that controlled TV production. He was right, they did.

THE GUARDIAN
Monday June 15 1992

COMMENT

De-romancing the Stones

As the police get set for Operation Summer Solstice, **Barbara Bender** and **Mark Edmonds** argue that we must confront the socio-political functions of sites like Stonehenge

A S USUAL, at this time of year, Stonehenge is about to be shrouded in razor wire and the arc lights and dog patrols are out. Our police will come in resemble their Third World counterparts in terms of the kind of control they will exercise over the environs of the site and general public movement around Wiltshire. If recent years are anything to go by, dawn on June 21 will witness either another bloody confrontation or a desolate silence.

As archaeologists, we could try to abdicate responsibility: our job, after all, is to study the past. But, alas, there is no neat dividing line between past and present. We know that the monuments that litter our landscape were once used and re-used by different peoples and that control over them was contested by different groups in struggles for position and power. These stones embody contradictory ideas and associations. But these processes did not terminate at some time in the past and the questions we ask about the broader socio-political functions served by these sites, or about how their meaning and power were controlled and sustained over time, are as relevant today as they were in prehistoric times. The violent confrontations at Stonehenge simply make it more imperative that we, as archaeologists, engage with the politics of the past in the present.

Whilst it is a truism that "every age has the Stonehenge it deserves", it is clear that the meaning of the site today is deeply contentious. What happens at the Solstice is not simply a physical confrontation but also a cultural clash: the stones provide a medium for the expression of the tensions and contradictions in contemporary society.

For the establishment Stonehenge is a pre-eminent trace of our great past (the "our" remaining unspecified). For the police it is presumably an unwelcome drain on resources and a public relations minefield. For the heritage industry it is a tourist honey-pot, and for advertisers a symbol which is used to sell everything from cigarettes to stereos. For at least some of the travellers it is a spiritual mecca and an important seasonal meeting point. In each case, one could sub-divide these far from homogeneous groups, highlighting fundamental differences of opinion and vision. English Heritage and the National Trust are crisscrossed by different interest groups, some focusing on conservation and preservation, others intent on meeting the needs of the tourist industry. Equally, as recent events in the Malvern Hills have shown, important distinctions need to be drawn between groups that the media lump together under the umbrella term "Travellers". We cannot assume a consensus within society regarding the focus on cosy vignettes of past historic sites.

Under these circumstances, current attitudes towards the political and material conditions under which people lived, and against which they struggled. It is usually left unstated that the grand avenues leading to many stately homes lead also to the slave plantations which provided the wealth for their construction and occupation.

These are rather more than semantic distinctions, of interest only to those occupying the beleaguered ivory towers of academia. As we walk through these landscapes, or visit ancient monuments and heritage centres, we take on board a variety of images which shape our understanding of both the past and present. For the majority of tourists, drawn from predominantly white, middle-class backgrounds, the notion of a common heritage, and of a landscape with deep historical roots, may seem unproblematic and part of the nature of things. But where does this leave large sections of Britain's population, for whom these traces may evoke different redolences and different histories?

I T IS perhaps inevitable that increasingly violent confrontations between a small section of the travellers and the police should come to command attention in the media. But amidst all the hyperbole we should not lose sight of the fact that, for many people in Britain today, the past is unavoidably political and undoubtedly contentious. It is a past to which they have little or no access. There can be no doubt that monuments such as Stonehenge are physically vulnerable, requiring active care and maintenance. But it is ludicrous to assume that the Solstice celebrations have been thus far the principal threat and cause of damage to the site. The entire region is full of ar-

chaeological remains, both above and below ground, all of which are much more deeply threatened by the firing ranges to the north and by the defences constructed to protect the monument. In the short term, the potential exists for arrangements to be made for controlled access to the site at the Solstice and for the placement of the Free Festival at some distance from the stones. In the longer term, and at a rather broader level, what is at issue is intellectual as well as physical access. Temporary road blocks, and the infringement of civil liberties that they constitute, may leave no mark in the archaeological record. But it remains to be seen how the archaeologists of the future will interpret the traces of barriers and trenches that define the perimeter of Stonehenge. Will they be taken as evidence for an increasing concern with problems of conservation? Or will they rather be seen as one more manifestation of how Stonehenge has been, and continues to be, an medium through which sectional claims to authority are made and reaffirmed?

Barbara Bender, Department of Anthropology, London University and Mark Edmonds, Department of Archaeology, Cambridge are supported by nine archaeologists from British universities.

Figure 28 An article in *The Guardian*
(*The Guardian* June 15th 1992)

A minibus of archaeologists attempted to enter the four mile exclusion zone thrown up around the stones at the Solstice. We were not allowed through the police barricades, and the police openly subverted the new law and order act. That act – punitive enough, though nothing in comparison to the Criminal Justice Act of 1994 – laid down that two people proceeding in a given direction can constitute a procession and can be arrested as a threat to civil order. We offered to go in with fifty yards between each person. They said they would arrest us anyway.[3]

Reproduced by kind permission of Pete Loveday

3. We went on to Avebury where, in the misty dawn, people were chilling out, dancing, dowsing. Not a policeman in sight. It felt great.

As a result of these various activities, I was contacted by a group of free festivalers and travellers. In *The Guardian* article Mark Edmonds and I had tried to address a range of issues to do with questions of heritage presentation and access, but the free festivalers focused on the one thing that mattered to them – that we had acknowledged their right to be heard. They had, in the aftermath of the Battle of the Beanfield in 1985 (see p. 203) formed The Stonehenge Campaign group. They met in London once a month.

I started going to their meetings. These are mainly about networking information on gigs, festivals, protests, and attempts to get to Solstices and Equinoxes. The networking is highly effective; but the meetings are, by definition, anarchic. Sessions start one/two/three hours late. There is an Agenda, but Any Other Business is dealt with first and takes up most of the time. People talk across each other, conversations within conversations, groups within groups, aggravation, a gentle subsidence into beer and weed. The group has, of course, almost no money, with all the limitations that that imposes. They have had dealings with English Heritage, meetings that fizzled into nothing (see p. 204). There are flickers of optimism: '... *this* year the Equinox will be different', 'Jocelyn Stevens (head of English Heritage) has promised ...' – but mostly they are profoundly sceptical. Their aim, at Equinox and Solstice, is to play cat-and-mouse with the forces of law and order, to take avoiding action, to get to events ... They recognise all too well the limitations of their actions.

Eventually, the question came up: what should be done at the next Solstice, and what, more precisely, would I, the 'outsider', do? Would I lead the students against the exclusion zone? Thinking of irate parents and the law-suits that would follow, I blenched. Then the idea of a travelling exhibition emerged. Would I co-ordinate it? I hesitated, then agreed. I wanted to support them. I wanted to see whether it was possible to find a way of creating space for different voices and of showing how exclusionary politics worked. Would it be possible to popularise without losing substance? Could one be involved and maintain a sense of perspective? How would it be to work with people who were non-academic and whose ideas were different from mine?

This chapter is about putting together the exhibition. But first, in the context, not so much of creating the exhibition, but of the issues concerning empowerment that were part of the reason for the exhibition, I want to touch on some theoretical matters.

Theoretical Matters

Mounting an exhibition such as this poses plenty of questions: about 'heritage' (how is it defined? who defines it, and for whom? what purpose does it serve?), about representation, and about power. I am not going to spend time on 'heritage' other than to suggest that it should be seen, not as separate from history, but as *a* form of history. A *commoditised* form, made – both consciously and unconsciously – *in* the present, *for* the present. Questions of representation come to the fore in the Dialogues in Chapter 8. What I want to focus on are slightly more abstract questions of *power* and *empowerment* (or lack of).

There is *power over* which is, by definition, about inequality (which need not always be negative, see pp. 60 and 99), and there is *power to*. *Power over* logically involves the *power to*. But the *power to* do things and think things (to act in and on the world) can also involve the circumvention, questioning, or finding alternative ways of being creative in the face of, or in the interstices of, unequal power relations.

Power over is never absolute and never fully achieved. Gramsci (1971) talks of hegemonic power as a moving equilibrium, a process, rather than a frozen embodiment. It is a process because although some form of consent has been achieved, it can never last. Consent is, at most, 'a tenuous mix of approval and apathy, resistance and resignation' (Warren 1993). There are multiple intersections to the structures of power: those with power (in power) are often at odds with each other (Mohanty 1991); and the same is true for those who contest.

Gramsci's notion of hegemonic power has often been depicted as something top-down, and imposed from above. It is supposedly very different from Foucault's notion of power as something not so much exerted over others, but as something that penetrates the total fabric of people's lived lives. People, Foucault suggests, are socialised into undertaking their own surveillance and policing (Foucault 1977: 228; 1981: 93), and power is omnipresent in the social body (Miller and Tilley 1984: 6). But, in fact, there is less to choose between the two positions than might seem. Here is Raymond Williams explicating the working of hegemony:

> The relations of domination and subordination, in their forms as practical consciousness, [are] in effect a saturation of the whole process of living – not only of political and economic activity, nor only of manifest social activity, but of the whole substance of lived identities and relationships, to such a depth that the pressures and limits of what can ultimately be

seen as a specific economic, political and cultural system seem to most of us the pressures and limits of simple experience and common sense (Williams 1994).[4]

But whether one talks in terms of hegemonic power or of self surveillance, there is always the possibility of resistance and alternative creativity.[5] The making of the Stonehenge exhibition, and the protesting voices and actions that form part of it, are not, in and of themselves, of major consequence, nonetheless they touch upon what De Certeau calls: 'the multiform, resistant, tricky and stubborn procedures that elude discipline without being outside the field in which it is exercised' (De Certeau 1984: 96). In his somewhat flowery evocation, De Certeau (1984: 96) talks of the 'Microbe-like, singular and plural practices . . . that, far from being regulated or eliminated by panoptic administration, have reinforced themselves in a proliferating illegitimacy, developed and insinuated themselves into the networks of surveillance.'

Such 'proliferating illegitimacies' often appear to be very local, sporadic, and anarchic. Harvey, following Williams, talks of 'militant particularism' – anger and frustration mobilising around particular, often local, issues (Harvey 1996: 32). Such militant particularism often appears to be ineffectual. But quite apart from the possibility of short-term local effectiveness, there is also the possibility that 'particularities' may join forces, may ally in ways that have greater disruptive potential. What happened, and happens, at Stonehenge are tiny acts of resistance, but, in the last few years, such acts have worked alongside other protests involving issues of access to land and sites, animal rights and environmental issues, road protests and so on (see pp. 169 and 205). The protests ramify, and move from local to regional to national and sometimes beyond. Contemporary compression of time and space,

4. I cannot resist quoting some more of this passage: 'Hegemony is the whole body of practices and expectations, over the whole of living. Hegemony can speak for example to the realities of electoral democracy, and to the signficant modern areas of "leisure" and private life. If the pressures and limits of a given form of domination are to this extent experienced and in practice internalised, the whole question of class rule, and of opposition to it, is transformed' (Williams 1994).

5. Blunt and Rose (1994) note the paradox that while 'the others' are marginalised and ignored, they are also given their own places – the slum, the ghetto, the harem, the colony, the closet, the inner city [and we could add the park-up site, the squat] , places [that] haunt the imagination of the master subject.

usually seen as a force promoting homogenisation, also creates the possibility of a networking of communication that promotes heterogeneity and subversion (Harvey 1989: 260–307).

Mohanty talks of ' "imagined communities" with divergent histories and social locations, woven together by the *political* threads of opposition'. Such communities are, she suggests, '"imagined" not because they are not "real", but because they suggest potential alliances and collaborations across diverse boundaries, and [are] "communities" because in spite of internal hierarchies . . . they suggest a significant, deep commitment to what Benedict Anderson calls "horizontal comradeship"' (Mohanty 1991). Mohanty is talking about alliances amongst Third World women, but there are many other such 'imagined communities', often fleeting but, while they last, just as real.

This notion of the mobility and 'globalisation' of resistance is reworked in a somewhat different way by Edward Said. He points out that people, whether they wish it or not, are increasingly on the move, and that resistance and opposition, have 'shifted from the settled, established, and domesticated dynamics of culture to its unhoused, decentred and exilic energies, energies whose incarnation today is the migrant' (Said 1993: 403). When he wrote this, Said was certainly not thinking about the Stonehenge 'marginals', but it is the case that mobility acts as a further bond between many disparate disaffected in contemporary Britain. And although one should not be too free with appropriating insights gained from very different historical and social conditions, when Clifford, in the context of diasporas, talks of 'Routes and rootedness . . . identifications not identities, acts of relationship rather than pre-given forms . . . 'tradition' [as] a network of partially-connected histories . . . globalisation from below' (Clifford 1994), it resonates with the local roots and inter-regional routedness of the hydra-headed protest movements. It also underlines a source of tension within these tentative alliances, for it is difficult to transcend:

> The narrow solidarities and particular affinities shaped in particular places – the preferred milieu of most grass roots activism – and adopt a politics of abstraction capable of reaching out across space, across the multiple environmental and social conditions that constitute the geography of difference in a contemporary world that capitalism has intensely shaped to its own purposes (Harvey 1996: 400).[6]

6. See also Jacobs (1993).

One further point before I return to the exhibition. I was the 'outsider', co-ordinating the exhibition, laying down a lot of the ground rules. Is this not just another form of power? One moment I am totally involved in putting together the exhibition, I am engaged and partisan. At another, the exhibition becomes this chapter, I don my ethnographer's hat, stand back from the action and try to account for what is happening.[7] What is concrete becomes abstract; what might seem objective to the groups involved, becomes subjective and relative. And then the chapter becomes a book: an offering to the Research Council, a claim to recognition. There is no easy answer to this dilemma. All one can do is recognise and reluctantly accept that one's thoughts and actions are ambiguous and often contradictory, but that one should try, as much as possible, not to speak for, but to speak with and to people – try to invest in dialogues, rather than subsume others within monologues (Spivak cited in Alcoff 1991).

To Return to the Exhibition

I brought a rough outline of how I thought the exhibition might work to the Stonehenge Campaign meeting. They accepted it. I was startled. Why was it not questioned? I think that, amongst themselves, when something has to be done, particularly something involving 'straights' (outsiders), people are delegated and allowed to get on with it. It is a question of temporary and quite unstable leadership (see Thomas, p. **). For this project I was temporary leader. Moreover, they were shrewd enough to recognise that I had some authority, could get things done, and would probably know how to present things to the outside world.

Most of them were in favour of the project but were not prepared to work on it, or with me, systematically. They provided materials, offered suggestions, and then wandered off. Out of fifteen or twenty regular Stonehenge Campaigners, three free festivalers (Hilary, Wesley, and Paul) worked consistently on it, and in the end the group consisted of them, an Arch Druid (Hugo Maughfling), a journalist who had been

---

7. Harvey expresses a somewhat similar sense of dis-ease about a time when, as an academic, he became involved in the Cowley motorwork closures and was asked by the people involved to contribute to a book. He found himself caught between the purely plant-based politics and a more abstract, more encompassing politics. There was, he admits, something 'problematic about imposing a politics guided by abstractions upon people who had given their lives and labor over many years in a particular way in a particular place' (Harvey 1996: 23).

following the free festivalers and travellers for a year (Annabel Edwards), an undergraduate (Vicky Larkin) from the Institute of Archaeology in London who had, independently, made contact with the group, and, towards the end, an anthropologist (Mandy Walker) whom I asked to come and help.

It was not easy. We wanted the exhibition to be on display by the Summer Solstice of 1993. We started just before the Christmas of 1992. We met at first once a month, then more frequently, in different combinations. We had no money. *They* had no money. I was unable to drum up grants: partly because I was very late, partly because the project fell between every conceivable stool. I used my own money and I used departmental resources. I estimate that it cost, approximately, £1500 (which, over the last three years, I have slowly recouped from the rent charged to museums and from the sale of T-shirts). The free festivalers provided timber when they could find it, sent out information on their mailing lists, used their own transport when available, and got hold of cartoons. They already had a huge, and invaluable, media database. They only ever asked for money for things they had to buy, and then accounted for their spending down to the last penny.

They could never have afforded to put up an exhibition of this size. They could never have organised it. They could have, indeed had once organised, something on a much smaller scale. But not on *this* scale. And they could not have got access to the places – the museums and libraries – where the exhibition was shown. I could use my position, affiliations, accent, perhaps my gender. I am not denigrating their activities. I am just stating the obvious, that there are monetary and institutional constraints on the various forms of potential subversion and resistance. As Morley put it, 'The weak are not entirely powerless, but given their lack of control over institutions and resources, they have to operate at the margins (temporal and spatial) left by those who do control such institutional resources' (Morley 1992: 275).[8]

I created the format. I tried to explain in the Introduction to the exhibition how the past is used over and over again, how there are different pasts at different times, and different pasts for different people (Figure 29). Multiple voices, multiple understandings, multiple engagements. We used a mirror so that people could see themselves and recognise that they, too, were part of the story (Figure 30). Very post-

---

8. Keesing (1994) notes, following Stuart Hall, that 'confrontational politics are inherently structured in the terms and categories of the dominant. In part . . . this is because of a strategic realization that one must meet the enemy on his own turf.'

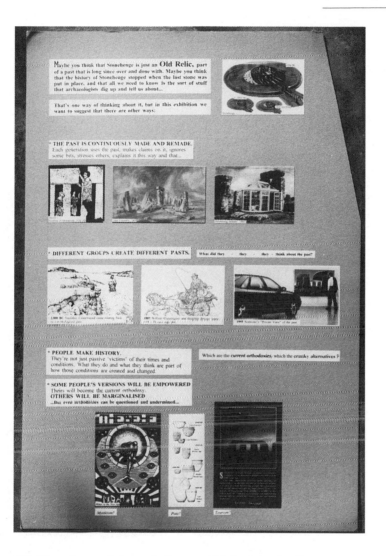

Figure 29 'Stonehenge Belongs to You and Me' – Introduction
(photo: Polly Farquharson)

modern. But also, less post-modern, we mentioned differential
empowerment: who among the multiplicity of voices gets to be heard,
and how and why?

The exhibition was mounted on nine great trilithons. The free
festivalers designed the trilithons. They had a very clear idea of the
shape and size that they should be. They did not approve of my original,
rather romanticised, design. Their's was realist-gothick. I had the
trilithons built; they painted them.

Figure 30 'Stonehenge Belongs to You and Me' – a mirror to pull you into the exhibition
(photo: Polly Farquharson)

I wrote the Introduction, and I wrote the sections on Prehistoric and Historic Appropriations and Contestations (Figure 31). With hindsight[9] I realise that I undermined part of my own thesis. I was presenting a particular version of prehistory and history, an archaeologist's version of the past. These sections should not have been neutrally positioned

9. And insights from Mike Rowlands.

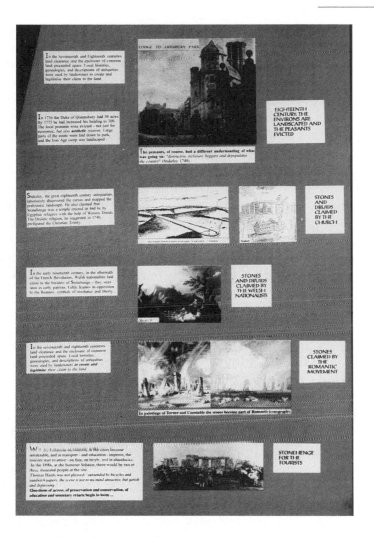

Figure 31 'Stonehenge Belongs to You and Me' – one of two boards on Historical Contestations and Appropriations
(photo: Polly Farquharson)

at the beginning of the exhibition, they should have formed part of the archaeological text.

The next trilithons were about present-day attitudes. The idea was that each interest group should write their own board. What did Stonehenge mean to them? How did they feel about how the site and the landscape were being used and presented? What did they want? We decided that English Heritage, archaeologists, free festivalers/travellers, Druids, locals, landowners and tourists should all be included.

I got in contact with a nice man from the education department of English Heritage. He was enthusiastic. He asked his superiors. They said the public relations department could handle it. We protested – it wasn't meant to be a public relations exercise. Reluctantly they agreed that he could write it but insisted on their right to censor what he wrote. We agreed. A week before the exhibition, he rang: they had told him to pull out. They said that they presented enough information in other places and forms, if anyone wanted anything they could apply directly to them. He was devastated, and so was I. They saw no need for debate. Just as, in their stewardship of the site, they saw no need for compromise (see The Dialogue that Never Happened, p. 174). So I wrote the English Heritage section. The free festivalers toned down my original, more acrimonious, text.

The free festivalers dragged their feet over their section. What was the problem? Eventually it emerged that they were not prepared to speak for each other. So it was agreed that they would provide me with a list of quotes and a history of their engagement with the site. I wrote it up; they carefully edited it (Figure 32).

The Druids provided their own materials (Figure 33). No problem there. They spent a lot of time and energy checking out details at the Public Record Office – dates of early Eisteddfods, royal charters of fairs, bardic celebrations and so on. They had a small problem with the photographic coverage. No picture could be earlier than 1987. There had, at that date, been a split in the Druid movement involving fisticuffs in muddy fields. The wrong photo could lead to more spilt blood.

I did the Archaeology board, and had almost as much trouble as the free festivalers. Who was I speaking for? I found that, once again, in a totally conventional way, I created a linear narrative. Just as the whole exhibition had a linear framework – contestations through time – so now I charted changing archaeological perceptions through time. It was only when I came to discuss more recent ways of thinking about the past that I managed to introduce the idea of a more reflexive circularity between past and present, present and past (Figure 34).

The other 'voices' showed interesting variations. Not surprisingly, the landowners expressed unmitigated hostility to the free festivalers.[10] They talked, to a *man*, about ownership and property, about threats to

10. Vicky Larkin sent letters and questionnaires to local landowners. She received nine replies.

Figure 32 'Stonehenge Belongs to You and Me' – one of two boards on the views of travellers, pilgrims, free festivalers
(photo: Polly Farquharson)

their land. On the other hand, local opinion was polarised.[11] Many people were against the exclusion zone and police action, partly because it affected their freedom of movement, partly because they had

11. Our sampling strategies left everything to be desired – we were simply interested in the *range* of potential opinion. Vicky Larkin interviewed local people in Amesbury, and several people wrote in response to a request for people's opinions placed in the local newspaper.

Figure 33 'Stonehenge Belongs to You and Me' – one of two boards on the views of druids
(photo: Polly Farquharson)

witnessed heavy-handed policing, but most often because it was their taxes that were being siphoned off for the police operations. Their priorities (education, housing) lost out to the escalating cost of containment.

The final sections were about how the different 'voices' were empowered. Or rather, more accurately, how some voices got

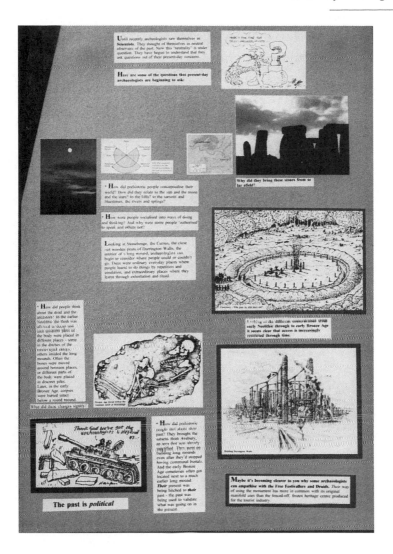

Figure 34 'Stonehenge Belongs to You and Me' – one of two boards on the views of archaeologists
(photo: Polly Farquharson)

marginalised. The free festivalers – Hilary, Wes, and Paul – created the media board (Figure 35). They had their own archive. They had clear ideas about how media misrepresentation worked. They also recognised that there was no conformity. Even the gutter press might run a pro-traveller piece in among the column inches of denigration. The journalist, Annabel Edwards, and I did the legal, juridical and police

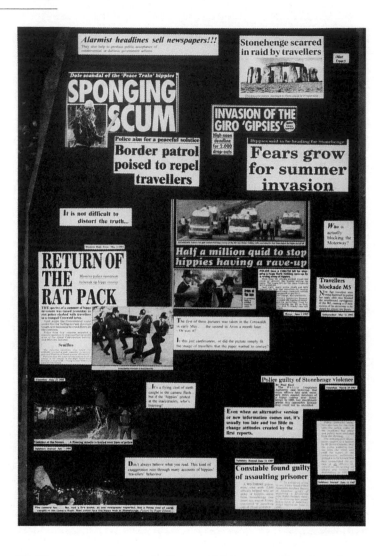

Figure 35 'Stonehenge Belongs to You and Me' – one of two boards on media coverage
(photo: Polly Farquharson)

sections. The focus was on containment, disempowerment and marginalisation as it worked itself out through the different, heterogeneous but interactive constituencies (Figure 36).

I recognise, again with hindsight, that whereas the contemporary boards were *relatively* even-handed, these last sections had more than a touch of agit-prop. I do not feel too guilty. After all, it is usually the other side that gets heard. But I acknowledge that there is a tension.

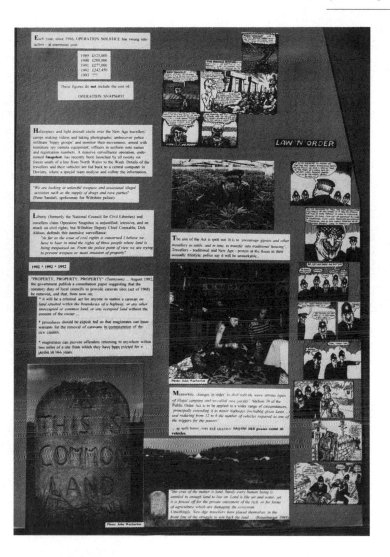

Figure 36 'Stonehenge Belongs to You and Me' – one of four boards on legal sanctions and police action
(photo: Polly Farquharson)

Perhaps we should have commented on this. We did point up other 'contradictions'. We had a little Asterix figure who signalled disagreements from the main text (Figure 37).[12]

12. When the exhibition arrived at the Museum of London, the Asterix figure had to be removed for copyright reasons. He was replaced by a character from Pete Loveday's *Russell. The Saga of a Peaceful Man* (1991).

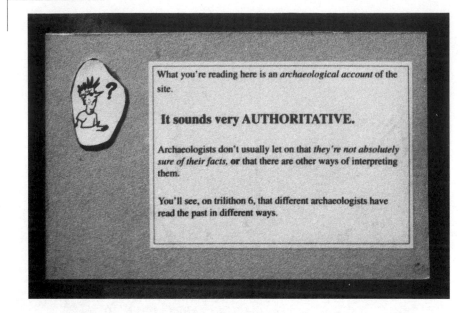

Figure 37 'Stonehenge Belongs to You and Me' – questioning the text (photo: Polly Farquharson)

There were also two boards with cartoons, and, in some venues, there was space for visitors to bring their own offerings. There were also large flip-charts so that people could write their comments on the exhibition, and their feelings about Stonehenge.

Although the exhibition was collaborative, I provided the structure and relativised and contextualised the different voices. But, in time-honoured fashion, practice fed into structure. It was, for example, exciting to discover, as the boards started to take shape, that different groups used different histories. The free festivalers evoked a short, epic, bloody history that centred on the Battle of the Beanfield. It was David (free anarchic spirit) versus Goliath (the overweening State). David usually lost, but he got up, dusted himself down, and started all over again. (This was my reading. Again, with hindsight, I assumed that the hero was male. In reality, in most of the present-day protest movements, the gendering is much more fluid and androgynous.)[13] There was also a strong sense of on-going history. Stonehenge was a

13. This would be a very interesting area of study. Thus Elenor, one of the heroines of the Fairmile road protest, is nick-named 'animal' (*The Guardian* February 1997).

living site, something ageless that meshed with the seasons.[14] The Druids had a quite different history. A wonderful, long, totally invented tradition. (Yes: *all* histories are a sort of invention. As Herzfeld says 'If any history is invented, all history is invented';[15] nonetheless the Druids' story was a particularly fine example of how quite disparate events can be strung together to create a narrative). They simply subsumed Welsh Eisteddfod, secular fair, and bardic orations into their genealogy. Until this exhibition, I'd never quite appreciated that within such an invented tradition each event may be accurate and documented, it is just the intercalations and subsumptions that are spurious. And the archaeologists, of course, have their form of history – linear, cumulative . . . Discovering these things, I added an extra board signalling these differences. I thought the free festivalers and Druids might feel uneasy about my doing this, that they might feel that, in relativising their histories, I was undermining the 'truthfulness' of their accounts and thereby their legitimacy.[16] But they did not seem to mind – maybe they have been quicker than archaeologists to recognise the subjective nature of their histories? Or maybe they recognise that people read themselves into these stories and find what they want to find.

I created the structure, but again, in the creative process, discourse and practice bounced off each other. The last boards, which I had thought to be an account of containment and differential empowerment, became, in the process of assembling the material and writing it up, a catalogue of a more general erosion and infringement of civil liberties, of the frequent illegalities of State action. And in at least one

14. Hetherington (1992) contrasts the Stonehenge of the archaeologists, 'sedimented in the past, a static place to be meticulously picked over, catalogued and mapped in order that we might come to know more about dead time', with the heritage tourists' 'dead space in living time . . . A space to be gazed upon but not changed, used or touched', and the Stonehenge of the New Age travellers who 'worship in effect the aura of the present . . . the living ambience created by the stones'.

15. As Herzfeld points out, the problem with the term 'invention of tradition' is that it suggests that there ought to be something else, another sort of history that represents the 'real' past. But since all pasts are constructed in the present they are all, to some degree, 'invented' (Herzfeld 1991: 12).

16. 'If one is involved in the construal and interpretation of ethnographic or historical realities, then one is bound on a collision course with others for whom such realities are definitive. Culture is supremely negotiable for professional culture experts, but for those whose identity depends upon a particular configuration, this is not the case. Identity is not negotiable. Otherwise, it has no existence' (Friedman 1992).

small incident these infringements moved from the text to lived reality. In June of 1993, while the exhibition was on in London, a group of free festivalers attempted, as they had done for many years, to walk from London to Stonehenge. There was an answer-machine at the back of the exhibition hall with up-to-date information on the walkers' whereabouts. Three days before the Solstice the phone was cut off. An obliging employee at British Telecom read out a message attached to the line. It had been cut off at the request of the Southern Intelligence Police Unit. Without an injunction, cutting off a phone is illegal.

Thus while I intended to create a structure, discourse and practice fed off each other, and in the process the structure altered.

Moreover, if I had, and have, an agenda, so did, and do, the free festivalers and Druids. Their news-sheets brought in visitors not usually seen in the august museums of Salisbury and Bristol. Their comments on the flip-charts elicited fierce responses – perhaps the most memorable being 'Go back to Russia – commie skiving gits'. Although I contracted for most of the venues, they took the show to Glastonbury twice, to the great protest meeting against the Criminal Justice Bill organised by the Levellers Band at the Rainbow Centre in April 1994, and to the Hackney Festival for the Homeless. For them, the exhibition became an icon, something that belonged to them, as well as something that worked for them vis à vis the Establishment. For me, I wanted to use it to question the theory/practice, academic/popular and presenter/viewer divides. (Just as in this book I want to see whether it is possible to mix styles and to use cartoons, and to ask people to respond, criticise, add their own stories, almost before the ink dries on the page).

This 'thing' then, this exhibition, takes on different valencies for the producers. And for the consumers. The custodians at the different venues had their own agendas. Why would a museum like Salisbury, in the Cathedral Close, take on a show like this? Was it, perhaps, because, although they are part of the intellectual Establishment, there is friction between the regions and the overweening, centralising English Heritage bureaucracy? And at each venue the exhibition accumulated new meanings. At Glastonbury it became something of a cult object, a thousand people tramped through it in four days. At Bristol, where the local Labour Council happened to be debating the possibility of a Free Festival and sites for travellers, it was seen as provocative and the police were rung up. At Guildford, one man objected, told a local councillor, who told the curator, who promptly removed the last four sections. A round-robin of protest against this action had no effect. Two months later the exhibition was back at

Guildford, uncensored, at the Friends Meeting House, as part of another protest campaign against the Criminal Justice Bill.

The visitors' responses were hugely varied. Over two hundred comments in the first year alone. Comments on access to Stonehenge ran 2:1 in favour of free access; comments on the exhibition ran 3:1 in favour. People used the flip-charts to argue with each other.[17]

After the first year we mounted two more boards with a cross-section of people's comments (Figures 38, 39 and 40). After the third year we

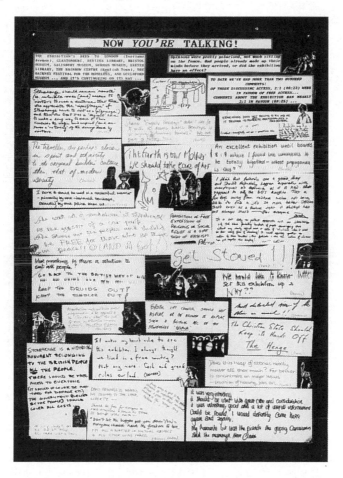

Figure 38 'Stonehenge Belongs to You and Me' – visitors' responses (photo: Polly Farquharson)

17. The variable readings of the exhibition lend considerable support to Barthes' and Ricoeur's insistence that any text may support a great number of meanings and that the intent of the author(s) is not necessarily privileged (Barthes 1977: 146–148; Ricoeur 1979).

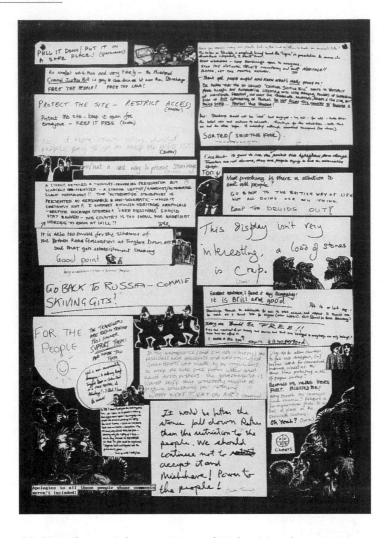

Figure 39 'Stonehenge Belongs to You and Me' – visitors' responses
(photo: Polly Farquharson)

added another new board (Figure 41). As we saw it, in the face of
increased State intervention and the promulgation of a Criminal Justice
Act which affects not just travelling people and access to public sites,
but *all* processions, *all* demonstrations, and *all* temporary sites, new
alliances have been forged between very disparate groups.[18] 'The CJB

18. As a result of the Act many of the travellers have moved on, to Portugal or Ireland.
Many have given up trying to get to Stonehenge, and some of the activities have moved
to Avebury (p. 186).

Figure 40 In the quiet setting of the Salisbury Museum in the close of the Cathedral, people used the flip-charts to argue – passionately – back and forth

[Criminal Justice Bill] is more like a JCB, bulldozing away basic democratic freedoms as if they were so many pieces of dispensable countryside' (*The Guardian* July 1994).

Whereas even five years ago the free festivalers were very much on their own, they now make common cause with gypsies, squatters, ravers, anti-road lobbyists, hunt saboteurs, and calf-transport protesters: De Certeau's 'proliferating illegitimacies'. Different groups have different but overlapping agendas, alliances are often temporary and fragile, but still the network ramifies across the land and the Internet. Stonehenge has now become one among many protest nodes.[19]

The new board covered some of these developments. It also returned to the theme of the present-past: the way in which different people draw on different pasts. The road protesters at Twyford Down, Solsbury, and Newbury recognise, in a way that archaeologists have only just

19. Interestingly, Monbiot, spokesperson for 'The Land is Ours', turns the argument round. As the group (an alliance of direct action groups – road protesters, environmentalists, travellers, and anti-CJB protestors), moved to reclaim a disused aerodrome at Wisley, he announced firmly: 'We are not protesting against anything. This action is intended to reassert people's control over how they live. We are challenging the Government's whole philosophy about the pre-eminence of property rights. We want the land to be well used. It's our common inheritance. We want our land back . . .' (*The Guardian* April 1995).

Figure 41 'Stonehenge Belongs to You and Me' – stop press
(photo: Polly Farquharson)

begun to, that what is under threat are not just a series of particular (historic, prehistoric) sites, but whole landscapes with their sedimented pasts and their environmental integrity, whilst those fighting against calf-transport often hark back to an imagined rural 'golden age', an arcadian landscape of small farms and market places.

Conclusions

The exhibition was amateur, it had too much text, and went off in too many directions. But it had an impact. And it created some space for people who do not usually get heard. It is important, as Mohanty puts it, for people to rewrite history and to write down memories, 'not merely as a corrective to the gaps, erasures and misunderstandings of hegemonic masculinist history, but because the very practice . . . of rewriting leads to the formation of a politicized consciousness and self-identity' (Mohanty 1991).

At a more practical level, I would suggest that there is much to be said in favour of small-scale, flexible, moveable exhibitions. Ephemeral exhibitions that can address particular issues, and issues of the moment. Where people can get involved on a temporary basis. When relatively little money is involved, and there are no major installations, it is much more likely that an exhibition can be used in different ways, can be altered, updated, made context specific. Places, venues, that cannot afford to create large exhibits can host them, and tailor them to suit their own questions and agendas (see pp. 230–231).

And academics can – temporarily – leave their ivory towers and join in. The legitimate boundaries for academic involvement are not clear-cut. But, just as the past cannot be unhooked from the present, so academia cannot be unhooked from the larger body politic. Passively or actively we are involved. We might as well be active; might as well get involved over issues which are not really about access to a particular place but about access to knowledge, access to the past and to the land, and, ultimately, about tolerance. We might as well play a part in creating, to adapt Foucault's terminology, 'a counter-archaeology of social knowledge' (Herzfeld 1991: 10).[20]

20. This quote is taken out of context from Herzfeld's subtle analysis of Cretan government attempts to create and preserve a heritage townscape frozen in time, and local resistance. The 'counter-archaeology' is, in this case, the evocation of a different sort of past 'in defiance of the etiquette of official history', and part of the ethnographer's role is to document the complex engagement of this counter-archaeology with the symbolism and meanings of official discourse (Herzfeld 1991: 10).

seven

Dialogues 3: Another Way of Telling. Stonehenge and Avebury

Who built Thebes of the Seven Gates?
In the books you will find the name of kings
Did the kings haul up the lumps of rocks?

Caesar beat the Gauls.
Did he not have even a cook with him?
Philip of Spain wept when his armada
went down.Was he the only one to weep?
Every page a victory,
Who cooked the feast for the victors?

Every ten years a great man,
who paid the bill?
So many reports.
So many questions.

from Berthold Brecht's
Questions from a Worker who Reads

Chapter 6 covered a great many different issues, so the Dialogues have been divided into two sections. In Dialogues 3 the emphasis is primarily on the contemporary situation at Stonehenge (and Avebury). In Dialogues 4 the discussion circles around exhibitions and multivocality.

A VERY SHORT DIALOGUE AT THE END OF A
STONEHENGE STUDY DAY AT THE
BRITISH MUSEUM AUTUMN 1996:

BB: If only we could have a modest interpretation centre at Stonehenge. Flexible. Easy to change and to add to. With places for people to put up their versions of the past and the present.

Julian Richards (English Heritage): If only we could have a modest building: a shed on skids ... Instead of a single palatial centre which becomes a focus for traffic, with erosion paths spreading into the landscape, why not several gateways into the landscape, each with a flexible gatehouse offering complementary but subtly different elements of the whole story?

BB: Or small encampments of large tents, with pennants flying. Like medieval fair-grounds.

Chris Chippindale: If only we could learn to tread lightly. If we could accept that what we build and what we say will soon be out of date. A fragile present. Why not create a contrast between the *durability* of the stones, and the *ephemerality* of the contemporary moment?[1]

Julian Richards: It'll never happen, these sorts of ideas would be seen as too homespun and folksy, as giving in to the woolly hat brigade – who generally had the right sort of ideas all along ...

The Dialogue that Never Happened

I wanted English Heritage to be one of the voices in the Stonehenge Belongs to You and Me *exhibition, but, despite the willingness of the man from the English Heritage education section, the people at Fortress House felt that they had already provided sufficient information elsewhere and therefore did not want to take part. The same happened again when I suggested that there should be a dialogue. Two polite post-cards from a secretary. Full-stop. So I decided to engage in a one-sided conversation.* This dialogue is my invention.

1. Three weeks later Chris Chippindale was appointed consultant to Madame Tussauds who looked set to win their bid to build the visitors' centre at Stonehenge, including the interpretative facilities. Would they 'tread lightly'? (but see p. 183).

BB: *As an outsider, I sense a considerable difference between the National Trust and English Heritage. Whilst both bodies have begun to change their attitude towards acquisition and to go for a much broader remit, the National Trust seems to be more prepared to consider radical changes in both style and content of management. I imagine that part of the reason is that English Heritage is a government quango, whilst the National Trust is more vulnerable to pressure from increasingly vocal and often disenchanted shareholders. It may also be that the National Trust is being pushed from inside by an influx of lower management, less Establishment-orientated, workers. Whatever the reason, the National Trust has begun to recognise that it can't just act as steward to its various properties, it has got to enter the political fray and make its voice heard over issues such as environment, transport, building and agricultural policies. This is bound, I imagine, to lead to some interesting confrontations. The National Trust has also recognised that it needs to talk* with, *rather than* to, *local communities and has published an important volume appropriately entitled* Linking People and Place.[2] *Its sensitive stewarding of the very difficult site of Avebury is a case in point (pp. 186–187). Again, maybe the National Trust's more political stance has something to do with the fact that it has begun to face a right-wing back-lash over the question of its stewardship of the big houses and the landscape. With everything else up for privatisation, National Trust stewardship has, in some quarters, been construed as a form of nannying, inimical to the private and individual ethos.[3] So there's been a subtle shift in allegiances and people who might have had reservations about the National Trust Stately Home/ Laura Ashley image find themselves rallying to its support as a bastion against privatisation and entrepreneurship.*

EH: Aren't you being a little starry-eyed? Given your credentials, doesn't it worry you that the National Trust is the biggest private land-owner in the country?

BB: *You're not wrong!*[4] *And while it's true that the National Trust is beginning to think about organic farming (on five out of 2,217 tenant farms!), and about car transport, houses in urban centres and so on, they never, as Monbiot points out, address the ethics of ownership. Monbiot suggests that the National Trust should encourage:*

2. The National Trust (1995).

3. Wright (1995).

4. 590,000 acres of land; 550 miles of coastline; 207 historic houses; 60 villages (Monbiot, *The Guardian* September 1995).

experiments in low-impact development on its property; help establish
local markets for local produce; allow us to reclaim our history . . . tell
the story of the enclosed and dispossessed, rather than that of the encloser
and the over-possessed; and help us to see that the rights of those who
do not own the land are a surer guarantee of its protection than the
privileges of those that do.[5]

I would have to agree with all that . . .

EH: Well, there you are. And you can hardly accuse us of being a
government satrap. As you know very well, we stood up against
the government over the new road proposals for the Stonehenge
area.

BB: *That's true. In 1995, when the government appeared to be opting for*
one of the cheaper and nastier of the road building options for the
Stonehenge area, both you and the National Trust went on the
offensive.[6] *You even allied yourself – briefly – with some of the*
alternative groups that you usually keep at arm's length! There was
some very effective networking, and at the official Government Inquiry,
to the dismay of the chairperson, you not only got the government option
rejected, but got the most expensive long tunnel option accepted.[7]
Admittedly it was only on paper, but the government has, at least
temporarily, thrown in the towel and announced that they will put the
road-building on hold. It was a good fight. But we all know that
hegemonic power is always riven with factions and fissions!

EH: All this stuff about 'hegemonic power' (pp. 150–151) is fine in
theory, but in practice it's all much less sinister. Most of the time
it's about getting by by the seat of one's pants.

BB: *It's not one thing or the other: you have power and you get by by the*
seat of your pants. There's a very apposite comment from Herzfeld:
'We can read the functionaries' necessary compromises between grand
ideology and exigent sociability in the spaces cleaned, excavated,
scratched, plastered, and painted on the architectonic landscape'.[8] *He's*
talking about Crete, but it'd be just as true for you. Of course you
fudge and compromise, but it doesn't stop you taking out injunctions
and laying down the rules.

5. ibid.

6. Wainwright (1996).

7. English Heritage and the National Trust opted for the two mile long tunnel option,
which would cost approximately £200,000 million, five times the cost of the Highway
Agency's preferred northern route.

8. Herzfeld (1991: 14).

EH: It's also very unfair to suggest that we haven't moved with the times. Look, for example, at our Education Programme.

BB: *I was coming to that. One of the really interesting things is that the English Heritage Education Programme is radical (more so than the National Trust's). But the trouble is that there seems to be a total split between the education department and the rest of management. My guess is that the education section has a degree of autonomy which has allowed it to be much more innovative. Maybe history for the kids is also seen as harmless – although that's patently a mistake. Maybe, too, it's about particular individuals that have stood up for a different way of doing things and thinking about things. There's no question,* the new A Teacher's Handbook to Stonehenge[9] *is excellent. On the one hand it hammers home how little we know:*

> We shall never be quite sure of what their homes and other buildings really looked like . . . nor . . . how often they moved house; or how many fields, sheep or cattle one family would expect to possess – if possession is even a concept they would have understood . . .[10]

And on the other, it confronts the issue of political controversy and alternative attitudes:

> Stonehenge has been at the centre of a great debate . . . on who controls the interpretation and presentation of – and access to – the monument. Who the site belongs to and what value(s) we attach to the past – and why.[11]

It gives a wonderful spread of opinions (Figure 42). OK, it's a bit slanted towards the English Heritage position but that's all right, the Stonehenge exhibition was slanted one way, this tips the balance the other. The handbook ends up suggesting that:

> The enormous volume of newspaper articles on conflict at Stonehenge makes this an ideal subject for studying conflict in society and media presentation.[12]

9. Anderson et al. (1996).
10. Anderson et al. (1996: 2).
11. Anderson et al. (1996: 3).
12. Anderson et al. (1996: 30).

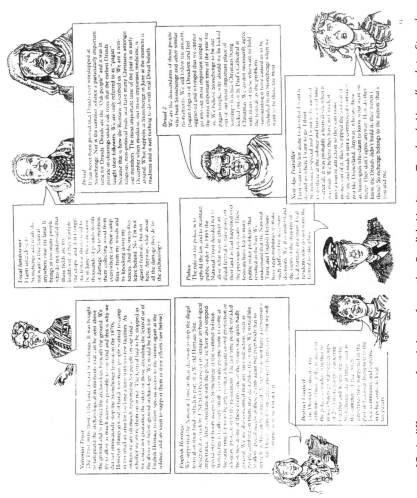

Figure 42 A difference of opinion – from the English Heritage *Teacher's Handbook to Stonehenge* (with kind permission of English Heritage)

EH: So what's the problem?

BB: *The handbook is really good. It encourages children to recognise that the interpretations of archaeologists are open to reinterpretation and revision. They're encouraged to attempt their own controlled speculations. They're even encouraged to 'listen to the wind in different parts of the landscape and to create their own music'. That's lovely.*

EH: Well, there you are!

BB: *If that sort of approach came through at other levels of management I might not have written this book. The problem is that it stays at the level of the Teacher's Handbook. It doesn't seem to filter down – or rather up. The minute management are involved, or more formal presentations, all the incertitudes and questions drop away and all the platitudes and desire to control reassert themselves. If only, as Cosgrove says, you'd recognise that 'conservation is itself a creative intervention, subject to the same individual and social negotiations and struggles over meaning and representation as any other action'.[13]*

I'll give you an example. At the end of the new volume on the twentieth- century excavations at Stonehenge, an English Heritage archaeologist wraps up the discussion of Late Neolithic/Early Bronze Age Stonehenge:

> *There were phases of insecurity or economic recession interspersed with rapid change. In response, society made a significant investment in the building of Stonehenge ... The building of Stonehenge was a political act and its massive physical presence must have invested it with a key role in legitimising power structures and, with the passage of time, in protecting traditional values from challenge by epitomising past achievements.[14]*

Phases of insecurity – economic recession – significant investment – political act – legitimising power structures – protecting tradition. It sounds more like a proposal for a new building for the Bank of England!

EH: Perhaps it was supposed to be a bit tongue in cheek.

BB: *I doubt it. But OK – I'll come to what has really riled me, as a statement of intent, a statement of management policy. It's a two page letter sent to people who write in with questions about the proposed developments at Stonehenge. It was written in 1996 and it's signed by Jocelyn Stevens.*

13. Cosgrove (1994).
14. Cleal et al. (1995: 494).

It's entitled Stonehenge – The Vision. *Let me spend a little time deconstructing its message.*

EH: Oh dear!

At this point, the dialogue, such as it was, deteriorates into a monologue – or perhaps a diatribe!

BB: *This open letter starts:*

> *Stonehenge is unique . . . Built between 5000 and 3000 years ago, its origins have recently been traced as far back as 8500 BC. It is the most important prehistoric monument in Britain. It is world-famous. It stands as a timeless testimony to the people who built it.*

Same old threnody: unique, incredibly old, British, world famous . . .

The letter then goes on to tell us how big *the protected area is (1,620 hectares, 450 sites); how* many *visitors it attracts (600,000 that pay, 100,000 that come under educational auspices, and – the undoubtedly regrettable – 250,000 who 'choose not to pay'). Then there's something on the problem of the roads and the inadequacy of the current visitors' centre.*

Then comes The Vision. *The vision is to acquire more land[15] as part of this World Heritage site, to get rid of the existing visitors' centre, car park, and slip road[16] and thus:*

> *return the greatest archaeological landscape in the world to chalk downland where the public will be encouraged to roam freely and in safety among the monuments and to walk among the stones as our ancestors did for thousands of years.*

---

15. The National Trust own 1,500 acres in the Stonehenge area. There is agreement in principle to buy a further 2,500 acres from private owners. The National Trust will receive £50 million from the Lottery, and match it from their own funds (*The Guardian* November 1996).

16. The locals are not happy with this removal of a much-used road. Already in 1992, the County Council, in a deeply Conservative constituency, voted overwhelmingly against the road change. They objected, as a local newspaper put it, to 'big shots' from London trying to tell them what was good for them. They'd also objected to the way in which English Heritage, presumably in the search for 'authenticity', had 'scalped' the trees at Old Sarum (just as at Chiswick House they cut down a fine avenue of yews because they did not conform to the original plan).

And it concludes:

> *The Stonehenge Millennium Park will be funded by English Heritage in partnership with the Millennium Commission and managed by the Stonehenge Trust with the Trustees appointed equally by English Heritage and the National Trust. Simultaneously, the new visitors' centre, which is to be called the Gateway to Wessex, will be funded, built and managed by the Private Sector under the Private Finance Initiative.*

In other words, whilst English Heritage and the National Trust will create and maintain the park, the Private Sector will create the visitors' centre which, by definition, must include the interpretative centre. Madame Tussauds and MacDonalds have put in bids. It looks likely that Madame Tussauds will get the contract (but see p. 183).

The visitors' centre is to cater for at least a million people a year. The site, at the Amesbury roundabout, is now so far from the stones that people will have to be transported up to the King Barrow Ridge. What happens then? It is still a good half mile to the stones. No doubt many visitors will simply look through the telescopes, spy out across the land, buy their postcards and go home. Or perhaps – a great little revenue-raiser – there will be little buggies pop-popping across the open landscape . . .

In this scenario, English Heritage and the National Trust busy themselves with the landscape, and abrogate all responsibility for the interpretations on offer. Will Madame Tussauds employ a wonderful and varied gamut of people to create an informative, wide-ranging, open-ended interpretative centre? Perhaps. Will it be modest and flexible? Will they stress how little we know, as well as how much? Will it make the point that 'the choice of pasts is negotiated in a shifting present'?[17] Will it create places for people to express their interests and their involvement? Or will it be yet another soft-edge, high-tech display, avoiding all controversy, all current debate? Will the audio-visuals cost millions and therefore be 'fixed' for years to come?

If the visitors' centre and the Stonehenge landscape are under entirely different managements how will people assimilate what is on offer in the interpretative centre with their perceptions and encounters as they walk the landscape? For the landscape, despite Jocelyn Stevens' letter, is decidedly not 'timeless'. It is cumulative and reworked. What nonsense to talk about 'returning the greatest archaeological landscape

17. Herzfeld (1991: 27).

in the world to chalk downland'. It is not an archaeological landscape, it's a contemporary landscape. What point in prehistory is it supposed to be returned to, since between the first bank and ditch and the last stone hole at Stonehenge, landuse, settlement, work areas, burial places, monuments, quarries all changed, and changed again? The one thing it never was was nice neat downland.[18]

And is it to be changed without any consideration of how local people may feel about their *landscape? Fielden, talking about a similar threat to 'return' the Avebury landscape to pasture, protests: 'The people who live [here] like to see the changing seasons reflected in the cornfields and the wild life they harbour; they do not want to be surrounded by a landscape 'fossilized' as an 'appropriate setting' for the monument.'[19]*

Today's landscape with its mixture of grassland and cornfield, with or without fences, can never be prehistoric, can only be contemporary. People are not stupid, why try and dupe them into a false sense of a golden, timeless, past landscape? Why not tell them about the processes at work, let them enjoy the profusion of landscapes, and the complexity of claim and counter-claim?

And let them enjoy some of the contemporary uses. In the Summer of 1996 there was a wonderful series of crop marks in the field opposite Stonehenge. Fake, but no less wonderful. When the crop-marks died away, they were replaced by a Stonehenge built out of straw-bales. It was terrific. Why is it impossible to have a field full of temporary tents and music? Our ancestors did not, as the English Heritage Visions letter suggests, simply 'walk among the stones'. They had great celebrations, probably drank a lot, and hallucinated.

EH: It's very easy for you, as an academic sitting on the side-lines, to make all these suggestions. If you're managing the site you have to think in terms of the future. Of preservation. And of the mass of the people who come to Stonehenge and don't want to have music and mess. And who does all the clearing up?

18. By the Early Bronze Age the landscape was open. It seems to have been mainly used for grazing rather than agriculture. But an 'open' landscape does not mean tidy rolling downland. It would have been a scruffy and scrubby landscape. If the reason for returning it to downland is because the soil is poor and easily eroded and returning it to grass would protect the archaeological remains, then this should be said, and the case for it argued.

19. Fielden (1996).

BB: *Things can be negotiated. Places and spaces can be created. More people's voices can be heard. It can't cost as much as the present-day policing, and Stonehenge, instead of – or as well as – being a symbol of past 'greatness' could be a flagship of contemporary tolerance and innovation.*

EH: (sigh; yawn)

POSTSCRIPT

Summer 1997:

Just as I'm about to hand my manuscript to the publisher, news of a major rethink begins to filter through on the network. None of it, I have to admit, due to my fulminations! More to do with a new government, economic machinations, and the perceived need to make a symbolic Millennium splash.

Rumour has it that Madame Tussauds was demanding, not just buggies, but a miniature railway running around the site. This was not well received. Then the Millennium Commission turned down the request for major funding. Now, it seems, the new Labour government is stepping in. Madame Tussauds is out. The visitors' centre is back under the wing of English Heritage. The Amesbury roundabout site has been abandoned. Larkhill – the original site for the centre – is back on the agenda. Already screened by trees, within reasonable walking distance of the stones, and with an approach that mirrors the original line of the Avenue, it makes infinitely better sense. The Ministry of Defence will – at last – be leant on to provide the land. Where the road will go remains a major problem. And as the Greenwich Dome goes up in London, (disputed) Millennium symbol of modernity, technology and the future, so (disputed) Millennium Stonehenge will be created, symbol and celebration of 'British' history. And who sets the agenda, who does the creating, of what, and when, and for whom, will depend, as always, upon a mix of politics, economics, ideology, and symbolism.

Another Dialogue with Ronald Hutton

Ronald Hutton is not only an expert on Medieval history (p. 133), he also works with contemporary pagan and Druidic groups. With Stonehenge 'shut' to the Druids and travellers, much of the action has shifted to Avebury. It seemed worth discussing what has been happening at Avebury, and how the question of access is being handled. I could not resist also including some of his comments on the contemporary roots of paganism, including eco-feminism, and the connections or disconnections with archaeology.

BB: *You're saying that whilst archaeologists like Glyn Daniel and Mortimer Wheeler were able to talk to people about archaeology and popularise it, by the late sixties this communication had broken down, and it was this breakdown that created a space for alternative viewpoints?*

RH: Yes, the new archaeology talked a language the public couldn't understand. Remember when Atkinson got the miners to tunnel into Silbury Hill? He got a lot of media attention but the results were a terrible anti-climax – a few flying ants, a bit of compost, and archaeologists doing their best to show they'd discovered something colossal with three phases of building. Well, along comes Michael Dames who's a lecturer in the history of art. Disgusted by the anti-climax, he comes up with a new vision. He looks up the great books of the fifties and sixties, finds Jacquetta Hawkes, Stuart Piggott, O.G.S. Crawford telling him the Neolithic was the time of the Great Goddess, finds that Silbury Hill was Neolithic, looks at it with an artist's eye and sees that, from above – from aerial photographs – it makes the figure of a Great Goddess. Most important, because flying ants are around at the end of July, and because Atkinson said maybe the construction commenced at the end of harvest, Dames notices that in the Scottish Lothians, in the eighteenth century, people built towers at Lamastide, and in Ireland, within living memory, there were gatherings around Lughnasagh to celebrate the potato harvest. So he has this vision of Silbury as a harvest tower. The Great Goddess – the harvest – the fertility of the land, it all comes together. Nearby is a spring that runs dry miraculously at certain times of year, like November – the menstrual blood of the Goddess, a sign of her power. Dames creates a sacred landscape of extraordinary power for the modern spiritual feminist. Just at the moment, in the mid-seventies, when spiritual feminism is looking for a home, he provides it with some of the greatest monuments of British prehistory.[20]

BB: *I've never heard any of this – it's a good story!*

RH: Then he wrote a sequel in 1977, called *The Avebury Cycle*,[21] in which the whole of the Avebury ritual landscape was tied into a cycle of ceremonies in honour of the Goddess. They were ceremonies which people could perform, and so, within a year, people were there. That's why women dance on Silbury Hill at the August full moon. The timing is brilliant – just at the moment that Dames is making these monuments spiritually accessible to a new generation in desperate need of a past, the monuments, Stonehenge and Silbury, are symbolically fenced off by the custodians.[22]

BB: *So Avebury becomes an alternative centre. What happens now? Will things go the same way as Stonehenge?*

RH: Something different has happened at Avebury, which shows you how paganism is maturing. Back in 1993, Druids gathered there for conferences, using National Trust property, and spilled out quite spontaneously to hold ceremonies among the stones. The ceremonies became regular, eight times a year. They became elevated to the status of Gorseddau (Druid gatherings), and in the last two years they've started to fulfil the role of religious ceremonies involving rites of passage for consumers. New Age pagans come there to have their children named and their marriages solemnised.[23] And the Druids find themselves in the position of pastoral clergy, administering, with increasing skills, to a congregation.

BB: *What's the distinction between pagans and Druids?*

RH: Increasingly Druidery is a branch of paganism . . .

BB: *And paganism?*

20. Dames (1976).

21. Dames (1977).

22. Somewhat more trenchantly, Pitts notes: 'an emerging archaeological fundamentalism, in which, deprived of relevant and comprehensible ideas and information, people revert to a pre-archaeological understanding whose power is increased by a touch of mysticism' (Pitts 1996).

23. Pitts (1996).

RH: ... is a huge umbrella which covers anybody who vaguely identifies with the monuments and the texts of ancient Britain. The biggest movement in modern paganism is Wicca, but Wiccans work or worship privately at night, and usually away from ancient monuments.

There was a fascinating schism among the Druids themselves this last Midsummer. The congregation shouted down the political Druids when they began giving speeches upon the progress of campaigns over Stonehenge and road building schemes. The vast majority of the people at Avebury wanted to have a spiritual experience, they wanted the processions, the ceremonies of naming and blessing, the music – they didn't want orators and soap-boxers shouting at them. The Druid Chiefs of Wessex, for whom this was their patch, found themselves, to their fury and their horror, being pushed to the side-lines, and the people who were being brought on by public demand were those gentle spiritual Druids who were best at invoking goddesses, talking to the sky, and, above all, working with people. Which is why, when the National Trust briefly appeared to threaten the existence of the Gorsedd, a terrific upswell of emotion occurred ...

BB: *At the Solstice?*

RH: No, the May Day weekend. The National Trust manager, Chris Gingell made a speech in public, witnessed by about a hundred people.

BB: *Why were the National Trust getting upset?*

RH: They were in an appalling position because more and more travellers were starting to camp in the Avebury area for the festivals. They weren't coming there because of the Druids or the Gorsedd, they were coming because of the spiritual impulse, the worship of the land. So more and more land owned by increasingly uncomfortable farmers was getting cluttered up, more and more villagers were being kept awake at night by people playing digeridoos. The National Trust was right in the middle and was getting the blame. And at the same time it also gets the blame from the New Age travellers and the Druids if it tries to remonstrate with them. What had bust Chris Gingell's blood vessels was that the night before May Day he saw fires lit on Silbury and he went scooting up there and found five urchins lighting them, with a Druid Chief looking on benevolently. He remonstrated – very effectively. The following morning he saw the five hooligans among the crowds milling around the Druids. So he felt he had to say something to warn people. Unfortunately, he said the wrong things to the company, went on far too long, and gave an impression of blaming the Druids collectively.

He provoked the very reaction he had been aiming to prevent. Some of the more 'political' Druids immediately began planning action to hold gatherings at Avebury in the event of a Trust ban and in the face of any police presence which would be called in to enforce the ban. I listened with my blood freezing because I could envisage the cost to both sides escalating as such a confrontation got under way. The perimeter of the henge is much bigger than at Stonehenge, the ritual landscape far more scattered, and I could see tempers fraying and violence growing as the forces of law enforcement struggled to create an exclusion zone. Fortunately a number of people went to see Dr Gingell, he listened to them, and since then, to his immense credit, his behaviour has been exemplary in dealing with Druids and Gorseddau, and he has won back a great deal of affection and support.[24]

BB: *Were you one of the people who interceded?*

RH: Yes.

BB: *What did you feel about mediating in this way?*

RH: Troubled. I thought I'd try it once. To be an eye-witness with a ringside seat for the Battle of Avebury would be a great position for a historian, but I love Avebury too much – just as Gingell does. I thought for once I would intervene even if it meant writing myself into my own history. I should emphasise, however, that others did more than I did, especially Philip Shalcrass, Chief of the British Druid Order.

BB: *Recently the stones at Avebury were daubed by 'vandals' – where do the Pagans fit into that story (Figure 43)?*

RH: What happened was that when the damage was done both pagans and National Trust people came on site. The National Trust people draped the damaged stones in sacking to protect them from the sunrise which would gel the bitumen paint on the stones. But when the National Trust had gone, some of the pagans took this for further vandalism and pulled the sacking down to mend the stones. They then found there was paint underneath. The

24. Gingell wrote recently, with some humour, 'Some planning has to be pragmatic and many things will remain imperfect. (In a place which has never been a managed estate and whose inhabitants do not wish to be managed at all, who is to say that imperfection is undesirable?)' (Gingell 1996).

Figure 43 Vandalised stones at Avebury
(with kind permission of The National Trust, Avebury)

National Trust was called back, explained the situation, and the pagans then co-operated in bringing in sacking and guarding the stones against further vandalism for the rest of the night. Since then word has gone out to ensure that if the culprits came from within paganism – which, given the nature of the symbolism, is extraordinarily unlikely – names are named and they're apprehended, and that some kind of vigilante process be mounted to watch ancient monuments near festival times.

BB: *The problem is how to keep the lines of communication open. And about tolerance and what's tolerable. But given that so many of the alternative groups are concerned with protecting the land – the spirit of the land – it makes good sense to have them on your side and work with them.*

RH: A small publication, *Walking the Talk. The Journal of Save Our Sacred Sites,* has been put together, with stuff written by pagans, academics, and the National Trust, asking people to work together to protect these spiritual places (Figure 44).

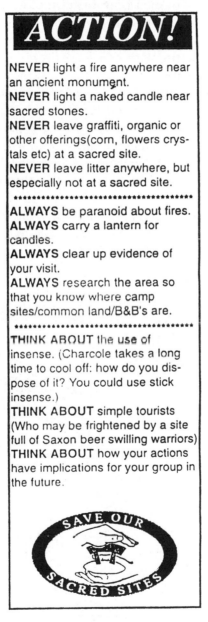

Figure 44 From *Save Our Sacred Sites*

Dialogue with Ian Hodder

Ian Hodder is one of the most post-modern of British archaeologists. His most recent book is The Domestication of Europe (1990). *I was interested to see how he would react to Chapter 6. He is working on the wonderfully complex tell site of Çatalhöyük in Turkey which, partly because of the numerous Mother Goddess figures, has attracted many alternative groups. Given the very different ways that people engage with the site, I had thought that we would concentrate on how he was going to present the findings and the material. As it happened, the conversation first took off in a very different direction concerning questions of empowerment and resistance. That part is presented here. Some of the questions that Ian posed are taken up in the dialogue with the free festivalers that follows on. Ian's thoughts on how to present the material from Çatalhöyük comes into the next chapter (p. 209).*

This conversation was by email, and it was my first attempt. I had not, at the time, grasped the simple principle that I could butt into Ian's text. The result is that the 'conversation' is somewhat staccato.

Reproduced by kind permission of Pete Loveday

IH [email 1]:   You asked me to comment on your chapter from a Çatalhöyük perspective. I would prefer to deal first with some underlying worries that seem relevant to both the Çatal and Stonehenge situations.

Your chapter and the exhibition deal with the problems of presenting a true multivocality. You present this as an issue of empowerment. You talk of your work as being about power and resistance, and about differential empowerment. As I think you know, I have doubts about discussing social relationships in terms of domination and resistance, which seem crude tools to deal with the complexities involved. I recognise the political need for such terms and for the analysis of power, but in the case you are concerned with I am worried that important dimensions of power are being masked by thinking in terms of domination and resistance. My suspicions were raised by your paragraph on page 154 in which you describe the inability of the travellers and free festivalers to organise the exhibition. 'They could', you say, 'never organise it'. In your account of meetings with them, there seems to have been a lack of direction, a lack of purpose on their part. You describe a multiplicity of aims, but it is difficult to pick up from your account a strong political agenda.

BB [email 1]:   *When I wrote 'they could never organise it', I was talking about the constraints on certain forms of resistance. In the case of the exhibition, I was making the point that exhibitions cost money, and they have no money. And even if they put together an exhibition, they would have problems persuading 'respectable' venues to put it on display.*

The Stonehenge Campaign Group is undoubtedly 'politically' committed. It has an obvious and limited agenda to do with free access to the Stonehenge and a Free Festival somewhere close at hand. But as you'll see, reading their account (p. 205), the free festivalers feel that the festival acts as an umbrella for a wide number of environmental and other causes. They are also networked into a loose alliance of protest groups, which, I believe, has some effect on mainstream politics.

IH [email 2]:   I want to respond strongly that it was not my intention to argue that the travellers and festivalers were not 'serious'. But you admit that the degree of political commitment is limited to single issues. Do you really think that resolving such issues is going to deal with the real miseries of the unemployed or the injustices of the Immigration Act?

BB [email 2]: *One has to start somewhere. You mention the Immigration Act, but what about the Criminal Justice Act? Questions about access – not just to the stones, but also the right to camp, to lead a nomadic life-style, to hold festivals and so on – are directly affected by that Act. And, of course, the Act spills over into quite other areas, and affects the right to demonstrate, hold processions . . .*

IH [email 1]: When I read your account or looked at the exhibition, I could not help but be struck by the difference with places in the world where the past is involved in life and death struggles about rights and resources. The repatriation of cultural materials and human remains in North America has helped to forge links between native peoples who have been the subject of genocide and of severe economic deprivation. In South Africa I was deeply moved to see how, in the archaeological excavation and museum in District 6 in Cape Town, communities torn apart by apartheid were rediscovering themselves. At Ayodya or in the Middle East people die over the ownership of cultural property and over the symbols of their religion and identity.

I was present for part of a wedding at Avebury attended by travellers, anarchists and New Age followers. What was going on there was very different from these examples, and what you are describing also seems different. I do not deny that the people you have been interacting with have aims and grievances, that they are marginal and 'undesirable'. But the right to participate in a New Age festival at Stonehenge seems of a very different nature to the struggles and injustices I have referred to on the world stage. Perhaps it is just a matter of degree. But I worry that it is more than that. I worry that the New Age movements you describe are themselves part of a dominant discourse.

BB [email 1]: *It's true we don't suffer from genocide, and people are not tortured (?) in Britain. We don't have a dictatorship, and there are places and spaces for dissent. Of course travellers don't suffer in the same way as North American Indians or Black South Africans, or even as other minorities within Britain. But nevertheless Britain has become a less democratic, less tolerant place. The Criminal Justice Act and the Immigration Laws are draconian. And the free festivalers, travellers, and a host of other groups are caught up in these developments. So there are plenty of good reasons why we should get involved in these debates and actions, and why we need to think through and apply our anthropological understanding of cultural variability and unequal representation. Of course there are more desperate contexts in which we (as archaeologists and human beings) need to get involved, but there's a lot to be said for starting at home. Maybe it's because we know (or think we know) a bit more about our own minorities, and recognise that there's no real uniformity, that we tend to feel more suspicious and less inclined to get involved.*

IH [email 1]: On page 155, you oppose your view to a simple postmodern account of multivocality. You claim to be taking a different tack because of your emphasis on empowerment. But in fact you tell us little about the background and social conditions of the travellers, and as already noted, the political agency does not seem strongly motivated. At least one component of the post-modern is the emphasis on pastiche – the endless play of signifiers without reference. Your travellers, you say, had little money, contacts, clout, resources. Yet 'they already had a huge media database'. I take this to mean that they had systematically collected information about themselves in the media. They *did* put resources into this area – into themselves as signs.

At least one view (superficial and simplistic as it may be) is that they used you and your exhibition as a part of that play of signifiers. You and the exhibit became part of the pastiche. [email 2] Do you not agree that it is precisely this sense of being (virtually) real which is the prime characteristic of the high- or post-modern form of dominant power?

BB [email 1]: *The database is significant in many different ways. Yes, I guess that the database does cost them some money, but not much. But are they really collecting all this stuff as part of a play of signifiers, part of a pastiche? My understanding of what happens is that, yes, seeing themselves in press – however misrepresented – makes them feel more 'real', more visible. Someone is taking notice. That in itself is empowering. More than that, combing the media is a way of collating information: finding out where police action is occurring, where court cases are being heard, and what the outcomes are. They know which County Councils are heavy, which more tolerant. It's an access to knowledge, which can then be deployed. They were, for example, very well briefed about the Stonehenge Road Inquiry last year, and had people there to keep tabs on the proceedings.*

The media coverage is part of a much larger networking tactic. And this is their great strength. They put out a free newsletter (see p. 204) which is packed with information on developments concerning Stonehenge and, more recently, concerning road protests and things like This Land is Ours *(see p. 169). Also, importantly, it carries detailed information on all activist networks, anti-Criminal Justice Act groups, alternative centres and services, and a calendar of festivals and events.*

IH [email 2]:   As regards the press coverage, I feel you confirm my view when you say it makes them feel 'real', 'visible'. News coverage is hardly 'real'. This is, as perhaps all realities are now, very virtual reality. At the same time that the flows of information create solidarity amongst marginal groups, so they entrap those groups within a dominant form of discourse.

BB [email 2]:   *But the entrapment is never complete, there's always the possibility that, from within the dominant discourse, one can turn things around and subtly subvert and resist.*

IH [email 1]:   Post-modernism is also about depthlessness, and few of those you have been interacting with seem concerned with Stonehenge and its 'deep time' interpretation in archaeology. Again, Stonehenge itself seems to have become part of a pastiche, a fragment in the play of New Age signifiers . . .

BB [email 1]:   *You seem to be saying that there's an 'unreality' about the New Age response to Stonehenge because it doesn't involve 'deep history'. But as you'll see (pp. 90–95), the ones I have talked to are often very well read in archaeology, they do take on the deep history. They're just suspicious of our particular interpretations. They question our emphasis on prehistoric social hierarchies – they think that the Stonehenge builders could have been much more egalitarian. But, then, we're beginning to question some of our own easy assumptions about hierarchy (p. 60). The free festivalers/travellers/Druids are also more interested in the spiritual dimensions of the stones. And we're heading in that direction as well. One of the things that emerged through putting the exhibition together was the different sorts of histories that different groups deploy. As archaeologists we may want to stay with our deep histories, but we have to recognise that our versions of deep history are wide open to question. They're all about our particular way of creating a sense of identity and rootedness. Other sorts of histories (North American Indian, Australian Aboriginal, eco-feminist, New Age . . .) respond to different conditions, different needs and perceptions. I would be very doubtful about labelling one sort of history as 'deep' and the other 'pastiche'.*

IH [email 1]: I would tend to agree with those that argue that we are moving into, or have moved into, a new global economy in which homogenisation is created by global markets, by information technologies and by global environmental issues. But a fascinating part of this globalisation is its simultaneous fragmentation. We see this localisation in the formation of new ethnicities and special interests. Within an optimistic viewpoint, this fragmentation occurs because the new technologies allow an empowering of marginals, a reawakening of local rights and identities. Within a pessimistic viewpoint, the fragmentation is itself the logic of the new economies and technologies. After all, we increasingly hear of 'niche marketing' or the 'constituency of one'. 'Everyone can participate in the new technologies' – but the technologies are produced at the centre.

At Çatal I have been struck by the evident emotion felt by eco-feminists and Mother Goddess worshippers when they experience the presence of 'the goddess'. These real experiences must, in my view, be catered for. But they are, I feel, part of the dominant culture. These experiences may play a central part in discovering personal and group identities as women. Perhaps in some ways such experiences help women to deal with domination and oppression. But those who come to Çatal are exclusively wealthy and educated women. While they and their cause may be helped by coming to the site, I think it is wrong to analyse the situation simply in terms of domination and resistance. Rather, these New Age movements which use the past are involved in contradictory ways in processes of globalisation and fragmentation. New identities and alliances are being formed. One of the characteristics of the internet is the formation of alliances between a myriad of special interest groups. Some empowerment may be going on here. But it is also in the interests of the global information technologies to create difference – as long, presumably, as the differences are harmless, depthless, pastiche.

BB [email 2]:   *So there's the (optimistic) possibility of empowerment through global alliances, but there's also the (pessimistic) possibility that fragmented politics and fragmented constituencies are actually part and parcel of the global market-place and global technology – that they form necessary niches which can then be catered for by the dominant global economies. But perhaps it's neither one nor the other, it's contingent, unstable, flips both ways . . .*

You rightly point out how variably constituted the alternative movements are. The eco-feminists who come to Çatalhöyük are, you say, 'exclusively wealthy and educated', but they're just a rather particular fraction of the American feminist movement. Some of the Stonehenge Campaign Group are out of work and live a fairly hand-to-mouth existence; some have been in higher education, others not. The people involved in the Road Protest Movement come from very mixed backgrounds. And you're quite right that these different movements, all constructing pasts in different ways, 'are involved in contradictory ways in processes of globalisation and fragmentation', and are forging new identities and alliances. These are surely some of the things we need to explore. And you, I guess, will tend to emphasise the way in which these protests and fragmentations are generated by and utilised by the global information technologies, and that the differences are often little more than 'harmless, depthless, pastiche', and I'll remain convinced that they can be, often are, sites of resistance!

Reproduced by kind permission of Pete Loveday

Dialogue with Hilary, Wes and Paul

Hilary Jones, Wesley Burrage, and Paul Aitken, were the three free festivalers that I worked with on the exhibition. I wanted to find out more about the background to their involvement with Stonehenge and with the Stonehenge Campaign Group (the protest group set up in the aftermath of the Battle of the Beanfield in 1985), as well as their reactions to working on the exhibition. Their comments begin to answer some of the questions posed by Ian Hodder (p. 193).

BB: *Wes, how did you get involved in Stonehenge and the Stonehenge Campaign Group?*

WB: As a teenager in the early eighties I was interested in non main-stream politics and non mainstream life-styles. I didn't hear about the Stonehenge Festival till '84. Then I saw what happened in '85 [the Battle of the Beanfield], and I saw an advert in *Time Out* about the Campaign meetings and that's how I got involved . . .

BB: *How did you get involved in alternative politics?*

WB: Music – punk rock. I was about ten or eleven when punk rock happened, and it was the big thing at the time. Punk rock's not just music, it is alternative politics.[25]

HJ: Punk rock was the backlash against the big industries of music. The whole thing about punk rock was that it was people in their bedrooms picking up guitars and making music. It spawned several small record labels, but then, unfortunately, the big companies stepped in and thought, 'God, this is marketable, it's enormous'. Then the fashion-designers stole the fashions that had grown round it, and it dissolved.

WB: It was the DIY thing of the seventies – you couldn't separate the politics out from it. And punk rock was really strongly involved with CND and anti-war issues . . .

BB: *So the fact that you lived in squats while you were a student – does that tie up with punk rock?*

WB: Yes, my squatting was as much a political decision as a financial one.

BB: *But you still went to university?*

WB: Yes, that was conventional behaviour – keeping my parents happy, doing what was expected of me. And at the same time doing things that I wanted to do alongside it. It was like a double life-style in a way. And to a degree I'm doing it again, because I'm working now, but it's not so polarised, there's a bit of a cross-over between the two. [Wes works for a firm that makes organic products. He cycles to work, seven miles each way.]

HJ: Wes came to Stonehenge because of his politics, I came to politics because of Stonehenge. I lived in the catchment area for the Stonehenge festival. For years I'd watch Bournemouth empty of

25. McKay cites Sarah Thornton that 'underground crowds are attached to sounds'. He also quotes Wally Hope, who started the first Stonehenge festival, 'Our temple is sound, we fight our battles with music . . . We have guitars instead of tommy-guns' (McKay 1996: 7).

young people for that couple of weeks. And then I became old enough to join the exodus. 1980, 1981. It literally was an exodus, I remember the first time I got on the bus and said, 'Salisbury, please', and the conductor said, 'Are you going to Stonehenge, because you can buy a through ticket?' They knew that anybody around seventeen, eighteen, nineteen, getting on the bus and asking for Salisbury was going to Stonehenge.

Up until then I'd gone to school ordinarily. Like Wes, I always felt detached from people around me, but I wasn't particularly disaffected, I wasn't particularly interested in the politics. It was going to Stonehenge and seeing alternative live-styles being lived that changed things. You go on site, and it is a different world. A completely different culture. And since that first year, I haven't missed a year, despite the clamp-downs. As far as I'm concerned, it's still mega-important to me, because that is where I suddenly switched . . .

BB: *What was the connection between the festival and the stones?*

HJ: The stones were meaningless to me when I first went to the festival. I went to the festival because everybody did, and I went over to the stones at the sunrise because it was such a big thing on site. There were even people going round saying, 'Get your acid! It's Solstice night tonight!' So right, I went over. From the festival field the stones were actually quite insignificant. It isn't until you actually leave the festival site and cross the road . . . That very first time that I watched the sunrise – the place is indescribable, it just blows you away. Suddenly the stones become more important than the festival – in fact they are inseparable really.

BB: *Did you go on with your A levels? Did you want to go to university?*

HJ: No, I didn't even want to finish my A levels.

BB: *Did you want to get a job?*

HJ: Oh god, no. I was much too interested in what I was doing then to knuckle down to a job. I was just hanging out with the core of people that went to Stonehenge. We were all dropping out of A levels, university. I was hanging out with a bunch of middle-class kids who all had parental pressures on them and were all kicking against them. One by one we stopped doing what we were doing and started doing something completely different which was living a nocturnal life-style and going round the festivals in the Summer. It did start to seem that we were living outside society – we lived different hours.

WB: The further I got into education the more I wanted to get out of
      it. And the same with me, there was no way I wanted a job when
      I'd finished. I wanted to live a life-style that I enjoyed . . .
      squatting, going to festivals . . .

BB: *And living on the dole?*

HJ: Yes, and obviously that makes you clash with the people outside
      because there's a lot of criticism for living on the dole. It's always
      been my argument that I was willing to work, there was just no
      work out there that I would have found fulfilling. Which I've
      now proved . . . [Hilary now works, for a pretty meagre salary,
      for a bird sanctuary. She usually works a seven day week.] I'm
      not a lazy person, and never have been, and yet that's always
      the argument that's levelled at you – that you're willing to live
      off society. But there just wasn't a single job available that
      wouldn't have mentally and spiritually crushed me if I'd taken
      it on. So it was easy enough to live on the dole and carve out an
      alternative existence that seemed – apart from that one connec-
      tion, going and signing on and receiving your cheque – totally
      unconnected to what the rest of society were doing.[26]

BB: *What happened to you in 1985?*

HJ: I wasn't actually there on the first of June [the Battle of the
      Beanfield]. So I missed that horrendous bit. But I was there a
      few days later, and I was there for that whole bit afterwards when
      people were nursing their wounds, the whole aftermath of shock
      (Figure 45). Walking to Westbury – I was walking alone – I got
      driven at, and almost knocked over, by a police range-rover and
      that was my very first clash with the police – I'd been there for
      years but there was no police involvement while the festival was
      going on. That was the real eye-opener, the real shock, and that
      was when my real cynicism with everything around me set in.

BB: *Paul, what about you, how did you get involved?*

PA: I suppose from a few different directions. I had this interest in
      archaeology in general. Prehistory was a particular interest. And
      apart from the archaeological sense, the Arthurian cycle. And in

26. Hakim Bey defines what he calls The Temporary Autonomous Zone: ' "pirate
economics", living high off the surplus of social overproduction – and the concept of
music as revolutionary social change – and finally their shared air of impermanence, of
being ready to move on, shape-lift, re-locate to other universities, mountain-tops, ghettos,
factories, safe houses, abandoned farms – or even other planes of reality' (cited in McKay
1996: 8).

another way it was again through music, but different music, the festivals that were before punk. In '74, I went to the last Windsor festival, and though I left before the place got trashed, obviously I identified with the events and went to the protest meeting that was held in Hyde Park. The Wallies were there and said, 'Come down to Stonehenge'.[27] So I did, and stayed with them for a while seeing what they were about. The first big festival was in '75, the year after Windsor. Unlike the later ones, it was very much linked to the stones. Partly because of its position in King Barrow woods, on the line of the Avenue. There was this continuous umbilical cord of people going to and from the stones, not actually on the Avenue – there's a particular route from the barrows that gets you down the scarp. The site was actually linked in a living way, and although it was ostensibly a music festival, there was a lot going on that was quite different.

Figure 45 After the Battle of the Beanfield

27. The first Stonehenge festival was the inspiration of Phil Russell a.k.a. Wally Hope. For a detailed description of Wally Hope's inspiration, and also his mysterious death see Stone (1996: 79–95).

BB: *Were you allowed into the stones?*

PA: Well, in the sense that we allowed ourselves in. At the Solstice we went down there in the afternoon rather than the sunrise – the real experience was the indescribable ceremony that took place in the afternoon. You were with the same people that you'd been living with, and everybody was suddenly completely different and the whole atmosphere was completely different. The stones were completely different, and there was really no turning back from there.[28]

BB: *What else were you doing at the time?*

PA: I had a job in the MoD – research and communications! And it just tended to get more military and things were happening in the family, and the work-place actually moved and – it left me rather than I left work.

BB: *Did you do A levels?*

PA: Oh yes, I did A levels; I did a year of university but . . .

BB: *Did the decision to give up work go hand-in-hand with getting more and more involved in the festivals?*

PA: Not really, because festivals other than Stonehenge were weekend things and one could fit that in. It was really after the Stonehenge festival was effectively banned that everything erupted. The amount of protest and work that was being done, and could be done, took up all the time.

HJ: It has been a full-time job. The amount of travel, the meetings we've had to travel to, the newsletters, the searching around for information and keeping abreast. It's been a full time job for many of us.

BB: *Paul, Hilary says that you more or less foresaw what happened in '85?*

PA: Not in detail, but it was generally feared that there would be bloodshed. It's a huge political question as to exactly why it ever happened, who was involved – and there are yet things to come out.

BB: *Do you think there was an ideological and political sea-change, an increasing intolerance, and that you were an obvious target?*

HJ: Of course. It was linked to the miners' strike. The Battle of the Beanfield and the miners' strike were so close to each other, and so similar, the way the police reacted to both . . .

28. There is a good description of the Stonehenge Free Festival 1974–76 in Stone (1996: 84–97).

BB: *Who set up the Stonehenge Campaign, and what was the idea behind it?*

PA: I don't suppose it was any different from a parents' group who object to a lack of a school crossing . . . a problem arises and you get together to do something about it.

HJ: It was an unwillingness to let go of the festival . . .

PA: People suddenly realised how much it meant to them . . .

BB: *When I came along (1992), the group was quite small . . .*

HJ: But it was enormous. At the first meeting we couldn't fit into the meeting house. That was September '85, and if you'd seen the diverse groups – there were theatre groups, community groups, housing groups, all the alternative things that went on at Stonehenge were represented. Obviously the momentum was greater in the first few years, and then people fell away because they couldn't see any results.

BB: *What were the tactics employed?*

WB: Setting up the Stonehenge Campaign enabled those people who felt they were denied their right to free access and the right to peacefully assemble to come together and work for a common purpose. This was in addition to the many individual efforts of people to resolve the supression of the festival and Solstice celebrations . . .

HJ: Opening up communications was a big thing. Opening up communications with the people that had done this to us. There wasn't a sense of 'Right, this is a call to arms, we're going to fight our way back', but rather, 'We've got to try and talk to these people. What the hell have they done, what do they think they're doing?' And there was also – 'If there are no communications, if that side doesn't move, then how are we going to do it anyway?' Hence the starting up of the Stonehenge Walk because everybody felt how can we get to Stonehenge without it seeming like a call to arms. If we pilgrimage from London to Stonehenge then nobody can say, 'Hey, these marauding yobos are storming the barricades.'

BB: *Was it difficult to get consensus about what to do?*

PA: Yes. There was a lot of discussion about what would be accepted as a compromise.

HJ: Endless hours of discussion about how far away would you be willing to have a festival. Whether one mile away, two miles away, a day's walking distance could count as a free Stonehenge festival.

PA: We thought that the more we were prepared to compromise, the more we'd get. But in practice when it came to talking to them about details, and new ideas, they had none.

BB: *Who went to the meetings with English Heritage?*

PA: Essentially anybody who wanted to . . .

HJ: As I recall we decided to keep numbers low . . .

PA: Yes, but the first time there was a room full of people, and what they essentially did was express their passion. And English Heritage sat white-faced and started to realise what sort of an impact they had on people. English Heritage said they'd try and find a site, talk to accommodating land-owners . . .

BB: *But nothing came of it?*

PA: No, they just repeated themselves. In the end we got disillusioned and stopped talking to them.

BB: *The Stonehenge Campaign newsletter is your most important means of communication. Where do you get all the information from?*

PA: For the Stonehenge news local people just keep on scanning the Wiltshire newspapers, checking on Council Meetings and so on.

WB: The rest comes in by mail, from individuals and groups and campaigns. We send stuff to them, and they send stuff back.

BB: *What's the mail out?*

PB: Five or six hundred.

BB: *So probably it gets read by a least four times that number.*

HJ: At least. We distribute about the same number by hand. And people photostat it and circulate it. And remember it's anti-copyright, so stuff gets lifted and re-used in other newsletters and Websites and so on.

BB: *Is it the most important thing that you do?*

HJ: Yes, in a way, because that's when we're talking to our type of people. But obviously the Campaign's also the point of contact with the other side, with the people who are trying to stop the festivals.

BB: *This is a more general question: what is the overall Stonehenge Campaign agenda?*

HJ: Well, it's written on the back of the Newsletter: 'to lobby, campaign, attend meetings, raise public awareness, maintain links with interested parties for the reinstatement of Stonehenge People's Free Festival and religious access to Stonehenge itself, and to protect the Stonehenge landscape and environment'. We're thinking of changing 'religious' to 'spiritual'!

PA: We're thinking that we should add something about respecting the stones, not climbing on them with boots on!

HJ: We've kind of tried to keep the question of the Free Festival and of access to the stones as a spiritual thing separate, because the clamp-down on the festival shouldn't have stopped the spiritual access. But we also view them as inseparable. For people in the Campaign Group one or other is more important, so we've got to keep both going.

BB: *There seems to have been a proliferation of protest in the last few years. Does that make any difference to your agenda?*

WB: Most of those movements have always been there – the animal rights, anti-war issues – they were always part of the festival, people were campaigning about them.

PA: But it is true that the Criminal Justice Act has thrown people together – more or less into the same cell if you like – and they've found intuitive links that aren't necessarily spelt out.

WB: More people have become active over the last few years – direct action has become a fundamental part of what people are doing. Previously, apart from some high profile environmental camp-aigns, direct action seemed to be the sole preserve of assorted radical/anarchist groups – often advocated as a tactic but rarely acted on!

HJ: And the direct action has brought the issues to public notice, because it's one of those things that the media can pick up on.

WB: It's become more fashionable. The issues were always represented on the festival sites, but people like you wouldn't have known.

PA: It's also true that large companies and the State, in looking for increased profits, have somehow crossed boundaries that people weren't really aware of, but that have pushed them into taking a stand. Like the live animal exports.

BB: *Do you think these various protests or campaigns can bring about political or other major sort of changes?*

HJ: We're not fighting for a change of government, or even to destroy English Heritage . . .[29]

29. This, of course, raises the question of the effectiveness of single-issue politics, even when they are widely networked. McKay suggests that 'The dangers of single-issue political action are that it diverts from class analysis, from economic challenge, or simply from having a wider perspective', but he also suggests that this fragmentation may also be its strength because it 'does operate outside the traditional framework of left and right. New spaces are opened up, which isn't always a comfortable situation, even for other political activists: what might be embraced with exhilaration is distanced with suspicion' (McKay 1996: 2; see also p. 151).

WB: We're campaigning for what we want to do, rather than destroy what they're doing. By its very nature these campaigns are very anarchic, they resist any formalised structure that will oppose pre-existing bodies.

BB: *Is that its strength, that it is anarchic?*

HJ: Yes, because we haven't got anything set in stone, because it isn't a political campaign, because we're not campaigning to bring down a government, more people can become involved, they can come in with their own versions. We can't have spokespeople. That's been a constant problem throughout. The bodies that we've talked to – conferences with the police, conferences with English Heritage and the like – they always want to tie us down to their formal structures, which is a hierarchy, with people who can give undertakings and make decisions at the meetings. We've always explained when we've gone into meetings that we can only represent ourselves, all we've ever said is that we're willing to go back and publicise through the newsletters and our channels of communication. We could never give undertakings.

BB: *That's always the problem, you're having to fight on their turf. They define the rules.*

HJ: Yes, and then what happens is that they offer tickets [to the Solstice] to those of us that are willing to speak to them – 'Here, have a ticket, you go in'. Or 'Here are 500 tickets', and we have to say 'How are we supposed to allocate 500 tickets among 5000 people?'.

BB: *They can't understand the problem. I've just read their side of this story. They think they're being reasonable, and you're being quite unreasonable:*

> *In 1987 we offered 500 free tickets but only about half of these were taken up. In 1988 English Heritage offered 1000 tickets of which only 500 were taken up. However an estimated 5000 people walked to the stones on the night of the Solstice and attempted to force their way into the site. Over the next few hours 1000 police were called in from seventeen different forces and the Chief Constable actually read the Riot Act to the crowd from the safety of a helicopter hovering overhead.*[30]

---

30. Anderson et al. (1996: 30).

They also maintain that the site can't hold more than 500 people.

HW: I know, they kept quoting the Hillsborough enquiry.[31] But you couldn't have a Hillsborough disaster at Stonehenge because people can move away from the stones.

BB: *So you'd say there can't be any curtailing of numbers and that people will sort themselves out?*

PA: We can also show that we've got ideas that would help. There can be different ceremonies going on in different parts of the Stonehenge triangle field and music so that you draw people away from the stones.

HJ: The permitted figures keep going down. They used to say there was a public order issue, now they've moved on and it's become a public safety issue . . .

PA: And yet, at Old Sarum, they want to have 15,000 people all at once at one of their violent re-enactments, this time of an American Civil War battle . . . It wouldn't occur to them that people should be herded in two hundred at a time.

HJ: They pay, of course! At the end of the day we can come up with suggestions but English Heritage are not interested in resolving the problems, they just want an excuse.

PA: Things are getting worse rather than better. 'The problem' is seen by everybody to be decreasing, it no longer occupies the banner headlines – 'the vandals at the gates' stuff – and yet the police are getting more and more agitated, using more and more powers. It just reflects the national picture, the police are just a symptom.

BB: *Let me ask you something about the Stonehenge Belongs to You and Me exhibition. Did you feel that I had too much control over what went into it?*

HJ: Not really, we were collaborating with you. It wasn't a Stonehenge Campaign exhibition. We were trying to fit our own opinions into your framework.

PA: We had an input, you created the flow, the theme ideas.

HJ: It was about raising the issues. It was an opportunity to express our opinions knowing that they would be circulating in an area which we wouldn't normally be able to reach. A different audience.

PB: It was a way of constructively doing something rather than just talking amongst ourselves.

31. The football stadium where the exits were closed and the football pitch sealed off so that when the crowd surged forward people were killed in the crush.

HJ: And because you express things in a different way from the way we would, it broadens our horizons . . .

WB: It modifies our view . . .

HJ: And it brought different people back in, who wouldn't otherwise have made contact with us.

WB: We've definitely had a lot of feed-back from it. The exhibition has gone beyond us and yourself and the Campaign.

HJ: It's a two-way thing – some of the people who have seen the exhibition would never have seen an exhibition put on by some-one like you. For you, it's gone to an alternative audience, for us to a mainstream one.

BB: *What was it like taking the exhibition round the different venues?*

WB: I really enjoyed it. Every venue was completely different.

HJ: It was always a nightmare.

WB: Yes, at the same time a nightmare.

BB: *Because of people's reactions to you?*

HJ: Everything about it. The logistics of getting it up and down. One forgets that it's pure hard labour. And the reaction. We were going to such an alien environment. The people who ran the venues that you booked it for were really taken aback, wondering who these scuzzy hippies in a beaten-up truck were, they probably thought you'd hired us for a fiver to set up the exhibition – we were the hired humpers!

BB: *It's true, I never thought to warn them!*

Dialogues 4: Other Places, Other Ways of Telling

A Short Dialogue with Ian Hodder

I have heard Ian Hodder talk about the complexity of view-points at the tell site of Çatalhöyük in Turkey, ranging from the Islamic Fundamentalist workforce who have mixed feelings about the female iconography and about the influx of scantily dressed tourists, to – among the tourists – eco-feminists (often American) determined to reclaim the 'Mother Goddess'. I wanted to know how he was going to find spaces and places for these – and many other – people's engagement with the past.

BB (email 2): *At Çatalhöyük, what ideas do you have about how to cater for all the divergent view-points that surround the meaning and use of the site?*

IH [email 2]: At Çatal I have felt that the important thing is to engage in the globalising process and to allow both sides of the dialectic to play themselves out – in ways that we cannot possibly predict. Of course, there are, in the Çatal case, clear issues of domination and resistance. In particular, how can I provide the means for poor rural Turks with limited education and few technologies to become involved in a dialogue about their past? There are clear issues of resources that have to be solved before inter-action can occur.

I had thought initially that the problem was simply to provide the data from the site so that the myriad of special interest groups could all then develop their own interpretations. These special interest groups range from amateur vulture specialists, to those carpet dealers interested in the origins of kilim carpets, to eco-feminists, Gaia theorists and Mother Goddess worshippers. But it became clear that my solution was inadequate because it was underlain by the fallacy that data can be separated from interpretation. Some of the special interest groups were able to articulate this – they said, 'But the data you provide us with have already been biased by you.' So what I am trying to do is to pull the interpretive process down into the data definition level. I believe it is possible to begin to do this using the new information technologies that are fast becoming available. For example, we take videos of the excavation and discovery process, digitise these and incorporate them into the database. This means that someone wanting to use the database can see discussions about the interpretation of the site and can see visually the context within which the data were produced. This makes reinterpretation more possible. We are also developing the use of hyper-text so that object and context information from the site can be referred across to narratives dealing with the discovery process. We are also using virtual reality in order to provide a fuller evaluation of the use and experience of space from different points of view.

Constructing a database like this, and putting it on the Web which is what we want to do, will have a dual purpose. First, it will mean that special interest groups will have a better chance to reinterpret the data from the bottom up. Second, it will break the boundary between the casual and the specialist involvement. Rather than having specialist books separated from 'popular' versions, an interactive multimedia database of this kind will allow browsing to any depth that is wanted. Even a casual visitor to the 'site' might be led into a deeper understanding of the data and the interpretive issues involved.

Certainly we are also planning to build a museum and to reconstruct parts of the site. Certainly we will provide multilingual displays designed for different levels and groups of interest. Certainly we are trying to engage local people as much as possible in this process. But in the end I think it is these new technologies which offer the best solution for breaking the mould of the fenced site, the guarded heritage, the privileged and educated tourist versus the theme park pastiche . . .

BB[email 2]:   *A sort of celebration of the indeterminate nature of technology which permits (rather than entraps) and allows people to create their own understandings? It sounds very generous, an opening up of doors within doors and layers within layers, though perhaps these aren't even the appropriate metaphors. So then, as you say, the problem remains that, for the present, these technologies are elitist. Who gets to tap in? Also, although this may say more about my own particular reluctance to experience the past with head-phones on and eyes fixed to a screen, it seems a rather solitary way of imbibing understanding . . .*

You could say that what you're attempting on the Web is the very opposite of the Stonehenge exhibition. It's hugely costly, requires a lot of capital investment, demands high level expertise. And yet it is utterly different from the usual grand, large-scale visitor-centre facility – the sort that's threatened for the new Stonehenge Centre. What your Web site offers, like the small, cheap, travelling exhibition, is flexibility, mobility, open-endedness, and spaces and place for people to answer back and to offer their ideas and interpretations . . .

Dialogue with Nick Merriman

Nick Merriman was a curator at the Museum of London, and is the author of Beyond the Glass Case (1991). *During the last few years the Museum of London has been changing its permanent exhibitions so that, for example, in the prehistoric gallery, the gender bias implicit in most depictions – visual and verbal – of Man the Hunter (active, virile, out-going) and Women the Gatherer (passive, domestic, home-based) has been questioned.*

Nick played an important part in the creation of a temporary exhibition entitled The Peopling of London *which worked with different communities in London and stressed that London has always, right from the beginning, been multicultural.*

The Museum of London was one of the few large museums that was prepared to host the Stonehenge Belongs to You and Me *exhibition. This dialogue took place whilst the exhibition was up.*

BB: *It is quite odd seeing the Stonehenge exhibition out in the hall of the Museum of London. A lot of people are stopping to look and there are lots of comments, in a multitude of languages, but I have to admit it looks a bit tacky in this very modern, clean environment.*

NM: To be honest, it's not so much the content but the appearance that makes it difficult to put on an exhibition of this sort in a place like this. It's not such a problem in local museums, but once you've got professional designers they want everything to look good. You could have a really radical exhibition and so long as it was extremely well designed there probably wouldn't be much problem.

BB: *That's a problem for people looking for venues for a travelling exhibition who don't have the money for smart presentation. I guess that, remembering research that shows that people's attention span in museums is incredibly short, you'd say we'd got too much text?*

NM: It is wordy . . .

BB: *Mind you, I've stood around watching people at the Stonehenge exhibition, and the thing is that if people are involved, if it matters to them, they'll spend hours and read everything. Didn't you find that was true for* The Peopling of London *exhibition?*

NM: That's the ironic thing . . . There were people saying it was far too wordy, and then people from the different communities complaining that there wasn't enough information!

BB: *With small exhibitions people are prepared to spend more time. They know they're not going to die of exhibition fatigue.*

NM: It's true. If people are taking in a whole museum it's incredible how little sticks. You'd be amazed what can be put in exhibitions and how few people will really notice. It suggests to me that large traditional exhibitions are very ineffective means of communication. In fact an exhibition about the size of the Stonehenge one is about the maximum that anyone can take in. Half an hour, and then your attention span is gone . . .

BB: *It depends on people's involvement – we've often had people staying for a couple of hours, pouring over the detail. But OK, too much text. What else?*

NM: Some of the language is a bit difficult. 'Appropriation/ Contestation' – very academic and intimidating. But on the other hand the mix of colour and black-and-white photographs, the cartoons, the broken-up text, the different voices, that all has a welcoming feel. Once you start getting into it, you feel quite involved and you can relate it to your own ideas. Maybe, though,

you could have tried for more interaction earlier on in the
exhibition, got people to comment on specific issues as they
went along, had some questions where people could lift flaps. It
is a bit passive . . .

BB: *The sequence of the exhibition is quite conventional: prehistoric,*
        historic, contemporary voices, questions of empowerment. I wonder if
        there'd have been better ways of structuring it?

NM: Well, you had to keep the voices separate because that's part of
        the agenda. But maybe you could have started with Stonehenge
        today: this place exists *now*, these views exist *now*, and this is
        how they project backwards into some mythical past. You could
        have kept the whole thing in the present.

BB: *Yes, the preliminary prehistoric board should have come later. It should*
        have come as part of the archaeological interpretation. That would
        have followed the logic of the exhibition. Different groups: different
        knowledges.

NM: Yes – we all tell stories, here's the archaeological story. What's
        good is that you can keep on bringing the protests right up to
        date.

BB: *Do you think that the last part of the exhibition is too didactic, too*
        much like agit-prop?

NM: Well, the tempo certainly changes. It starts off being pretty even-
        handed and calm and then it begins to get more emotive and to
        take a particular line. I suppose that if I'd been doing this as a
        Museum of London exhibition I'd feel the need to put another
        viewpoint. I would have tried very hard to get a statement from
        English Heritage about what they're trying to do.

BB: *I should have taken their PR job (see p. 158). At the time it seemed*
        pointless, I wanted them to be self-critical. Now I can see that I could
        have included it and then let people make up their own minds.

NM: Maybe you could have looked at some other sites. Why doesn't
        the confrontation happen at Avebury? You'd get back to the
        question of Stonehenge as national icon, a symbol of Britishness.
        Or you could have said 'This section is biased – what do *you*
        think? What have we left out?'

BB: *Yes, all good ideas. Let's talk a bit about* The Peopling of London
        exhibition. It was all about different ethnic communities in London,
        past and present. I know that you worked with some of the
        communities – did that process of consultation change the shape of
        the thing?

NM: Yes it did. Originally we wanted to put in stuff about the reception of different immigrant groups, racism and so on, and about contemporary discrimination. But one of the messages we got very clearly from talking to people was that, from their point of view, everybody knew that stuff, they'd read about it in the papers – crime, unemployment, poverty and what have you. They wanted a more celebratory thing . . .

BB: *What did they want to celebrate?*

NM: They were all saying that, within the high-status context of the museum, they wanted to show the contribution they'd made, they didn't want to show the negative thing – the negative stereotype – they wanted to show that they contribute to the economy and so on. And we had to respect their wishes, though then, of course, we were criticised in some quarters for not being critical enough. Our detached, rather academic, curatorial position was that we should have a fairly comprehensive view which pointed up some of the hardship, but theirs was a personal view – because they were involved, and because they had a stake in being shown in the right light. I felt that we had to recognise their way of thinking and, at least at this stage, because we were contacting many of these groups and working with them for the first time, say 'Yes, we want to accommodate you. Maybe later on we can talk in more detail about some of these other issues'. So this was a case of us not being even-handed as part of the overall brief of the project.

BB: *Do you think there are tensions, when you're involved in a more radical exhibition of this sort, between throwing it open for different voices to be heard, acting as mediator or enabler, and creating the overall structure (see p. 153)?*

NM: That's a difficult one, and it's one I've agonised over quite a lot. One of the ideas, with at least some of our recent exhibitions, is that the curatorial authority should recede into the background. That, in some way, the curator should act as an enabler for other people. But ultimately so much of it comes down to practicalities. Somebody has to take the lead and get things done to deadlines and raise money and so on. So, inevitably, even by coming up with the idea of being an enabler, you're more seriously involved than you might originally have wished to be. My thinking now is that you're acting much more like an editor, or a conductor of an orchestra. The exhibition is very much shaped by how you envisage it, but you have to work with that. You have to be explicit to the people you're working with about your agenda.

Then, if they can persuade you to alter it, that's fine. Maybe it's slightly wishy-washy, but I think that if you're working from a critical perspective, and you're aware of the position you're adopting, and you're willing, as part of that, to embrace as many points of view as possible, and to discuss it with people, then it's OK. Discussing it is important – some of our projects have changed just through talking to people. So long as you're receptive, I don't think it matters that you're quite heavily involved in creating the overall shape. Ultimately, in a way, it's your job to do this, and you have to be prepared not to hide behind people.[1]

BB: *One of the great things about smaller, temporary exhibitions is that they can more easily focus on a particular issue.*

NM: Yes. In the case of *The Peopling of London* exhibition, I didn't want a multivocal approach. I wanted it to be quite didactic, I wanted to ram home a very basic point, one which most people were unaware of, which is that London's always had a mixed population (Figures 46 & 47). Whereas with the Stonehenge exhibition you really wanted to open it out as widely as possible, because there are different viewpoints and they need to be heard. We could, I suppose, have had an alternative – bigoted – viewpoint, but that would have insulted the people we worked with.

BB: *Actually I think* The Peopling *exhibition is multivocal. You're letting the voices that are usually muted come through, you're proposing an alternative reading of London's history which goes against the grain of what most people have been taught . . .*

NM: Yes, some of that came out in the comments on the flip-chart – 'Thank you very much, at last I feel that I'm a Londoner', 'Shows me that what we learnt at school was very biased', 'This exhibition should be made permanent; what a shame that the people who most need to see it, probably won't'.

BB: *How explicit was the message?*

NM: Right near the beginning we had a section called 'A Liberal City?' which displayed both racist and anti-racist material, and then we put the Museum's line which was obviously anti-racist (Figure 48). We tried to show that there was a correlation between cycles of economic decline and cycles of hatred against foreigners right

1. 'We are obliged to share authority with both subject and reader, but equally cannot evade the authority of authorship' (Cosgrove & Domash 1993).

Figure 46 Part of the 'Peopling of London' exhibition
(with kind permission of the Board of Governors of the Museum of London)

from the earliest records, from the reign of King Edgar in the Anglo-Saxon period, and that economic problems are the root cause, not the inherent racial characteristics of different immigrant groups. It was a fairly overt sub-text all the way through the exhibition.

BB: *90,000 people saw the exhibition, how many came specifically to see The Peopling?*

NM: Something like 28 per cent came specifically to see *The Peopling* exhibition, and about 64 per cent of the people who came to the museum went to see it as well.

BB: *And presumably a lot of them didn't usually visit museums?*

Figure 47 Part of the 'Peopling of London' exhibition
(with kind permission of the Board of Governors of the Museum of London)

Figure 48 A Liberal City? – from 'The Peopling of London' exhibition
(with kind permission of the Board of Governors of the Museum of London)

NM: We certainly got a much larger percentage of people from ethnic minority groups.

BB: *Do you think the fact that you asked people to contribute items made them feel more involved (see p. 223)?*

NM: That was only a modest component. People that we interviewed did lend objects, and, yes, they came and brought all their friends and relatives.

BB: *There was a by-election being fought at the time in which a British National Party [ultra right-wing, overtly racist] candidate was running. Did people make any connections?*

NM: Yes, on the flip-charts there were lots of slogans saying 'Smash the British National Party' or 'One in the eye for Derek Beacon'. And we got a lot of publicity in the local paper. In fact I was a bit concerned that we might see some action. We discussed with the security staff what we might do if anything happened . . . but nothing did. I suppose it shows that museums are fairly well removed from most people's political consciousness! In North America, museums are getting swept up in political controversies. Perhaps if we'd been a very local museum, if we'd been in Tower Hamlets, we'd have had a few windows smashed.

BB: *Was that a one-off exhibition, or are you going to take on other sacred cows?*

NM: We've put in a Lottery bid to develop our rotunda building, and one of the proposals is that we have a permanent exhibition on 'London as a Financial Centre'. We'd certainly get funding from the City of London. But the big question for us is how far would we be able to push our own critical line – after all, most of us have read Will Hutton's *The State We're In* . . .[2]

BB: *It is difficult. Big institutions and organisations seem to find it quite impossible to be self-critical. I guess it would be the perfect setting for a multivocal exhibition: there'd be a Will Hutton-type critique; the City PR job; and all stations in-between.*

NM: That's what the working group came up with. What we'd like is a series of different spins on the City. There'd have to be stuff on Insider Dealing, on the effect of the City on Third World countries . . . But the question is whether the City would find that acceptable. Ultimately it comes down to who is going to pay for it? It would have to be subtle.

2. W. Hutton (1996) *The State We're In*, London: Vintage. This book provides a critical analysis of banking and investment institutions.

BB: *Who funded* The Peopling?

NM: It came from our own museum budgets . . .

BB: *There you go. Maybe it's these sorts of financial restraints that again make small, cheap, exhibitions more effective, harder hitting. You don't end up in hock to the people with money.*

NM: It's true that a lot of the more radical exhibitions are done outside the museum structure, because they're not constrained by institutional parameters. The first exhibition of the Black History of London, 'Black Presence', was put on by the GLC [Greater London Council – disbanded by Thatcher] in the early eighties. It used to go round all the anti-apartheid rallies. But there are things going on in the museums too. There's Springburn Museum outside Glasgow. It's a district of Glasgow where they made railway locomotives, a tight-knit working-class community. The works closed down, mass unemployment, the terraced houses were razed to the ground and the people were decanted into high-rise buildings. European Community funds were put in to develop a museum, and the curator deliberately didn't build up any collections, he just went out into the community. So, for example, he worked with teenagers – who wouldn't normally come near a museum – he lent them cameras, they went and photographed themselves and did some historical research, and then he did an exhibition about teenagers. He learnt to knit, and did an exhibition about knitting circles. Lots and lots of community history, he didn't care whether it involved artefacts or not, he built up this place as an exhibition centre, but also a healing centre whereby a community that had been severely dislocated could try and heal some of the wounds of its history. People would just drop in and have a cup of tea. In the end, it's not necessarily the subject matter that's radical, it's the approach.

Dialogue with Dolores Root

Dolores Root is director of exhibits and programmes at the New England Science Centre which is an environmental museum in Worcester, Massachusetts. She spent six years as a programme director at the Massachusetts Foundation for the Humanities where she worked on new approaches to the long-term histories of New England Native People. She was also director of the Brattleboro Museum, and whilst she was

there she created, amongst other things, a travelling exhibition, Seeing
Japan. *I never saw it, but it certainly influenced my thinking on the
importance of engaging with other people, both in the making and in
the viewing.*
    We talked by email.

BB: *When I started on the* Stonehenge Belongs to You and Me *exhibition
      I remembered, though not in any detail, a travelling exhibition that
      you'd put on about Japan. In fact, I pinched the idea of incorporating
      a mirror – so that the visitors saw themselves and began to recognise
      that they were part of the exhibition – from you. Tell me a bit about
      how your exhibition came into being?*
DR: It was called *Seeing Japan.* I was working at the Brattleboro Museum
      and Art Centre in Vermont, and we used to put on eight or nine
      exhibitions each year . . .
BB: *How big is Brattleboro?*
DR: Not big, but we served communities within a fifty mile radius.
      There's a wonderful mix of people, with a working-class commun-
      ity that cohabits with 'flatlanders' – people who've come from
      large urban areas and suburbs and are artists, writers, musicians,
      back-to-landers, trust fund hippies and Summer/weekend people.
      There are extraordinary people hidden up in the hills . . .
BB: *Flatlanders?*
DR: Vermont is steep, hilly, mountainous in parts. According to the
      'truc' Vermonters, the transplants from New Jersey and New York
      come from where the land is flat . . .
BB: *OK!*
DR: In the context of an exhibition season on American perceptions
      of Japan, we wanted one exhibition that would examine critically
      how Americans form ideas and images of another country and
      culture, and what these images tell us about our own cultural
      attitudes and values.
BB: *Was there a particular reason for being interested in Anglo-Japanese
      relations in the eighties?*
DR: Until recently most Americans had little first-hand exposure to
      Japan. They tended to learn about Japan from the popular media,
      from the Second World War, and from Japanese imports. In the
      1950s and '60s the label 'Made in Japan' meant made cheaply; in
      the '80s that same label tended to mean well made and in
      competition with America. In the mid '80s trade relations had

eased up, things Japanese were popular with American audiences, and more and more Americans could afford to travel to Japan. It seemed like a good opportunity to explore American–Japanese relationships in terms of how people form, use, manipulate and perpetuate cultural stereotypes. More or less unconsciously we chose a country and culture which were not part of the Brattleboro cultural heritage, so people were less likely to feel defensive.

In creating the exhibition, the first thing we had to do was to find a hook – an exhibition about how people create and maintain cultural stereotypes is not an obvious block-buster! There was a group of people known as Ex-Com – that's community people and staff – that would get together and brainstorm ideas. We played with the idea of travel and then we hit on the idea of suitcases: what did travellers to Japan bring back in their suitcase at different historical moments?

BB: *A brilliant idea!*

DR: I started researching American images in the popular media. I found there were an abundance of images right through from 1860, and that, at any given historical moment, there was a repetition of images in different forms. The major theme was the way in which, over time, the images of Japan and the Japanese flip-flop between Japan as delightful and as frightful.

I was fortunate to work with some of the most well-respected American scholars of Japanese–American relations: John Dower, an historian at MIT who has written extensively on Japanese history and had just completed a very powerful book that exposed the Second World War in the Pacific as a war about race for both sides; Carol Gluck, an historian at Columbia University; and Theodore Bestor who's an anthropologist, also at Columbia. Ted Bestor and Victoria Lyon-Bestor co-curated the exhibition with me and taught me a great deal about popular culture and contemporary Japan.

BB: *The suitcase is a wonderful image: objects moving between contexts and taking on new meaning along the way . . .*

DR: Yep. But in order to show how the objects embodied changing cultural values and attitudes we had to create a context. I researched 150 years of images in the American popular media, focusing on the covers of magazines such as *Life, Time, Fortune, Harper's Illustrated*, assuming these most visibly captured prevailing American attitudes. With the help of my scholars I narrowed the search to specific historic moments when Japan was in the American news. I started with the 'opening' of Japan by Perry.

BB: *Perry?*

DR: Commodore Matthew Perry ended almost 250 years of self-imposed isolation from the world on the part of Japan. In 1853 his squadron of 'Black Ships' (that's what the Japanese called them) cruised into Japanese waters on the first of two voyages to 'open' Japan to America for trade.

BB: *Right.*

DR: The first installation in Brattleboro was very, very modest. Visitors entered the exhibition through a 'tunnel' of travel posters and on the title poster was a plexi-holder with 'Take One' written above it. In the holder was a facsimile of a travel brochure which introduced the exhibition. This way of presenting the exhibit text was repeated throughout the exhibition. We wanted to minimise the text on the wall so people could concentrate on the visual images. Also it meant that people didn't have to buy a catalogue, and they could take the packet of travel brochures representing the different historical moments home to read. Each of the text/travel brochures had a format and image appropriate to its period.

    The exhibit was organised chronologically and at Brattleboro we kept the images and objects separate. The key element was a series of headlines asking why, at different historical moments, Americans saw Japan in certain ways: 'Is Japan a strange alien land?' 'Why do we often picture Japan as an exotic paradise?' 'How did we portray the enemy?' 'Why do Americans see Japan as the land of contrasts?' 'Do our images today evoke the battlefield?' and so on (Figures 49 & 50). Underneath each headline were images from the popular media.

BB: *I remember that you got people to lend their souvenirs ...*

DR: Yes. We solicited objects from the community for two reasons. First, we were a non-collecting museum which meant we didn't have any stuff. And, second, I knew from past experience that people love to see their own stuff or their neighbour's in a museum context. It was another hook to get people to really explore the exhibition – the illusion of travel *and* seeing Mrs. Jones's teapot. Initially I thought I would only be able to collect objects from the Second World War and later. I was wrong! Being good Yankees, many people had kept mementoes belonging to relatives who had travelled to Japan in the late nineteenth century and in the twentieth century prior to the Second World War.

Figure 49 Themes in the 'Seeing Japan' exhibition
(with kind permission of Dolores Root)

Through researching who would have been visiting Japan at
different historical moments, we created five representative
personae. We didn't want to focus on specific individuals, so we
created an elegant Victorian woman; a missionary couple ('20s
and '30s); a GI ('40s); Mom, Dad and the two kids ('60s); and a
college student ('80s). We worked out a list of the kind of items
these representative travellers would have brought home and used
the newspaper to solicit objects for each suitcase setting. We had

Figure 50 Themes in the 'Seeing Japan' exhibition
(with kind permission of Dolores Root)

an extraordinary response, and of course people had amazing and
wonderful stories. So we also put on an evening 'Show and Tell'
programme . . .

The objects were displayed uncovered, spilling out of period
suitcases – a between-context moment before the traveller put
them on display and made them something more precious
(Figures 51 & 52). There were certain items that were brought
back in every period. One was the kimono and it was wonderful

how it varied over time – from the authentic to fantasy to souvenir. This reflected the fact that right through the one hundred and fifty years Japanese women were only portrayed or alluded to as geisha girls.

   Observing visitors and reading their comments, it was clear to me that they liked being asked questions, were surprised by the history of images and many took time to reflect on these images.

BB: *When did the suitcases start to travel?*

Figure 51 Unpacking the suitcases – from the 'Seeing Japan' exhibition (with kind permission of Dolores Root)

Figure 52 Unpacking the suitcases – from the 'Seeing Japan' exhibition
(with kind permission of Dolores Root)

DR: I was intrigued with the concept of making travelling exhibitions
     that packaged the ideas without the objects. To me, it was
     pragmatic and cost-effective. To many in the museum profession
     it was heresy to make a travelling exhibit without the objects!
     Two years later I accomplished it . . . I had a good sense of what
     had worked and what needed improvement. We had to find a
     better way to mesh the contents of the suitcases and the images
     from the popular media, and we had to make people more
     critically aware of how stereotypes were created. I put together a
     team of museum professionals – an exhibition developer and
     Japanese specialist from the Boston Children's Museum which
     does innovative exhibitions, a freelance designer, and a visual
     artist who had worked with me on the Brattleboro installation. I
     kept my academic consultants and added a few. We met over a
     six-month period to rethink the presentation and to package
     Seeing Japan for travel.
BB: *Was it hard to raise the money?*
DR: Yes, getting money from American sponsors for the Brattleboro
     exhibition – let alone the travelling exhibition – was really hard.

American funders, like most Americans, had definite ideas about Japan. They tended to like 'Japan the Beautiful' images and thought there were many wonderful aspects of Japanese culture that we could focus on, instead of challenging popular ideas and images. Too many funders have narrow and conservative ideas of what museums should be doing. Moreover, the Brattleboro Museum's approach to a topic was multidimensional, so that in the context of our annual exhibition theme on American perceptions of Japan, we produced an exhibition on kites, and another which compared indigenous architectures where we had a team of carpenters working side by side, each team framing a post and beam farmhouse, and contemporary Japanese sculpture and more. The sponsors didn't understand all that, so, in the end, the Brattleboro installation was funded from general operating funds and cost, for materials and publicity, about $6000 (I'm guessing).

After that, the scholars with whom I worked, as well as individuals important in the world of Japanese–American relations, who appreciated this approach to American perceptions of Japan, were instrumental in opening doors to Japanese funders. You have to appreciate the kind of ambitious and dynamic exhibits that we produced at Brattleboro were highly unusual, and we were a small museum with no 'history'. We were upstarts! The process of soliciting support from Japanese funders for the travelling exhibition was fascinating because I used visuals that showed images of the delightful and the frightful. In one instance, showing these images to the head of marketing at JAL (Japan Airlines), he said (his voice controlling rage), 'You show me these images and ask me to support this exhibition!' I (in my determined and forthright manner!) said, 'Yes! and let me explain'. Within half an hour he agreed to give the project $10,000 and me a round-trip to Japan! Most Japanese are very aware of the duality of images that Americans hold of their country and people, and feel it is unfair. It took me a year to raise $75,000 to cover the costs of making a travelling exhibit and a small catalogue. With one exception, all the funders were Japanese based. The Massachusetts Foundation for the Humanities, the State programme of the National Endowment for the Humanities, gave the project $25,000, whereas the Vermont Council gave none!

Later on, when the Smithsonian Institution's Traveling Exhibition Service tried to raise funds for a national tour – after I had produced and successfully toured it to three museums – they couldn't raise a dime. It was 1991 and 1992, a period of intense trade antagonisms, and both funders and museums were afraid to touch it. One museum said, 'If we take this exhibit, we'll lose all our corporate funding . . .'

BB: *Another flip-flop – just as the exhibition showed! Was the travelling exhibition different from the original installation?*

DR: Well, yes. This time we had an exhibition designer and that enabled us to work on more effectively communicating the main ideas visually. One question we struggled with was how to present the very images we want people to question. We solved that by creating five leitmotifs, recurring images of Japanese men and women and of the landscape. Some of these images appear, disappear and reappear over the hundred and fifty year period without changing their form (for example, women as geisha), others change their form but not their character (thus samurai sometimes means strong and noble, other times fierce and cruel). In each historical context, we introduced each leitmotif, 'lifting' them from the original image, reducing them in size, coding with colour, repeating this 'shadow image' over time, so it functions like a code conveying continuity, contrast, or recurrence.

The other big issue we grappled with was the entrance and how to pull the viewers into the story. Here again, creative design became the instrument. We abandoned the creation of the illusion of travel that we had had in Brattleboro. Instead, we thought about how images of another country and culture are like a tape that reels through our minds. We also wanted to clearly communicate that perception is always from the point of view of the viewer, and that embodied in perceptions are cultural attitudes and values, and finally, we wanted to communicate the time depth of images. The metaphor for the design was a ribbon strung along with images which reference the array of typical images of Japan and the Japanese that loop through people's minds on a subliminal level. The physical lay-out of the exhibition was a looping ribbon (a double helix) constructed with nine modular units arranged chronologically. The five period suitcase settings were interspersed among the popular media panes, thus making them part of the contours of the ribbon. We used plexiglas for the popular media images because it is transparent, durable and permits layers of images. Through the design we created an environment which enabled the viewer to see backwards and forwards in time, as well as an array of conflicting images.

BB: *And in each venue the local people brought in their objects?*

DR: Yes, they loved it! But the museum curators, especially art curators, initially were appalled. It was so alien to most museum practice. Nonetheless, in the late '80s and '90s American museums became increasingly concerned about reaching beyond their traditional audiences and increasing attendance. So some curators saw the merit in soliciting objects from their community. On the other hand, most museums have a much greater level of bureaucracy than Brattleboro which greatly increased the amount of paper-work. In challenging the established museum practice, I felt it was important to explain to the host sites the underlying pedagogy and thinking, as well as the history of Japanese–American relations, and to list the objects to be solicited for each suitcase setting. The handbook made it simple – so I'm told – at least conceptually.

Some curators couldn't fathom leaving objects exposed – uncovered. We had to compromise by building a plexi screen in front of the suitcase settings – a sneeze guard. Too, the curators wanted to arrange the suitcase objects with a museum aesthetic – each object to be fully viewed – and found it difficult to have artefacts spilling out, touching each other, half-covered. Never-theless, in the three cities in which *Seeing Japan* toured, the curators accomplished the task beyond their expectations. They had no problem collecting the necessary objects, nor in getting their community excited about the project. At one venue – Louisville, Kentucky – there was the possibility of a different response: it was the site of one of the first Toyota plants in the USA with American workers. But, in the end, the range of responses to the exhibition did not seem to differ from the other venues.

BB: *We must stop! What do you see as the advantages of this sort of small, flexible, travelling exhibition?*

DR: The Brattleboro Museum was unusual in terms of our approach to exhibits. We had a professional staff of two, yet through collaboration with guest curators, designers and scholars, we prod-uced well researched exhibits. Most small or mid-size museums don't have the staff, resources, or, frankly, the vision. On the other hand, given the amount of resources, mainly human, that it took to mount the exhibition, it would be criminal to have it on display for three months, six months or whatever. What we packaged was an interpretive framework, and a process. The cost of shipping and mounting the exhibition was relatively modest and certainly affordable for small/mid-size museums. Another advantage is that the host site is involved in the production, creating a sense of ownership, which does not happen for typical travelling exhibitions. Certainly, I had my mission, modelling for other museums ways of doing exhibits – ways that actively engage the local community in the ideas and production.

Sad, but worth mentioning, when I turned *Seeing Japan* over to the Smithsonian Institute's Traveling Exhibition Service (SITES), it did not succeed, in part because the increased bureaucracy, more expensive and stringent packing and shipping requirements, and other costs added to the mounting of the exhibition. Its flexibility and simplicity were sacrificed!

BB: *Last question. I have to know – was there a mirror in the exhibition?*
DR: No – but as you can see, the concept of mirror, mirroring back, reflecting the tape in our heads, is embedded in the design.
BB: *How strange: so I internalised an image, a concept, and then, in our exhibition, externalised it and used a real mirror! Still, internal or external, it is about getting people to recognise their own involvement.*

Notes and Comments Page

If you feel that you, too, must have your say, you can write to Barbara Bender, c/o the publishers.

Bibliography

Alcoff, L. (1991), 'The problem of speaking for others', *Cultural Critique* 5–32.

Anderson, C., P. Planel & P. Stone (1996), *A Teacher's Handbook to Stonehenge*, London: English Heritage.

Ascherson, N. (1988), *Games with Shadows*, London: Radius/Century Hutchinson.

Atkinson, R. (1967), 'Silbury Hill', *Antiquity* XLI 259–62.

Baker, F. (1988), 'Archaeology and the heritage industry', *Archaeological Review from Cambridge* **7(2)** 141–44.

Bakhtin, M. (1984), *Rabelais and his World,* trans. H. Iswolsky, Bloomington, Ind.: Indiana University Press.

Barrell, J. (1972), *The Idea of Landscape and the Sense of Place 1730–1840*, Cambridge: Cambridge University Press.

Barrett, J. (1991), 'Later prehistoric landscapes: a biography of place', Paper presented to the Conference of the Theoretical Archaeology Group, Leicester, 18 December 1991.

—— (1994), *Fragments from Antiquity,* Oxford: Blackwell.

—— (1998), 'Chronologies of landscape', in R. Layton & P. Ucko (eds), *Shaping Your Landscape*, London: Allen & Unwin.

Barthes, F. (1987), *Cosmologies in the Making: a Generative Approach to Cultural Variation in Inner New Guinea*, Cambridge: Cambridge University Press.

Barthes, R. (1977), *Image, Music, Text*, New York: Hill & Wang.

Basso, K. (1983), '"Stalking with stories": names, places, and moral narratives among the western Apache', in E. Bruner (ed.), *The Construction and Reconstruction of Self and Society*, Illinois: Waveland Press Inc.

Bender, B. (1985), 'Prehistoric developments in the American mid-west and in Brittany, northwest France', in T. Price & J. Brown (eds), *Prehistoric Hunter-Gatherers. The Emergence of Cultural Complexity*, New York: Academic Press.

—— (1992), 'Theorising landscapes, and the prehistoric landscapes of Stonehenge, *Man* **27** 735–55.

—— (1993), 'Introduction: landscape – meaning and action', in B. Bender (ed.), *Landscape. Politics and Perspectives*, Oxford: Berg.

—— (1998a), 'Subverting the western gaze: mapping alternative worlds', in R. Layton & P. Ucko (eds), *Shaping Your Landscape*, London: Allen & Unwin.

—— (1998b), 'The living giant', in T. Darvill & K. Barker (eds), *The Cerne Giant: An Antiquity on Trial*, Oxford: Bournemouth University School of Conservation Sciences. Occasional Paper 5.

—— M. Edmonds, S. Hamilton, C. Tilley (in press), 'The rituals of routine practice', in G. Cooney & J. Gardiner (eds), *Interpreting, Preserving and Managing Ritual Landscape*, Proceedings of the Prehistoric Society Monograph.

—— S. Hamilton & C. Tilley (1997), 'Leskernick: stone worlds; alternative narratives; nested landscapes', *Proceedings of the Prehistoric Society*.

Bewley, B. et al. (1996), 'Notes. New features within the henge at Avebury, Wiltshire: aerial and geophysical evidence', *Antiquity* **70** 639–46.

Bloch, M. (1962), *Feudal Society*, trans. L. Manyon, vol. 1. London: Routledge and Kegan Paul.

Bloch, M. (1995), 'People into places: Zafimaniry concepts of clarity', in E. Hirsch and M. O'Hanlon (eds), *The Anthropology of Landscape*, Oxford: Clarendon Press.

Blunt, A. & G. Rose (eds) (1994), *Writing Women and Space. Colonial and Postcolonial Geographies*, New York: The Guildford Press.

Bommes, M. & Wright, P. (1982), 'Charms of residence, the public and the past', in R. Johnson et al. (eds), *Making Histories: Studies in History Writing and Politics*, London: Hutchinson.

Bourdieu, P. (1977), *Outline of a Theory of Practice*, Cambridge: Cambridge University Press.

—— (1984), *Distinction*, London: Routledge & Kegan Paul.

—— (1990), *The Logic of Practice*, trans. R. Nice, Cambridge: Polity Press.

—— (1991), *The Political Ontology of Martin Heidegger*, Cambridge: Polity Press.

Bradley, R. (1984), *The Social Foundations of Prehistoric Britain*, London: Longmans.

—— (1991), 'Ritual, time and history', *World Archaeology* **23(2)** 209–19.

—— (1993), *Altering the Earth*, Edinburgh: Soc. of Antiquaries of Scotland. Monograph Series number 8.

—— (1996), 'Ancient landscapes and the modern public', in D. Evans, P. Salway & D. Thackray (eds), *The Remains of Distant Times: Archaeology and the National Trust*, Woodbridge: Boydell for the Society of Antiquaries of London and the National Trust.

Britton, S. (1991), 'Tourism, capital and place: towards a critical geography of tourism', *Environment and Planning D: Society and Space* **9** 451–78.

Brunton, R. (1992), 'Mining credibility', *Anthropology Today* **8(2)** 2–5.

—— (1996), 'The Hindmarsh Island Bridge and the credibility of Australian anthropology', *Anthropology Today* **12(4)** 2–7.

Burke, P. (1980), *Sociology and History*, London: George Allen & Unwin.

Burl, A. (1979), *Prehistoric Avebury*, New Haven: Yale University Press.

—— (1987), *The Stonehenge People*, London: J.M. Dent.

Carmichael, D., J. Hubert, B. Reeves, & A. Schanche (eds) (1994), *Sacred Sites, Sacred Places*, London: Routledge.

Chamberlin, R. (1986), *The Idea of England*, London: Thames & Hudson.

Chatwin, B. (1988), *The Songlines*, London: Pan Books.

Chippindale, C. (1983), *Stonehenge Complete*, London: Thames & Hudson.

—— (1986), 'Stoned henge: events and issues at the Summer solstice', *World Archaeology* **18(1)** 38–58.

—— et al. (1990), *Who Owns Stonehenge?* London: Batsford.

Clark, G. et al. (1994), *Leisure Landscapes*, Lancaster: Centre for the Study of Environmental Change.

Cleal, R., K. Walker, & R. Montague (1995), *Stonehenge in its Landscape. Twentieth-century Excavations*, London: English Heritage.

Clifford, J. (1994), 'Diasporas', *Cultural Anthropology* **9** 302–38.

Conkey, M. (1991), 'Contexts of action, contexts of power: material culture and gender in the Magdalenian', In J. Gero & M. Conkey (eds), *Engendering Archaeology*, Oxford: Basil Blackwell.

—— & R. Tringham (1995), 'Archaeology and the Goddess: exploring the contours of feminist archaeology', in D. Stanton & A. Stewart (eds), *Feminisms in the Academy*, Ann Arbor: University of Michigan Press.

—— (1996), 'Cultivating thinking/challenging authority: some experiments in feminist pedagogy in archaeology', in R. Wright (ed.), *Gender and Archaeology*, Philadelphia: University of Pennsylvania Press.

Connerton, P. (1989), *How Societies Remember*, Cambridge: Cambridge University Press.

Cosgrove, D. (1990a), '. . . Then we take Berlin: cultural geography 1989–90', *Progress in Human Geography* **4** 560–68.

—— (1990b), 'Landscape studies in geography and cognate fields of the humanities and social sciences', *Landscape Research* **15(3)** 1–6.

—— (1994), 'Should we take it all so seriously? Culture, conservation, and meaning in the contemporary world', in W. Krumbein et al (eds), *Durability and Change*, Chichester: John Wiley & Sons.

—— & M. Domash (1993), 'Author and authority. Writing the new cultural geography', in J. Duncan & D. Ley (eds), *Place/Culture/Representation*, London: Routledge.

Crang, M. (1994), 'On the heritage trail: maps and journeys to Olde-Englande', *Environment and Planning D: Society and Space* **12** 341–55.

Dames, M. (1976), *The Silbury Treasure*, London: Thames & Hudson.

—— (1977), *The Avebury Cycle*, London: Thames & Hudson.

Daniels, S. (1988), 'The political iconography of woodland in later Georgian England', in D. Cosgrove & S. Daniels (eds), *The Iconography of Landscape*, Cambridge: Cambridge University Press.

—— & D. Cosgrove (1993), 'Spectacle and text: landscape metaphors in cultural geography', in J. Duncan & D. Ley (eds), *Place/Culture/Representation*, London: Routledge.

Darvill, T. (1997), 'Ever increasing circles: the sacred geographies of Stonehenge and its landscape', in B. Cunliffe (ed.), *Science and Stonehenge*, London: Proceedings of the British Academy **92** 167–202.

De Certeau, M. (1984), *The Practice of Everyday Life*, Berkeley: University of California Press.

Deloria, V. (1995), *Red Earth, White Lies: Native Americans and the Myth of Scientific Fact*, Hemel Hampstead: Prentice Hall.

Deutsche, R. (1991), 'Boys town', *Environment and Planning D: Society and Space* **9** 5–30.

Eagleton, T. (1989), 'Introduction', in T. Eagleton (ed.), *Raymond Williams: Critical Perspectives*, Cambridge: Polity Press.

Ecco, U. (1980), *The Name of the Rose*, London: Secker & Warburg.

Edmonds, M. (1993), 'Interpreting causewayed enclosures in the past and the present', in C. Tilley (ed.), *Interpreting Archaeology*, Oxford: Berg.

—— (1995), *Stone Tools and Society*, London: Batsford.

Eliade, M. (1962), *The Forge and the Crucible*, trans. S. Corrin, London: Rider.

Fielden, K. (1996), 'Avebury saved?', *Antiquity* **70** 503–7.

Flannery, K. (1976), *The Early Meso-American Village*, NewYork: Academic Press.

Fleming, A. (1996), 'Total landscape archaeology: dream or necessity?', in F. Aalen (ed.), *Landscape Study and Management*, Dublin: Office of Public Works.

Foch-Serra, M. (1990), 'Place, voice, space: Mikhail Bakhtin's dialogical landscape', *Environment and Planning D: Society and Space* **8** 255–74.

Foucault, M. (1977), *Discipline and Punish*, New York: Vintage Books.

—— (1980), 'Questions on geography', in C. Gorden (ed.), *M. Foucault: Power/Knowledge*, New York: Pantheon.

—— (1981), *The History of Sexuality*, Harmondsworth: Penguin.

—— (1984), 'Panopticism. An interview with Paul Rabinow', in P. Rabinow (ed.), *The Foucault Reader*, 206–13, New York: Pantheon.

—— (1986), 'Of other spaces', *Diacritics* **16** 22–7.

Fowler, P. (1990), 'Academic claims and responsibilities', in C. Chippindale et al. (eds), *Who Owns Stonehenge?* London: Batsford.

Friedman, J. (1992), 'The past in the future: history and the politics of identity', *American Anthropologist* **94** 837–59.

Gell, A. (1995), 'The language of the forest: landscape and phonological iconism in Umeda', in E. Hirsch & M. O'Hanlon (eds), *The Anthropology of Landscape*, Oxford: Oxford University Press.

Geoffrey of Monmouth (1966), *The History of the Kings of Britain*, trans. L. Thorpe, Harmondsworth: Penguin.

Gero, J. & M. Conkey (eds) (1991), *Engendering Archaeology*, Oxford: Basil Blackwell.

Giddens, A. (1981), *A Contemporary Critique of Historical Materialism. Vol. I: Power, Property and the State*, London: University of California Press.

—— (1985), 'Time, space and regionalisation', in D. Gregory & J. Urry (eds), *Social Relations and Spatial Structures*, London: Macmillan.

Gilroy, P. (1987), *There Ain't No Black in the Union Jack: the Cultural Politics of Race and Nation*, London: Hutchinson.

Gingell, C. (1996), 'Avebury: striking a balance', *Antiquity* **70** 507–11.

Gold, M. (1984), 'A history of nature', in D. Massey & J. Allen (eds), *Geography Matters*, London: Macmillan.

Golding, F. (1989), 'Stonehenge – past and future', in H. Cleere (ed.), *Archaeological Heritage Management in the Modern World*, London: Unwin Hyman.

Gosden, C. & L. Head (1994), 'Landscape – a usefully ambiguous concept', *Archaeol. Oceania* **29** 113–16.

Gramsci, A. (1971), *Prison Notebooks*, New York: International Publishers.

Greber, N. (1979), 'A comparative study of site morphology and burial patterns at Edwin Harness mound and Siep mounds 1 and 2', in

D. Brose & N. Greber (eds), *Hopewell Archaeology. The Chillicothe Conference*, Kent: Kent State University Press.

Grinsell, L. (1976), *Folklore of Prehistoric Sites in Britain*, Newton Abbot: David & Charles.

Gurevich, A. (1988), *Medieval Popular Culture; Problems of Belief and Perception*, Cambridge: Cambridge University Press.

Hall, S. (1980), 'Cultural studies and the centre: some problematics and problems', in S. Hall, D. Hobson, A. Love, P. Willis (eds), *Culture, Media, Language*, London: Hutchinson.

Haraway, D. (1991), *Simians, Cyborgs and Women: the Reinvention of Nature*, London: Free Association.

Harding, J. (1991), 'Creating the landscape, monuments and social space', Paper presented to the Conference of the Theoretical Archaeology Group, Leicester, 18 December 1991.

Harding, S. (1993), 'Rethinking standpoint epistemology: what is "strong objectivity"?', in L. Alcoff & E. Potter (eds), *Feminist Epistemologies*, London: Routledge.

Harvey, D. (1989), *The Condition of Postmodernity*, Cambridge: Blackwell.

—— (1996), *Justice, Nature and the Geography of Difference*, Cambridge, Mass.: Blackwell Publishers Inc.

—— & D. Haraway (1995), 'Nature, politics and possibilities: a debate and discussion with David Harvey and Donna Haraway', *Environment and Planning D: Society and Space* **13** 507–27.

Hawkes, J. (1967), 'God in the machine', *Antiquity* **41**, 174–80.

Hawkins, G. (1965), *Stonehenge Decoded*, New York: Dorset Press.

Heidegger, M. (1962), *Being and Time*, trans. J. Macquarrie & E. Robinson, Oxford: Blackwell.

—— (1971), 'Building, dwelling, thinking', in D. Krell (ed.), *Martin Heidegger: Basic Writings*, London: Routledge.

Helgerson, R. (1986), 'The land speaks: cartography, chorography, and subversion in Renaissance England', *Representations* **16** 51–85.

Herzfeld, M. (1991), *A Place in History. Social and Monumental Time in a Cretan Town*, Princeton: Princeton University Press.

Hetherington, K. (1992), 'Stonehenge and its festival. Spaces of consumption', in R. Shields (ed.), *Lifestyle Shopping. The Subject of Consumption*, London: Routledge.

Hewison, R. (1987), *The Heritage Industry: Britain in a Climate of Decline*, London: Methuen.

Hill, C. (1982), 'Science and magic in seventeenth-century England', in R. Samuel & G. Stedman Jones (eds), *Culture, Ideology and Politics*, London: Routledge and Kegan Paul.

Hobsbawn, E. (1983), 'Introduction: inventing traditions', in E. Hobsbawn & T. Ranger (eds), *The Invention of Tradition*, Cambridge:
Cambridge University Press.

Hodder, I. (1990), *The Domestication of Europe*, Oxford: Blackwell.

Hoskins, W.G. (1954), *Devon*, Newton Abbott: David & Charles.

—— (1985), *The Making of the English Landscape*, Harmondsworth:
Penguin (First published 1955).

Hunter, M. (1975), *John Aubrey and the Realm of Learning*, London:
Duckworth.

Hutton, R. (1991), *Pagan Religions of the Ancient British Isles*, Oxford:
Blackwell.

—— (1994), *The Rise and Fall of Merry England*, Oxford: Oxford University Press.

—— (1995), 'The English Reformation and the evidence of folklore',
Past and Present **148** 89–116.

—— (1996), *The Stations of the Sun: a History of the Ritual Year in Britain*,
Oxford: Oxford University Press.

Hutton, W. (1996), *The State We're In*, London: Vintage.

Inglis, F. (1977), 'Nation and community: a landscape and its morality',
Sociological Review **25** 489–514.

Ingold, T. (1993), 'The temporality of landscape', *World Archaeology* **25**
152–74.

—— (1996), 'Hunting and gathering as ways of perceiving the environment', in R. Ellen & K. Fukui (eds), *Redefining Nature: Ecology, Culture
and Domestication*, Oxford: Berg.

Jackson, J.B. (1984), *Discovering the Vernacular Landscape*, New Haven:
Yale University Press.

Jackson, P. (1991), 'Repositioning social and cultural geography', in C.
Philo (compiler), *Reconceptualising Social and Cultural Geography*,
Aberystwyth: Cambrian Printers.

Jacobs, J. (1993), '"Shake 'im this country": the mapping of the aboriginal sacred in Australia', in P. Jackson & J. Penrose (eds), *Construction
of Race, Place and Nation*, Mineapolis: University of Minnesota.

—— (1994a), 'Negotiating the heart: heritage, development and identity
in postimperial London', *Environment and Planning D: Society and
Space* **12** 751–72.

—— (1994b), 'The Battle of Bank Junction: the contested iconography
of capital', in S. Corbridge, R. Martin & N. Thrift (eds), *Money, Power,
Space*, Oxford: Blackwell.

—— (1996), *Edge of Empire. Postcolonialism and the City*, London:
Routledge.

Johnson, M. (1993), 'Notes towards an archaeology of capitalism', in C. Tilley (ed.), *Interpreting Archaeology*, Oxford: Berg.

Jones III, J. & P. Moss (1995), 'Guest editorial. Democracy, identity and space', *Environment and Planning D: Society and Space* **13** 253–57.

Jones, R. (1990), 'Sylwadau cynfrodor ar Gôr y Cewri; or a British aboriginal's land claim to Stonehenge', in C. Chippindale et al. (eds), *Who Owns Stonehenge?* London: Batsford.

Joyce, R. (1992), 'Images of gender and labor organization in Classic Maya society', in C. Claassen (ed.), *Exploring Gender through Archaeology*, Monographs in World Archaeology no. 11. Madison, Wisconsin: Prehistory Press.

—— (1993), 'Women's work. Images of production and reproduction in pre-Hispanic Southern Central America', *Current Anthropology* **34(3)** 255–74.

—— (1996), 'The construction of gender in Classic Maya monuments', in R. Wright (ed.), *Gender and Archaeology*, Philadelephia: University of Pennsylvania Press.

Keen, I. (1992), 'Undermining credibility', *Anthropology Today* **8(2)** 6–9.

Keesing, R. (1994), 'Colonial and counter-colonial discourse in Melanesia', *Critique of Anthropology* **14(1)** 41–58.

Kuchler, S. (1993), 'Landscape as memory: the mapping of process and its representation in a Melanesian society', in B. Bender (ed.), *Landscape. Politics and Perspectives*, Oxford: Berg.

Lefebvre, H. (1991), *The Production of Space*, trans. D. Nicholson-Smith, Oxford: Blackwell.

Le Goff, J. (1980), *Time, Work and Culture in the Middle Ages*, trans. A. Goldhammer, Chicago: University of Chicago Press.

Legg, R. (1986), *Stonehenge Antiquaries*, Sherborne: Dorset Publishing Co.

Loveday, P. (1991), *Russell. The Saga of a Peaceful Man*, London: John Brown Publishing.

Lowenthal, D. (1979), 'Age and artefact', in D. Meinig (ed.), *The Interpretation of Ordinary Landscape*, New York: Oxford University Press.

—— (1991), 'British national identity and the English landscape', *Rural History* **2(2)** 205–30.

—— (1996), *The Heritage Crusade and the Spoils of History*, London: Viking.

Lumley, R. (ed.) (1988), *The Museum Time-Machine*, London: Routledge.

Mahfouz, N. (1997), *Echoes of an Autobiography*, trans. D. Johnson-Davies, London: Doubleday.

Massey, D. (1991), 'Flexible sexism', *Environment and Planning D: Society and Space* **9** 31–57.

—— (1995), 'Thinking radical democracy spatially', *Environment and Planning D: Society and Space* **13** 283–8.

McKay, G. (1996), *Senseless Acts of Beauty. Cultures of Resistance since the Sixties*, London: Verso.

McVicar, J. (1984), 'Change and the growth of antiquarian studies in Tudor and Stuart England', *Archaeological Review from Cambridge* **3:1** 48–67.

Merriman, N. (1991), *Beyond the Glass Cage: the Past, the Heritage and the Public in Britain*, Leicester: Leicester University Press.

Miller, D. & C. Tilley (1984), 'Ideology, power and prehistory: an introduction', in D. Miller & C. Tilley (eds), *Ideology, Power and Prehistory*, Cambridge: Cambridge University Press.

Mohanty, C. (1991), 'Introduction. Cartographies of struggle: Third World women and the politics of feminism', in C. Mohanty, A. Russo & L. Torres (eds), *Third World Women and the Politics of Feminism*, Bloomington: Indiana University Press.

Morley, D. (1992), *Television Audiences and Cultural Studies*, London: Routledge.

Morphy, H. (1989), 'From dull to brilliant: the aesthetics of spiritual power among the Yolngu', *Man* (N.S.) **24** 21–40.

—— (1993), 'Colonialism, history and the construction of place: the politics of landscape in Northern Australia', in B. Bender (ed.), *Landscape: Politics and Perspectives*, Oxford: Berg.

—— (1996), 'Proximity and distance: representations of Aboriginal society in the writings of Bill Harney and Bruce Chatwin', in J. MacClancy & C. McDonaugh (eds), *Popularizing Anthropology*, London: Routledge.

Mouffe, C. (1995), 'Post-Marxism: democracy and identity', *Environment and Planning D: Society and Space* **13** 259–65.

Munn, N. (1992), 'The cultural anthropology of time: a critical essay', *Annual Review of Anthropology* **21** 93–123.

Murray, T. (1989), 'The history, philosophy and sociology of archaeology: the case of the Ancient Monuments Protection Act (1882)', in V. Pinsky & A. Wylie (eds), *Critical Traditions in Contemporary Archaeology*, Cambridge: Cambridge University Press.

Naipaul, V.S. (1987), *The Enigma of Arrival*, Harmondsworth: Penguin.

Nairn, T. (1977), *The Break-up of England*, London: NLB.

National Trust, The (1995), *Linking People and Places. Background Papers*, The National Trust.

Newham, C. (1964), *The Enigma of Stonehenge*, Tadcaster.

Olivier, E. (1951), *Wiltshire*, London: Robert Hale.

Olwig, K. (1996), 'Recovering the substantive nature of landscape', *Annals of the Association of American Geographers* **86** 630–53.

Piggott, S. (1941), 'The sources of Geoffrey of Monmouth. II. The Stonehenge story', *Antiquity* **15** 305–19.

—— (1985), *William Stukeley. An Eighteenth Century Antiquarian*, London: Thames & Hudson.

Pitts, M. (1996), 'The vicar's dewpond, the National Trust shop and the rise of paganism', in D. Evans, P. Salway, & D. Thackray (eds), *The Remains of Distant Times: Archaeology and the National Trust*, Woodbridge: Boydell for the Soc. of Antiquaries of London & the National Trust.

Pred, A. (1990), *Making Histories and Constructing Human Geographies*, Boulder, San Francisco: Westview Press.

Rappaport, J. (1988), 'History and everyday life in the Colombian Andes', *Man* **23** 718–39.

Richards, C. & J. Thomas (1984), 'Ritual activity and structured deposition in later Neolithic Wessex', in R. Bradley & J. Gardiner (eds), *Neolithic Studies*, BAR British Series **133**.

Richards, J. (1984), 'The development of the Neolithic landscape in the environs of Stonehenge', in R. Bradley & J. Gardiner (eds), *Neolithic Studies*, BAR British Series **133**.

—— (1990), *The Stonehenge Environs Project*, English Heritage Archaeological Report **16**.

—— (1991), *Stonehenge*, London: Batsford/English Heritage.

Ricoeur, P. (1979), 'The model of the text: meaningful action considered as text', in P. Rabinow & W. Sullivan (eds), *Interpretive Social Science, a Reader*, Berkeley: University of California Press.

Robinson, D. & C. Garrett (1996), *Ethics for Beginners*, Cambridge: Icon Books.

—— (in press), *Descartes for Beginners*, Cambridge: Icon Books.

Rose, G. (1993), *Feminism and Geography*, Cambridge: Polity Press.

Rosenberger, A. (1991), 'Stones that cry out', *The Guardian* June.

Rowlands, M. (1993), 'The role of memory in the transmission of culture', *World Archaeology* **25** 141–52.

—— (1994), 'The politics of identity in archaeology', in G. Bond & A. Gilliam (eds), *Social Construction of the Past. Representations as Power*, London: Routledge.

Rowntree, L. (1996), 'The cultural landscape concept in American human geography', in C. Earle, K. Mathewson & M. Kenzer (eds),

Concepts in Human Geography, Lanham, Maryland: Rowman & Little-field.

Royal Commission on Historical Monuments (1979), *Stonehenge and its Environs. Monuments and Landscape*, Edinburgh: Edinburgh University Press.

Said, E. (1989), 'Jane Austen and empire', in T. Eagleton (ed.), *Raymond Williams: Critical Perspectives*, Oxford: Polity Press.

—— (1993), *Culture and Imperialism*, London: Vintage.

Salmond, A. (1982), 'Theoretical landscapes. On cross-cultural conceptions of knowledge', in D. Parkin (ed.), *Semantic Anthropology*, London: Academic Press.

Samuel, R. (ed.) (1975), *Village Life and Labour*, London: Routledge & Kegan Paul.

Scully, V. (1962), *The Earth, the Temple and the Gods*, New Haven: Yale University Press.

Sibley, D. (1992), 'Outsiders in society and space', in K. Anderson & F. Gale (eds), *Inventing Place. Studies in Cultural Geography*, Australia: Longman Cheshire Ltd.

Smith, L. (1994), 'Heritage management as postprocessual archaeology?', *Antiquity* **68** 300–309.

Soja, E.W. (1989), *Postmodern Geographies*, London: Verso.

Startin, B. & R. Bradley (1981), 'Some notes on work organisation and society in prehistoric Wessex', in C. Ruggles & A. Whittle (eds), *Astronomy and Society during the Period 4000–1500* BC, BAR British Series **88.**

Stewart, L. (1995), 'Bodies, visions, and spatial politics: a review essay on Henri Lefebvre's *The Production of Space*', *Environment and Planning D: Society and Space* **13** 609–18.

Stilgoe, J. (1982), *Common Landscape of America 1580 to 1845*, New Haven: Yale University Press.

Stone, C. (1996), *Fierce Dancing*, London: Faber & Faber.

Stone, P. (1994), 'The re-display of the Alexander Keiller Museum, Avebury, and the National Curriculum in England', in P. Stone & B. Molyneaux (eds), *Presented Past*, London: Routledge.

Strang, V. (1997), *Uncommon Ground: Cultural Landscapes and Environmental Values*, Oxford: Berg.

Stukeley, W. (1740), *Stonehenge: a Temple Restor'd to the British Druids*, London: Innys & Manby.

Taçon, P. (1991), 'The power of stone: symbolic aspects of stone use and tool development in western Arnhem Land, Australia', *Antiquity* **65** 192–207.

Thom, A. (1967), *Megalithic Sites in Britain*, Oxford: Oxford University Press.

Thomas, J. (1991), 'Reading the Neolithic', *Anthropology Today* **7** 9–11.

—— (1993a), 'After essentialism: archaeology, geography and postmodernity', *Archaeological Review from Cambridge* **12** 13–27.

—— (1993b), 'The politics of vision and the archaeologies of landscape', in B. Bender (ed.), *Landscape. Politics and Perspectives*, Oxford: Berg.

—— (1996), *Time, Culture and Identity. An Interpretive Archaeology*, London: Routledge.

—— (1997), 'An economy of substances in earlier Neolithic Britain', in J. Robb (ed.), *Material Symbols: Culture and Economy in Prehistory*, Carbondale: Centre for Archaeological Investigation.

—— & C. Tilley (1992), 'The torso and the axe: symbolic structures in the Neolithic of Brittany', in C. Tilley (ed.), *Interpretative Archaeology*, Oxford: Berg.

Thomas, K. (1983), *Man and the Natural World*, Harmondsworth: Penguin.

Thompson, E. (1974), 'Patrician society, plebian culture', *Journal of Social History* **7** 382–405.

Thorpe, I. (1984), 'Ritual, power and ideology: a reconstruction of earlier Neolithic rituals in Wessex', in R. Bradley & J. Gardiner (eds), *Neolithic Studies*, BAR British Series **133**.

—— (1989), 'Neolithic and Earlier Bronze Age Wessex and Yorkshire', PhD thesis: University of London.

Thrift, N. (1991), 'Over-wordy worlds? Thoughts and worries', in C. Philo (compiler), *Reconceptualising Social and Cultural Geography*, Aberystwyth: Cambrian Printers.

—— & A. Pred (1981), 'Time-Geography: a new beginning', *Progress in Human Geography* **5** 277–86.

Tilley, C. (1994), *A Phenomenology of Landscape*, Oxford: Berg.

—— (ed.) (in press), *Interpretative Archaeology*, Oxford: Berg.

Tringham, R. (1991), 'Households with faces: the challenge of gender in prehistoric architectural remains', in J. Gero & M. Conkey (eds), *Engendering Archaeology*, Oxford: Blackwell.

—— (1994), 'Engendered places in prehistory', *Gender, Place and Culture* **1(2)** 169–203.

Tse-Tung, M. (1972), *The Poems of Mao Tse-Tung*, trans. W. Barnstone, London: Barrie and Jenkins.

Ucko, P., M. Hunter, A. Clark & A. David (1991), *Avebury Reconsidered: from the 1660s to the 1990s*, London: Unwin Hyman.

Urry, J. (1990), *The Tourist Gaze*, London: Sage Publications.

Wainwright, G. (1996), 'Stonehenge saved?' *Antiquity* **70** 9–12.

Warren, S. (1993), 'This heaven gives me migraines', in J. Duncan & D. Ley (eds), *Place/Culture/Representation*, London: Routledge.

Weldon, F. (1984), 'Letter to Laura', in R. Mabey, S. Clifford, A. King (eds), *Second Nature*, London: Jonathan Cape.

Whittle, A. (1996), 'Review article: Eternal Stones: Stonehenge Completed', *Antiquity* **70**, 463–5.

—— (1997), 'Remembering and imagined belongings: Stonehenge in its traditions and structures of meaning', in B. Cunliffe (ed.), *Science and Stonehenge*, London: Proceedings of the British Academy **92**.

Willett, J. & R. Manheim (eds) (1976), *Bertolt Brecht Poems 1913–1956*, London: Eyre Methuen Ltd.

Williams, R. (1963), *Culture and Society 1780–1950*, Harmondsworth: Penguin.

—— (1973), *The Country and the City*, London: Chatto & Windus.

—— (1980), *Problems in Materialism and Culture*, London: Verso.

(1994), Selections from 'Marxism and Literature', in N. Dirks, G. Eley and S. Ortner (eds), *Culture/Power/History: a Reader in Contemporary Social Theory*, Princeton: Princeton University Press.

Wolf, E. (1982), *Europe and the People without History*, Berkeley: University of California Press.

Wright, P. (1985), *On Living in an Old Country*, London: Verso.

—— (1995), 'Faulty Towers', *The Guardian* January.

Wright, R. (ed.) (1996), *Gender and Archaeology*, Philadelphia: University of Pennsylvania Press.

Wylie, A. (1992a), 'The interplay of evidential constraints and political interests: recent archaeological research on gender', *American Antiquity* **57(1)** 15–35.

—— (1992b), 'Feminist theories of social power: some implications for a processual archaeology', *Norwegian Archaeological Review* **25(1)** 51–68.

Index